Recommended

ROMANTIC INNS™

of
America

by

Julianne Belote • Brenda Boelts Chapin
Doris Kennedy • Eleanor Morris • Sara Pitzer
Bob Puhala • Elizabeth Squier

(the Authors of the
Recommended Country Inns™ Series)

A Voyager Book

The Globe Pequot Press

Old Saybrook, Connecticut

Library of Congress Cataloging-in-Publication Data

Recommended romantic inns of America / by the authors of the Recommended country inns series. — 1st ed.
     p.   cm.
  "A Voyager book."
  Includes indexes.
  ISBN 1-56440-129-4
  1. Hotels, taverns, etc. —United States—Guidebooks.
TX907.2.R434   1992
647.947301—dc20   92-39760
                                                        CIP

Manufactured in the United States of America
First Edition/First Printing

Contents

Indexes

Romantic Inn-Sights

When the mind and body have been kept too long to the tasks and worries of the workplace and, yes, even to those of the old homestead, the spirit rebels and begs for attention. "Ah, but for a little romance," your inner voice may sigh. This book is for you.

Describe romance in any terms you like, and unless your tastes range toward the very strange, you're likely to find an inn in these pages to satisfy all your yearnings. Take the hand of your partner and prepare to soak up delight after delicious delight at one of these most soul-soothing hostelries.

Researched and selected by seven of the most incurable romantics on the planet, the inns profiled here define and redefine romance. If you are looking for starlight and moonglow, soft rain and sea breezes, shimmering sunsets and breathtaking vistas, Mother Nature will provide them. If you need candlelight, bubble baths, champagne, firelight, porch swings, whirlpools, fabulous food, beautiful flowers, linens and lace, breakfast in bed, carriage rides, secluded picnics, country lanes, grand staircases, turret bedchambers, and pampering of the most gracious sort, the inns will provide them. And when you've put down the luggage and all the other baggage of life at home and work, if you need whispered promises, urgent kisses, and passion of any sort these inns inspire you to kindle, *you* will provide them. True romance, after all, is what you bring with you. Just let these gentle innkeepers encourage you.

Among these romantic establishments are inns at the seashore and inns in the mountains; inns miles (but not too many miles) from nowhere and inns close to hubs of culture and entertainment; inns with room for scores of travelers and inns with room for just a few (or even only two). The authors have chosen island inns, city inns, inns where you may ride horseback or soar in a hot-air balloon, inns that provide gourmet meals and inns that will guide you to fine restaurants. Many of the inns are in historic structures; you might choose an eighteenth-century New England tavern, a Cape May Victorian, a Pennsylvania German barn, an Italianate palazzo, a Georgian Revival mansion, an antebellum plantation home, a honeymoon cottage in a former chapel, a rustic lodge with hand-hewn beams. Some inns are new or nearly new, but all share the ambience that harkens back to quieter times.

As in other volumes of the Globe Pequot Press *Recommended Country Inns* series, every inn in this book has been personally visited by the authors. Their inclusion depends on meeting the highest standards of atmosphere, service, comfort, hospitality, history, and location. Essentials include welcoming innkeepers and special personal touches designed for your pleasure. These are the elements that make inn travel unique. Where but at an inn can you relax near a crackling fire, sipping wine or feeding each other strawberries? Where else can you stroll through glorious gardens to secluded benches and arbors specially placed so that none but the roses will hear your murmurs? Where else can you expect a host's polite but oh, so very warm appreciation of your special celebration?

These innkeepers have endeavored to ensure your pleasure, delight your senses, renew your spirit, and relight your passion. Our authors have endeavored to share their experience that, for any excuse at all, you can rendezvous most romantically at each and every one of these memorable inns.

About This Inn Guide

This in guide contains descriptions of 140 inns in seven regions of the United States. These inns were selected by the authors of The Globe Pequot Press's seven regional *Recommended Country Inns* guides as the most romantic inns in their regions. *All inns were personally visited by the authors. There is no charge of any kind for an inn to be included in this or any other Globe Pequot Press inn guide.*

The guide is arranged geographically by region, beginning along the Atlantic Ocean. These regions, in order, are: New England; Mid-Atlantic and Chesapeake Region; the South; the Midwest; Arizona, New Mexico, and Texas; Rocky Mountain Region; and the West Coast. Within each region, the states are listed alphabetically; within each state, the towns are arranged alphabetically.

Preceding each region's listings is a regional map and a numbered legend of the eighteen family inns found in that region. The map is marked with corresponding numbers to show where the inns are located.

Indexes: At the back of the book are various special-category indexes to help you find inns located on a lake or at the seashore, inns with golf or tennis, inns with skiing, inns with swimming pools, and more. There is also an alphabetical index of all the inns in this book.

Rates: The guidebook quotes current low and high rates to give you an indication of the price ranges you can expect. They are more than likely to change slightly with time. Be sure to call ahead and inquire about the rates as well as the taxes and service charges. The following abbreviations are used consistently throughout the book to let you know exactly what, if any, meals are included in the room price.

> *EP:* European Plan. Room without meals.
> *EPB:* Room with full breakfast. (No abbreviation is used when continental breakfast is included.)
> *MAP:* Modified American Plan. Room with breakfast and dinner.
> *AP:* American Plan. Room with breakfast, lunch, and dinner.

Credit cards: MasterCard and Visa are accepted unless the description says "No credit cards." Many inns also accept additional credit cards.

Reservations and deposits: These are so often required that they are not mentioned in any description. Assume that you'll generally have to pay a deposit to reserve a room, using a personal check or a credit card. Be sure to inquire about refund policies.

Pets: No pets are allowed unless otherwise stated in the description. Always let innkeepers know in advance if you are planning to bring a pet.

Wheelchair access: Some descriptions mention wheelchair access, but other inns may be feasible for the handicapped. Therefore, if you're interested in an inn, call to check if there is a room suitable for a handicapped person.

Air conditioning: The description will indicate if an inn has rooms with air conditioning. Keep in mind, however, that there are areas of the country where air conditioning is totally unnecessary. For example, in the Rocky Mountain region, where the inn is at a high elevation (stated in the description), you will be comfortable without air conditioning.

Television: Some inns offer televisions and VCRs in guest rooms; the room description will mention if the rooms are so equipped. Sometimes there's a television or VCR in a common room. *Note:* Most innkeepers say there is so much to do at the inn or in the area that guests generally don't watch television. In addition, most inns inspire true romantics to engage in pleasures the television can't enhance.

Telephone: Assuming that when you yearn for romance you want to get away from it all, the descriptions do not state if you will find a telephone in your room.

Smoking: Unless otherwise specified, smoking is permitted.,

BYOB: It is often acceptable to bring your own bottle, especially if an inn has no bar service. If you see no mention of BYOB or a bar in the description, you may want to check in advance.

Meals: Most of the inns profiled offer dinner as well as breakfast. Those that do not are more than happy to make reservations for you at fine, nearby restaurants. Some inns also offer brunches, lunches, hors d'oeuvres, or afternoon tea. The authors often indicate some favorite foods they enjoyed at an inn, but you should not expect the menu to remain the same forever. Menus usually change seasonally or monthly. The description of the inn's food should give you a general idea of the meals served; with notice, innkeepers and chefs are happy to fill special dietary requests or create celebration cakes or the like.

Author additions: The comment preceded by a big initial (standing for the author's name) occasionally found at the end of the inn description is one more personal statement from the author about an inn.

A final word: The authors have convinced the editors that these innkeepers are themselves the soul of romance. Drink deeply of their sweet ministerings and renew the promises romance makes so easy to whisper.

New England

by Elizabeth Squier

New England is a very special place, and you the visitor are in for a special treat whatever season you decide to come. Spring is so romantic; the trees bud and flowers poke up from sometimes-lingering snow. The birds do their mating dances; beautiful swans sit on their nests. Oh, yes—romance is all around. Country inns are a special part of the romance of New England—after all, this is the region where they started. For this book I have selected some of the most romantic country inns I have visited. Each has been chosen for one romantic reason or another—a quiet corner, wonderful dinners, breakfast in bed, a walk in the snow. Just remember they are off the beaten track (there's even one on an island off the beautiful coast of Maine), and romance is everywhere. Winter brings its own magic—the snow, the glow of a fire. I know of nothing more romantic than sitting by a fire, a glass of wine and someone very special by your side.

Many of the inns have common areas with magazines and newspapers for guests to read—even whole libraries to browse in. There are puzzles to put together, games to play, televisions, and VCRs for movies. Special touches in the rooms are also important criteria for romance—fluffy pillows, good mattresses, extra blankets, good lighting, and chairs for reading. For bed readers like me, good bed lamps are a must.

In the fall, when the leaves are turning glorious colors, what a romantic feeling it is to turn up the driveway of a beautiful inn, meet a welcoming innkeeper, relax near a crackling fire, and enjoy a lovely, romantic interlude.

I can remember a few occasions when my husband and I were caught in one of these lovely inns either by rain or snow. We sat by the fire, played some gin rummy, and sipped some fine concoction to warm the tummy. Oh, what romantic times we had.

Well, by now you know it—I am a romantic, and I love my inns and their innkeepers. All inns in their own way are romantic. Come on up to New England and enjoy.

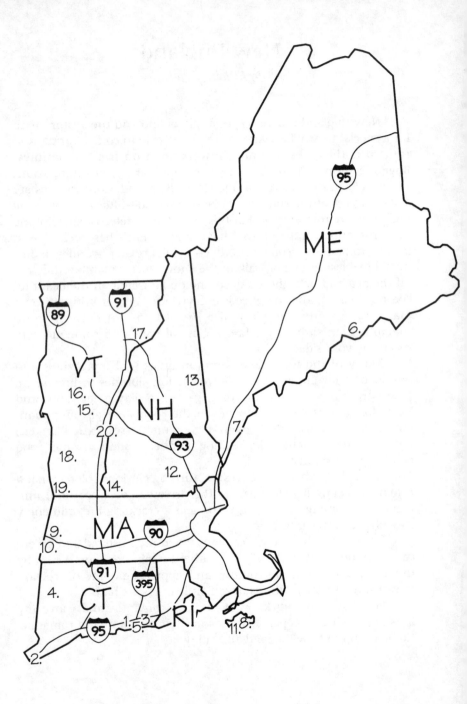

New England

Numbers on map refer to towns numbered below.

The Homestead Inn
Greenwich, Connecticut
06830

Innkeepers: Lessie Davison and Nancy Smith
Address/Telephone: Field Point Road; (203) 869–7500
Rooms: 17, plus 6 suites; all with private bath, color TV, clock radio, phone.
Rates: $127 to $152, double; $167, suites; continental breakfast.
Open: All year.
Facilities and activities: Full breakfast, lunch Monday through Friday, dinner
seven days a week, Sunday brunch. Dining room closed Christmas
Day, New Year's Day, and Labor Day. Bar, small conference center.

There are very good reasons why this lovely 1799 inn has been
chosen as the best country inn in the country. Jacques Thiebeult is
the French chef who oversees the superb food served here. The
entire staff makes you feel like royalty. I think we all need this kind
of treatment once in a while.

The dining room is elegant in a rustic fashion; hand-hewn
chestnut beams, brick walls, fireplaces, skylights, and well-spaced
tables with comfortable chairs. A simple bunch of flowers is on each
table.

The inn's rooms are beautifully refurbished and each has a
name. William Inge wrote *Picnic* while staying at the inn in the
1950s, and the name of the room he stayed in is the Picnic Room. I
stayed in this one, too. The Poppy Room is a single with the smallest bathtub I believe was ever made. The Tassel Room has his and

her desks, the Sleigh Room has old sleigh beds, and the Robin Room has delicate stencils on the walls. They were found under six layers of wallpaper dating back to 1860. The Bride's Room has a queen-sized canopy bed.

The Independent House is the newest addition to the inn. There are eight glorious rooms out here. The bathrooms are large and have tub, shower, and bidet. All the rooms have porches, and the furnishings are wonderful. The cottage has a lovely suite and two other bedrooms, all very nice and quiet.

La Grange is the dining room and the food is fabulous. Besides the extensive menus, there are many specials. One that I had was poached fresh Dover sole, the best I have ever eaten. The inn is noted for its fresh fish and wonderful, tender veal prepared many interesting ways. Another dinner offering is "Black Angus" sirloin béarnaise. A real winner is *mélange de fruits de mer au safran*—lobster, shrimp, scallops, and mussels in a creamy saffron sauce. The presentation of the food is so picture perfect, you could almost eat the plate. The ironstone place settings in Wedgwood's Chinese Bird pattern and the beautiful stemware are exquisite.

Luncheon on the lawn in season is a joy. One of the luncheon dishes is escallops of veal, served with chestnuts, cream, and cognac. Some of the hors d'oeuvres are fresh poached Arctic salmon or a pot of snails with cream, Pernod, and herbs. The desserts, needless to say, are spectacular.

Do I like it here! I just wish I lived a bit closer.

How to get there: From New York take I-95 north to exit 3. Turn left at the bottom of the ramp, then left again at the second light onto Horseneck Lane. Turn left at the end of the lane onto Field Point Road. The inn is in ¼ mile on the right.

Copper Beech Inn
Ivoryton, Connecticut
06442

Innkeepers: Eldon and Sally Senner
Address/Telephone: 46 Main Street; (203) 767–0330
Rooms: 4 in inn, 9 in carriage house; all with private bath.
Rates: $100 to $160, double occupancy, continental breakfast.
Open: All year.
Facilities and activities: Restaurant closed on Mondays, Christmas Eve, Christmas Day, and New Year's Day. Dinner, full license. Greenhouse cocktail lounge open Saturdays.

One of the most beautiful copper beech trees in Connecticut shades the lawn of this lovely old inn and is the reason for the inn's name.

The grounds are beautiful. Eldon, who really is a gardener, has done wonders with the property. There is an authentic English garden, many bulbs are in bloom at different times of the year, and everything is just breathtaking.

Sally is an interior designer, and her expertise really shows in this inn. There is a lovely parlor on the first floor with bookcases and a table for playing cards or writing or whatever. Very warm and comfortable.

Accommodations at the Copper Beech are wonderful. There are four rooms in the inn itself, and they have unbelievable old-fashioned bathrooms. The towels are soft and fluffy. Nine more guest rooms are in the carriage house, and each one has a Jacuzzi tub, so wonderful after a day of exploring the lovely town of Essex, Mystic, and other area attractions. The carriage house has an elegant country atmosphere. The halls have very nice early nineteenth-century botanical prints. In fact, there is nineteenth-century art all over the inn and a wonderful collection of fine oriental porcelain.

The four dining rooms have comfortable Chippendale and Queen Anne chairs. The Garden Porch, which is a favorite place for me, features white wicker and nice Audubon prints on the walls. The spacious tables are set far apart for gracious dining. Fresh flowers are everywhere, and the waiters are friendly and courteous.

The hors d'oeuvres menu is a beauty. When I come here I love to sample the ten or more choices offered. The lobster bisque is always spectacular, and there are about twelve more hors d'oeuvres to choose from. Good fresh fish is used for entrees. The lobster is always easy to eat; no struggling with it here. My friend Lucy Goodale and I ordered different veal dishes. The veal was so tender we didn't need to use a knife. Beef Wellington and roast rack of lamb are always winners here and so are the fresh sweetbreads and a very different breast of chicken—a little French and a little oriental. Desserts are super. I love chocolate and raspberries, so I had some in the form of a cake and mousse and berries. No matter what you order, it is good at the Copper Beech and always exquisitely presented.

How to get there: The inn is located 1 mile west of Connecticut Route 9, from exit 3 or 4. Follow the signs to Ivoryton. The inn is on Ivoryton's Main Street, on the left side.

The Inn at Mystic
Mystic, Connecticut
06335

Innkeeper: Jody Dyer

Address/Telephone: Routes 1 and 27; (203) 536–9604; restaurant, (203) 536–8140

Rooms: 5 in 2 houses; all with private bath.

Rates: $155 to $195, double occupancy, EP.

Open: All year.

Facilities and activities: Breakfast, lunch, Sunday brunch, dinner every night except on Christmas Eve. Bar, lounge, room service, swimming pool, tennis, canoes, sailboats, walking trails. Nearby: museums, Mystic Seaport, Mystic Marinelife Aquarium, charter boats and tours, miniature golf and driving range; Foxwood Casino is about a half hour north in Ledyard.

Every time I think about this beautiful spot, I want to go back there. The views from the inn extend from Mystic Harbor all the way to Fishers Island; they are absolutely breathtaking.

The inn and gatehouse are situated on eight acres of land amid pear, nut, and peach trees and English flower gardens. From the Victorian veranda—furnished, of course, with beautiful old wicker—the view of the natural rock formations and ponds (I watched birds have their baths) and beyond to the harbor is worth a trip from anywhere.

Built in 1904, the inn is elegant. The large living room has walls covered with magnificent pin pine imported from England

and contains lovely antiques and comfortable places to sit. The rooms in both the inn and the gatehouse are beautifully done. Some have fireplaces. My room had a canopy bed, and was it ever comfortable! They all have interesting baths with whirlpool soaking tubs or Thermacuzzi spas. One has a view across the room to the harbor. Now that's a nice way to relax. Look south out the windows and you'll see Mason's Island; on a clear day you can see Long Island and Montauk.

The Flood Tide restaurant has a wonderful executive chef, Bob Tripp, who orchestrates the Tableside Classics prepared or carved at your table. Never have I seen a whole roast chicken for two on any menu except here. What a nice idea. I had baked stuffed two-tail Maine lobster—two claws and two tails and very good. Pork tenderloin with lingonberries almost got me. On my most recent visit, my friend Arneta Dow and I had chateaubriand for two, which was exquisite. All the food is memorable. The luncheon buffet is lavish, or ask for a picnic basket to take out sightseeing. They have thought of everything to make your stay pleasant. Sunday brunch, as you can imagine, is a bountiful affair.

The lounge is pleasant for lighter fare and is right at the swimming pool. A piano player provides music on a parlor grand piano every night and Sunday brunch. A wedding up here would be ambrosia.

How to get there: Take exit 90 from I-95. Go 3 miles south through Mystic on Route 27 to Route 1. The inn is here. Drive up through the motor inn to the inn at the top of the driveway.

Olive Metcalf

Boulders Inn
New Preston, Connecticut
06777

Innkeepers: Kees and Ulla Adema
Address/Telephone: Route 45; (203) 868–0541
Rooms: 17, including 2 suites and 8 guest houses; all with private bath.
Rates: $175 to $225, double, MAP. EP rates available.
Open: All year.
Facilities and activities: Breakfast, dinner. Sunday brunch. Bar, tennis court.
Nearby: swimming, boating, bicycling, hiking, cross-country skiing.

The stone boulders from which the inn was made jut right into the inn, and so the name, Boulders Inn.

If you have the energy, take a hike up Pinnacle Mountain behind the inn. From the top of the mountain, you'll be rewarded with a panorama that includes New York State to the west and Massachusetts to the north. Nice to enjoy the woods without having to go very far.

If you're not a hiker, you can enjoy the marvelous countryside right from the inn. There is an outside terrace where, in summer, you may enjoy cocktails, dinner, and spectacular sunsets. The spacious living room has large windows, and its comfortable chairs and couches make it a nice place for tea or cocktails. The dining room is octagonal in shape and provides a wonderful view of the lake. Some very good food is served here. There are some different appetizers like artichoke hearts with smoked trout mousse, sweetbreads with watercress sauce, and squid or leeks vinaigrette. And the entrees—oh my. Native roast leg of lamb au jus with shiitake mushrooms. Venison with lingonberries and chestnut puree. Quail. The list goes on and on. Kees serves very interesting wines by the glass.

All the guest accommodations have a view either of the lake or of the woods and are tastefully furnished. There are eight cozy guest houses, all with fireplaces. Say hello to Mouse and Fred, the inn cats.

How to get there: From New York take I–84 to Route 7 in Danbury; follow it north to New Milford. Take a right onto Route 202 to New Preston. Take a left onto Route 45, and you will find the inn as you round onto the lake.

E: *Kees and Ulla have added lovely touches to the inn. They have interesting paintings, Quimper pottery made in France, and cut and pierced lampshades all made by Ulla.*

Olive Metcalf

Bee and Thistle Inn
Old Lyme, Connecticut
06371

Innkeepers: Bob and Penny Nelson and Jeff and Lori Nelson
Address/Telephone: 100 Lyme Street; (203) 434–1667
Rooms: 11, plus 1 cottage; 10 with private bath.
Rates: $64 to $115, double occupancy; $175 to $195, cottage; EP.
Open: All year except Christmas Eve, Christmas Day, and first two weeks of
   January.
Facilities and activities: Breakfast. Lunch and dinner every day except Tues-
   day. Sunday brunch. Afternoon tea, November 1 to May 1. Bar,
   lounge, library.

What could be more romantic than breakfast in bed! Especially
here, where the guest rooms are all tastefully decorated. Your bed,
maybe a four-poster or canopy, is covered with lovely old quilts or
afghans. The bath towels are big and thirsty. How I love them. The
cottage is air-conditioned and has a reading room, bedroom with
queen-sized bed, kitchen, bath, and a large TV room. A deck goes
around the outside.

This lovely old inn, built in 1756, sits on five and one-half
acres bordering the Lieutenant River in historic Old Lyme. Of the
six fireplaces in the inn, the one in the parlor is most inviting—a
nice place for a cocktail or just good conversation. A lovely carved
staircase leads from the welcoming center hall to the guest rooms
on the upper floors. Cozy nooks are found everywhere—you can
curl up with a book or just dream.

The dining rooms are charming, and the food is wonderful. Fresh scones served with honey at dinner are delicious. Lunch is interesting and inventive. Try the wild mushroom lasagne, Maryland-style crabcakes, or the Bee and Thistle shepherd's pie. Sunday brunch is really grand. Fresh rainbow trout, chicken hash, three different omelets, baskets of sticky buns—I could eat the menu. And, of course, dinners here are magnificent. Candlelit dining rooms, a good selection of appetizers and soups, and entrees such as spiced breast of chicken, pork medallions, shrimp, scallops, salmon, trout, filet of beef, veal, and rack of lamb. The list goes on and on—and changes three times a year, each time bringing new delights. Leave room for desserts; they are spectacular.

Afternoon tea is served in the parlor from November 1 to May 1 on Monday, Wednesday, and Thursday from 3:30 to 5:00 P.M. The tea service is beautiful; English tea and assorted finger sandwiches and traditional scones are offered. Coffee and aperitifs are also available.

This is a fine inn in a most interesting part of New England. You are in the heart of art, antiques, gourmet restaurants, and endless activities. Plan to spend a few days when you come.

How to get there: Traveling north on I-95, take exit 70 immediately on the east side of the Baldwin Bridge. At the bottom of the ramp, turn left. Take the first right at the traffic light, and turn left at the end of the road. The inn is the third house on your left.

Traveling south on I-95, take exit 70; turn right at the bottom of the ramp. The inn is the third house on your left.

olive Metcalf

Blue Hill Inn
Blue Hill, Maine
04614

Innkeepers: Don and Mary Hartley
Address/Telephone: Route 177; (207) 374–2844
Rooms: 11; all with private bath. No smoking inn.
Rates: In-season, $120 to $160, double occupancy, MAP. Lower rates in off-season. One room specially equipped for handicapped.
Open: All year.
Facilities and activities: Restaurant closed Monday through Thursday in off-season. Wheelchair access to dining room, parlor. Full license. Nearby: cross-country skiing, swimming, boating, golf, tennis, concerts.

Blue Hill Inn is another no smoking inn. This is really nice. The inn was built in 1830 as the home of Varnum Stevens. It has been an inn since 1840. It is located just up the hill from the head of the bay. There are tall beautiful elms all around the property. The garden area is lovely, and during the summer cocktails are so nice out here.

There are two common rooms to relax in. You can feel free to curl up in a chair and read—the fireplaces are so nice up here on a cold night. A variety of accommodations is available. All the rooms are comfortable, and all have their own private bath. You'll find some queen- and king-sized beds and some fireplaces in the rooms. The furnishings are nineteenth-century antiques.

Every evening before dinner guests are invited to the innkeepers' reception, where hors d'oeuvres are served and cocktails are

14

available. The inn guests enjoy meeting each other and making new friends. Dinner is a six-course affair served by candlelight. (Look for the twenty-candle chandelier.) The first course might be lobster bisque or squash-orange soup or warm quail and wheatberries. The entree could be fresh Maine salmon with honey and fennel, swordfish in citrus marinade, or noisettes of lamb with balsamic vinegar. Fresh fish is special here. All this is followed by a grand dessert: poached pears dipped in chocolate, frozen white chocolate mousse, white chocolate gateau with raspberry, among others, and a cup of hot coffee or tea. The inn has a fine wine list to accompany your meal. And in the morning your breakfast is a hearty and filling one.

How to get there: From Belfast, follow Route 3 East through Searsport to Bucksport. Bear right after crossing the Bucksport Bridge. After a few miles, turn right onto Route 15 South to Blue Hill. Turn right on Main Street, then bear right again onto Route 177 West. The inn is the first building on your left at the top of the hill.

Olive Metcalf

Captain Lord Mansion
Kennebunkport, Maine
04046

Innkeepers: Beverly Davis and Rick Lichfield
Address/Telephone: Ocean Avenue (mailing address: P.O. Box 800); (207)
    967–3141 or (800) 522–3141
Rooms: 22, plus 1 suite; all with private bath, 17 with working fireplace.
Rates: $100 to $249, double occupancy, EPB.
Open: All year.
Facilities and activities: Breakfast only full meal served. Afternoon tea. BYOB.
    Gift shop. Nearby: Perkins Cove and Rachel Carson Wildlife Refuge.

This is a truly grand inn. The mansion was built in 1812 and has had such good care that the front bedroom still has the wallpaper that dates from that year. Another room has wallpaper that dates back to 1880. Some of the original Lord furniture is in the house. For example, the handsome dining room table with carved feet and chairs belonged to Nathaniel Lord's grandson, Charles Clark, and is dated 1880. Throughout the inn are portraits of past owners in the Lord family.

A three-story suspended elliptical staircase, a hand-pulled fireplace that works, a gold vault, and double Indian shutters are but a few of the wonderful things to be found in the inn. There are fireplaces, oriental rugs, old pine wide-board floors, and claw-footed tables. It's almost a comfortable museum. Rick knows the history of the house and loves to tell it.

Seventeen of the guest rooms in the inn have working fireplaces. Most of the rooms have padded, deep window seats, a great place to relax and daydream. One of the beds is a four-poster 12 feet high. Rugs and wallpaper, thanks to Beverly's eye for decoration, are well coordinated, thirsty towels are abundant, and extra blankets and pillows help make your stay better than pleasant.

Breakfast is the only meal served in the inn, but what a meal! It is family style. Two long tables in the kitchen are set with Wedgwood blue. There are two stoves in here side by side, a new one and an old coal one about a hundred years old. The breakfast bell is a hundred-year-old music box. You'll start your day with good baked food like rhubarb nut bread, French breakfast puffs, pineapple nut upside-down muffins, oat and jam muffins, or strawberry bread. The recipes are available in the lovely gift shop, so now I can bake some of these yummies at home. In addition you'll have eggs, cereal, and fruit—all this, plus an exquisite mansion, good staff, and great innkeepers.

The Captain's Hideaway is a secluded cottage three houses from the inn. The Garden Room has a private entrance from a brick patio, a working fireplace, a nice sitting area, a queen-sized four-poster bed, cable television, whirlpool tub, and private phone. The Captain's Room, which is really a suite, has a tremendous private bathroom with a two-person whirlpool tub, large shower, and a fireplace. A queen-sized canopy bed, fireplace, and sitting area are in the bedroom. A full gourmet breakfast is served to Captain's Hideaway guests in the lovely parlor, by candlelight.

This is a bring-your-own-bottle inn, and from the scenic cupola on its top to the parlors on the first floor, you will find many great places to enjoy a drink.

How to get there: From I–95 take exit 3 of the Maine Turnpike to Kennebunk. Turn left on Route 35 and drive through Kennebunk to Kennebunkport. Turn left at the traffic light at the Sunoco station. Go over the drawbridge and take first right onto Ocean Avenue. Go ³/₁₀ mile and turn left at the mansion. Park behind the building and take the brick walkway to guest entrance.

Olive Metcalf

The Charlotte Inn
Edgartown, Massachusetts
02539

Innkeepers: Gery and Paula Conover
Address/Telephone: South Summer Street; (508) 627–4751
Rooms: 21, plus 3 suites; all with private bath, some with fireplace.
Rates: In-season, $195 to $295; interim-season, $125 to $205; off-season,
$95 to $175; suites, $195 to $450; double occupancy; continental
breakfast.
Open: All year.
Facilities and activities: In-season, dinner. Off-season, dinner on weekends.
Sunday brunch year round. Reservations a must. Gift shop and gallery.
Nearby: sailing, swimming, fishing, golf, tennis.

The start of your vacation is a forty-five-minute ferry ride to
Martha's Vineyard. It's wise to make early reservations for your
automobile on the ferry. There also are cabs if you prefer not to
take your car.

When you open the door to the inn, you are in the Edgartown
Art Gallery, with interesting artifacts and paintings, both watercolor
and oil. This is a well-appointed gallery featuring such artists as Ray
Ellis, who has a fine talent in both media. The inn also has an
unusual gift shop.

Four of us had dinner in the inn's lovely French restaurant
named L'Etoile. The food was exquisite. Capon breast stuffed with
duxelles, spinach, and sun-dried tomatoes with coriander mayon-

18

naise was the best I have had. I tasted everyone's food—nice occupation I have. Rack of lamb, served rare, with red wine–rosemary sauce, and accompanied by potato and yam gratin was excellent. They also have a special or two, but then everything is so special, the word does not fit. At brunch the cold cucumber soup was served with chives and followed by entrees like blueberry soufflé pancakes with crème fraiche. For breakfast I had a strawberry crepe that I can still remember vividly. Freshly squeezed juices and fruit muffins. . . . Heaven!

The rooms are authentic. There are early American four-poster beds, fireplaces, and the carriage house is sumptuous. The second-floor suite with fireplace I could live in. Paula has a touch with rooms—comfortable furniture, down pillows, down comforters, and all the amenities. As an example, the shower curtains are of eyelet and so pretty. As a finishing touch, there are plenty of large towels.

Across the street is the Garden House, and it is Edgartown at its best. The living room is unique and beautifully furnished, and has a fireplace that is always set for you. The rooms over here are just so handsome. The Coach House is magnificent, furnished with fine old English antiques, a marble fireplace, and a pair of exquisite chaise longues in the bedroom. It is air-conditioned.

Paula, by the way, has green hands, and all about are gardens that just outdo each other.

How to get there: Reservations are a must if you take your car on the ferry from Woods Hole, Massachusetts. Forty-five minutes later you are in Vineyard Haven. After a 15-minute ride, you are in Edgartown, and on South Summer Street is the inn.

olive Metcalf

Wheatleigh
Lenox, Massachusetts
01240

Innkeepers: Susan and Linfield Simon
Address/Telephone: West Hawthorne; (413) 637–0610
Rooms: 17; all with private bath, air conditioning, phone.
Rates: $110 to $435, double occupancy.
Open: All year.
Facilities and activities: Dinner. Grill room, lounge. Swimming, tennis, cross-country skiing.

In the heart of the beautiful Berkshires, overlooking a lake, amid lawns and gardens on twenty-two self-contained acres stands the estate of Wheatleigh, former home of the Countess de Heredia. The centerpiece of this property is an elegant private palace fashioned after an Italian palazzo. The cream-colored manse re-creates the architecture of sixteenth-century Florence. You must read the brochure of Wheatleigh, for it says it all so well.

Patios, pergolas, porticos, and terraces surround this lovely old mansion. The carvings over the fireplaces, cupids entwined in garlands, are exquisite. In charming contrast, the inn also has the largest collection of contemporary ceramics in the New England area. There are many lovely porcelain pieces on the walls. In the dining room are tile paintings weighing over 500 pounds. They are Doultons from 1830; this was before it became Royal Doulton. They are just beautiful.

The grill room provides an a la carte menu of light fare prepared to the same high standards of the dining room. Its casual ambience features an elegant black and white color scheme—the plates are beautiful.

There is a service bar in a lovely lounge, and boy, you sure can relax in the furniture in here. It has a wonderful fireplace, and the views from here are glorious. And imagine a great hall with a grand staircase right out of a castle in Europe. There are also exquisite stained-glass windows in pale pastels, plus gorgeous, comfortable furniture. From the great hall you can hear the tinkle of the fountain out in the garden.

The rooms are smashing with lots of white dotted swiss and eyelet material for the canopy beds. Do you long for your own balcony overlooking a lovely lake? No problem. Reserve one here.

At the entrance to the dining room, the homemade desserts are beautifully displayed along with French champagne in six sizes from a jeroboam to a small bottle for one. This is very nice indeed. I chose grilled quail on young lettuce leaves and raspberries for a dinner appetizer; it was superb. Tartare of fresh tuna was so beautifully presented, just like a Japanese picture, and delicious. I also had chilled fresh pea soup with curry and sorrel, followed by monkfish coated with pistachios, sautéed, with red wine sauce. Homemade sorbets are very good, but then, so is everything here.

How to get there: From Stockbridge at the Red Lion Inn where Route 7 turns right, go straight on Prospect Hill Road, bearing left. Go past the Stockbridge Bowl and up a hill to Wheatleigh.

From the Massachusetts Turnpike, take exit 2, and follow signs to Lenox. In the center of Lenox, take Route 183, pass the main gate of Tanglewood, and then take the first left on West Hawthorne. Go 1 mile to Wheatleigh.

E: *Susan's description of the inn is "elegance without arrogance," and Lin's is "the ultimate urban amenity." Mine is "a perfect country inn."*

olive Metcalf

The Williamsville Inn
West Stockbridge, Massachusetts
01266

Innkeepers: Gail and Kathleen Ryan
Address/Telephone: Route 41; (413) 274–6118
Rooms: 14, plus 1 suite; all with private bath.
Rates: $90 to $165, double occupancy, EPB.
Open: All year.
Facilities and activities: Dinner. Tavern, swimming pool, clay tennis court.
   Nearby: hiking, biking, skiing, golf, Tanglewood, Shaker Village.

   Built in 1797 as a farmhouse, this inn is the second oldest house in the hamlet of Williamsville. It is a charmer, now run by a mother-daughter duo.

   You will find fireplaces all over the inn—so important in this part of the world where there is so much winter. The fireplaces in the dining rooms are raised hearth and especially warming. There also are fireplaces in two bedrooms, the sitting rooms, and the tavern.

   The garden room is a lovely sitting room with a puzzle going most of the time, books, television, and a music center with stereo and tapes. The comfortable chairs and couches make this such a cozy room. Tom Ball's Tavern, which is a delight, has nice stencils on the walls.

   The guest rooms are so attractively styled and furnished with a sense for old-fashioned grace and comfort. The suite boasts a lovely four-poster canopy bed.

Three of the four candlelit dining rooms have fireplaces. In all four, the service is unhurried and the food outstanding. The menu changes four times a year, so you may not find what I had, but I am sure your choices will be delicious. A vegetable terrine appetizer is three layers of vegetable pâtés served chilled over a fresh tomato and ginger coulis. Another appetizer is chèvre cheese ravioli served with shiitake mushrooms and cream sauce. Entrees include chicken, pasta, roast duck, and rack of lamb—all so good. A nice selection of French and California wines will add to your enjoyment of your meal.

Desserts, of course, are freshly made. Lemon angel pie is so good, and nice liqueur parfaits are always in order. Eating my way through New England is so much fun.

So much to do in this area, from skiing, theater, and antiques, to just loafing at this lovely inn.

How to get there: Take the Massachusetts Turnpike to exit 1, which puts you on Route 41. Turn left toward Great Barrington. The inn is 4 miles south of the turnpike on your right. From the New York Thruway, follow directions for Berkshires Spur, exit 33. Go south on Route 22 to Route 102, east on Route 102 to Route 41, south on Route 41 toward Great Barrington.

E: *The glass-enclosed dining room is lovely all year, and there is so much to see on the beautiful grounds.*

Lambert's Cove
Country Inn
West Tisbury, Massachusetts
02568

Innkeepers: Ron and Kay Nelson

Address/Telephone: Lambert's Cove Road (mailing address: Box 422, RFD, Vineyard Haven, MA 02568); (508) 693–2298

Rooms: 15; all with private bath.

Rates: In-season, $105 to $130; off-season, $65 to $95; double occupancy; continental breakfast. 7-day stay in summer preferred, but 3-day minimum possible.

Open: All year.

Facilities and activities: Dinner daily in-season, Thursday through Sunday off-season. Sunday brunch. BYOB, tennis court. Nearby: swimming, cross-country skiing, ice skating.

At the end of a tree-shaded country road you will find this gem of an inn. It provides quiet and seclusion amid a country setting of tall pines, vine-covered stone walls, spacious lawns, gardens, and an apple orchard.

It's for romantic folks who seek a place where both mind and body can be restored far from the noise and crowds of the rest of the world. The original house was built in 1790. Over the years it was enlarged, and a carriage house and barn were added. Today they have been beautifully renovated for guest use; half of the rooms are here.

Each room has distinctive charm. Many open onto individual decks. One of the rooms in the carriage house has a greenhouse sitting room at one end. Nice to have your cocktails in here and look up at the stars. All of the rooms in the inn are done with imagination. The mattresses are new, and there are plenty of pillows and lush color-coordinated towels. All baths are private.

When you enter the inn, you are in an elegant center hall done in soft beige. Up a magnificent staircase and you are in a restful sitting area with wicker furniture and bookcases full of books. There also is a delightful library, a huge room with walls lined with volumes of books, and furnished with tables for games and really comfortable furniture. On a cold day a fire in the fireplace here feels good.

A big deck opens from the library and dining room and looks out on an apple orchard. There are five decks in all at this inn. The English garden is lovely, and flowers are everywhere you look.

The food here is glorious. Cioppino is one of the dishes served. This Italian seafood stew is prepared with salmon, scallops, scrod, swordfish, clams, and mussels. The omelettes are different, such as fresh salmon and tomato or asparagus, or tomato with smoked mozzarella. Maybe you'd like to come for dinner. Roast duckling is glazed with honey and Grand Marnier. Breast of chicken Francis comes with pine nuts and lemon butter. All the desserts are made right here. The one I had on my last visit was white and chocolate mousse with fresh raspberries. It was hard to make a choice, because they also serve Key lime pie and strawberries Romanoff. No matter what you order, it will be good.

This is real country—so peaceful. Walk twenty minutes to the Lambert's Cove beach, or just walk anywhere. It's a beautiful part of the world, and it would be a wonderful spot for a wedding. There is tennis, golf, shopping, and fishing nearby.

How to get there: Take the ferry to Martha's Vineyard from Cape Cod. After driving off the ferry, take a left, then a right at the next stop-sign intersection. Stay on this road for 1½ miles to Lambert's Cove Road, on your right. Three miles from this point look for the inn's sign, on the left.

olive Metcalf

The Inn at
Crotched Mountain
Francestown, New Hampshire
03043

Innkeepers: John and Rose Perry
Address/Telephone: Mountain Road; (603) 588–6840
Rooms: 13; 8 with private bath, 4 with fireplace.
Rates: $50 to $60, per person, double occupancy, MAP.
Open: All year except first three weeks in November, weekdays in winter, and after ski season until Mother's Day.
Facilities and activities: Wheelchair access to inn and dining rooms. Bar, tennis, swimming pool, cross-country skiing. Nearby: golf, fishing, summer theater.

This 150-year-old Colonial house is located on the northern side of Crotched Mountain. There is a 40-mile view of the Piscataquog Valley, complete with spacious skies. Both innkeepers have gone to school to learn their trade, and what a charming house to practice it in. They are both pretty special themselves. Rose is from Singapore, and John is a Yankee.

Come and stay, there are many things to do. There are three golf courses in the nearby valley, fishing is great, and there is a wading pool for the young, as well as a 30-by-60-foot pool for real swimmers. Two areas provide skiing, one at the front door, and another down the road. Two clay tennis courts eliminate that tiresome waiting for a playing area. And come evening there are two summer theaters, one at Peterborough and another in Milford.

There are two English cockers who live here, Winslow and Anan. There are numerous streams, ponds, and lakes for fishing and mountains for hiking. Golf is nearby. Come and enjoy this wonderful countryside with Winslow and Anan. They would love to have you.

How to get there: Take 101A from Nashua to Milford, Route 13 to New Boston, and Route 136 to Francestown. Take Route 47 2¹/₂ miles, then turn left onto Mountain Road. The inn is 1 mile up the road.

E: *Any house that has nine fireplaces needs a wood lot and a man with a chain saw. Four of the bedrooms here have a fireplace, so remember to request one when you reserve.*

Snowvillage Inn
Snowville, New Hampshire
03849

Innkeepers: Frank, Peter, and Trudy Cutrone
Address/Telephone: P.O. Box 176; (603) 447–2818 or (800) 447–4345
Rooms: 18; all with private bath, 4 with fireplace.
Rates: $65 to $85, per person, double occupancy, MAP. $10 more during
fall and Christmas. $45 to $65, per person, EPB; $10 less from May 1
to June 18 and November 1 to December 20. Special package rates
available.
Open: All year except April.
Facilities and activities: Bar, lounge, sauna, cross-country skiing, tennis,
nature trails. Nearby: swimming, fishing, canoeing, hiking, downhill
skiing.

The view from the inn is breathtaking. Mount Washington
and the whole Presidential Range, plus the rest of the White Mountains, greet your eyes everywhere you look. In summer at the top
of Foss Mountain, right at the inn, you can eat your fill of wild
blueberries.

When I arrived at the inn this time, my car died in the driveway. The Cutrones were so helpful and made me feel right at home
while finding someone to work on the car. We found out in the
morning how sick my car was . . . oh, dear. Remember, these
innkeepers would be just as welcoming and helpful to you, too.

The guest rooms are comfortable and spacious, with tons of

towels in luscious colors. Each room is named after a favorite author of the innkeepers. The living room, with its huge fireplace and nice couches all around, makes this an inn for rest and relaxation. There are a service bar and a lounge and plants and books everywhere. A huge porch surrounds the inn. I could sit here all day and enjoy the incredible view.

The cooking has an Austrian flavor. One entree is served each evening. You may find pork tenderloin with sauerkraut, curried chicken with peaches, beef tenderloin, chicken or veal piccata, and shrimp scampi, just to name a few. All breads and desserts are made here, and the soups also are homemade. This does make a difference. Cookies, made right here, are placed in your room in a cookie basket as a welcome to the inn.

Nice animals are here. The cats are Skunk, Elvira, and Virginia. Boris and Natasha, the inn dogs, are Samoyeds. Igor is a gorilla (he's stuffed) who holds the menu outside the restaurant.

How to get there: Out of Conway on Route 153, go 5 miles to Crystal Lake. Turn left, follow sign to Snowville, go about 1¹/₂ miles, turn right at the inn's sign, and go up the hill ³/₄ mile to the inn.

The Chesterfield Inn
West Chesterfield, New Hampshire
03466

Innkeepers: Judy and Phil Hueber

Address/Telephone: Route 9; (603) 256–3211, (800) 365–5515

Rooms: 11, plus 2 suites; all with private bath, air conditioning, refrigerator, phone, and 8 with fireplace, 1 with wheelchair access. Pets welcome.

Rates: $99 to $159, double occupancy, EPB.

Open: All year.

Facilities and activities: Dinner Tuesday through Saturday. Wheelchair access to dining room. Full license. Ice skating. Nearby: fishing, boating, skiing, swimming.

The inn was a tavern from 1798 to 1811, and then it became a farm. In 1984 the inn opened after extensive renovations by architect Rod Williams of The Inn at Sawmill Farm, and he is the best around. Exposed beams, many of them part of the original structure, and walls paneled with boards that came from an old barn make for a warm and friendly atmosphere.

The guest rooms are spacious. Some rooms have balconies or garden patios, others have a fireplace, and all are scrumptious. They are done in soft shades of blues, greens, and pinks. They are air-conditioned and have clock radios and telephones (all different), including one in the bathroom. Good fluffy towels and an assortment of toiletries are here. To top it all off, each room has a refrigerator with juice, bottled spring water, beers, and wine. I found a welcoming split of champagne in mine. Oh my.

The foyer has a large fireplace holding a bright red wood stove, and nice couches. It's a good place for cocktails. The entrance to the dining room is through the kitchen. It was designed this way as a tribute to the chef, Carl Warner. It shows he is proud of his kitchen and his staff. He is a four-star chef, and when you dine you will believe it. The menu changes often, and many unusual dishes are served. Try the scallop kabob with basil and lime sauce. Fettucine with four cheeses is unbelievable. So are grilled vegetables with aioli. A different soup is featured every day. Duck is served with homemade apricot chutney; coho salmon comes with garlic, ginger, and tomatoes; and lamb tenderloin is stuffed with leeks and Vermont goat cheese. The chef always has a fish of the day. Desserts are wonderful. Come and try this food. There are three dining rooms to choose from, all with wonderful views.

The inn's grounds are full of perennial, herb, and vegetable gardens. The beautiful Connecticut River is a short walk from the inn, so bring along your canoe or fishing pole. Lake Spofford has boats for rent. Pisgah Park has hiking trails and two spring-fed ponds for swimming. In winter skiing is close at hand, and the inn's pond is lighted for night skating under the stars. (Watch for Ellie, the inn cat.) And all year, you'll find good antiques shops and arts and crafts shops.

How to get there: Take exit 3 off I–91. Take Route 9 east, going over the border from Vermont to New Hampshire. The inn is in 2 miles on your left.

Olive Metcalf

Tulip Tree Inn
Chittenden, Vermont
05737

Innkeepers: Ed and Rosemary McDowell
Address/Telephone: Chittenden Dam Road; (802) 483–6213
Rooms: 8; all with private bath, 5 with Jacuzzi.
Rates: $144 to $200, double occupancy, MAP.
Open: All year except April and most of May.
Facilities and activities: Full license. Fishing. Nearby: swimming, hiking, golf,
  tennis, canoeing, bicycling, skiing.

In 1989 this inn was selected as one of the top ten country inns in the nation. You can't beat that! You arrive and a lovely front porch with wicker chairs beckons you at once. Beautiful woods surround you. You hear a brook babbling and a feeling of sheer peace comes over you. Guinness, the old English sheepdog, or Hoover, the cat, may greet you. Inside you find a nice living room with a fireplace, a small bar and library, a den with a fireplace, and a great assortment of chairs, love seats, and couches throughout.

The rooms are the sort you never want to leave. Puffy comforters on the beds are inviting to curl up under, and the Jacuzzi tubs in five of the rooms feel so great after a long day. There are nice antiques, including a huge pine bed with a pineapple on top.

Dining is very special here at the inn. Pretty, too, with yellow and white napery in the summer and red, white, and blue in the winter. Rosemary's breakfasts are full Vermont style. That means you'll find cold cereals; yogurt; juices; sweet breads; and apple, cheese, or blueberry pancakes or French toast, all with pure maple syrup.

If you think that's good, come back at dinnertime and Rosemary really shines. There are homemade breads and soups like zucchini and curried carrot. Salads are interesting, especially with Rosemary's dressings. A sorbet is brought to you to cleanse your palate, and then it might be medallions of pork with apricot-orange sauce or chicken with curry sauce or filet of beef with béarnaise. Oh my, and her desserts. . . . Well, just save some room, because they are so good.

The inn is only a mile from the Chittenden Reservoir, where the fishing and swimming are superb. East Brook runs right by the house. Trout anyone?

How to get there: From Rutland, drive north on Route 7. Just outside Chittenden, you will see a red-brick power station on the left. Just beyond it is a Y in the road with a red country store in the middle. Keep right of the store and follow the road approximately 6 miles. Just past the fire station, go straight ahead ½ mile to the inn, which will be on your left.

Blueberry Hill
Goshen, Vermont
05733

Innkeeper: Tony Clark
Address/Telephone: Blueberry Hill, R.D. 3; (802) 247–6735, (802) 247–6535,
(800) 448–0707
Rooms: 12; all with private bath. One room specially equipped for handi-
capped. No smoking inn.
Rates: In summer, $76 to $100 per person; in winter, $105 per person; dou-
ble occupancy, MAP.
Open: All year.
Facilities and activities: Packed lunch available, BYOB. Sauna. Cross-country
skiing, swimming, fishing.

The inn is a cross-country skier's dream come true. It is nestled
at the foot of Romance Mountain in the Green Mountain National
Forest and is surrounded by good clean air and well-groomed
snowy trails. From the inn brochure I quote: "The Blueberry Hill
Ski Touring Center, across from the inn, devotes itself to cross-
country skiers of all ages and abilities. Inside the fully equipped Ski
Center are retail and rental departments, a waxing area, repair
shop, and an expert staff to see that you are skiing better with less
effort. Upstairs you can relax, make friends, and share the day's
events in our lounge with its large windows, comfortable seating,
and old wood stove. Surrounding the Ski Center are 75 kilometers
of both challenging and moderate terrain. A loop around Hogback,

a race to Silver Lake, or just making tracks in a snow world all your own . . . the activities never cease—from seminars, waxing clinics, night and guided tours, to the 60-kilometer American Ski Marathon."

In the summer the ski trails are used for hiking, walking, or running. There are a pond for swimming and streams and lakes for fishing.

The inn is a restored 1813 farmhouse. Dinner is served family style in a lovely, candlelit dining room. There are four courses served in an unhurried, comfortable way. While I was here dinner included such delicious things as cold cantaloupe soup, scallion bread, broiled lamb chops with mint butter, stir-fried asparagus, lemon meringue tarts, and homemade ice creams. Tony's son made strawberry ice cream, and it was so good. The greenhouse just off the kitchen is full of glorious plants. Three of the guest rooms and a new wing are out here, just beyond the greenhouse.

Their upside-down gardens hanging from the ceiling beams are a colorful and imaginative use of straw flowers, and the brick patio overlooking Dutton Brook is so restful and nice. There are plenty of books to read, and the rooms are comfortable with many antiques, quilts, and hot water bottles on the backs of the doors. Honest, they are there.

How to get there: From Rutland take Route 7 north to Brandon, then Route 73 east for 6 miles. Turn left at the inn's sign, and follow the signs up the mountain on a dirt road to the inn.

Olive Metcalf

Rabbit Hill Inn
Lower Waterford, Vermont
05848

Innkeepers: John and Maureen Magee
Address/Telephone: Route 18, Box 55; (802) 748–5168 or (800) 76BUNNY
Rooms: 16, plus 4 suites; all with private bath, radio, and cassette player; 6
    specially equipped for handicapped. No smoking inn.
Rates: $149 to $219, double occupancy, MAP. EPB rates available.
Open: All year except April and first two weeks in November.
Facilities and activities: Bar, library, wheelchair access to dining rooms, snow
    shoeing, tobaggoning, cross-country skiing, trout fishing, lawn games.

In 1834 Rabbit Hill became an inn. It has had a few owners
over the years; however, this pair has really done justice to this
lovely old inn.

Each of the inn's rooms is done according to a theme. Some
are the Doll Chamber, the Toy Chamber, and Carolyn's Room,
which has a blue-and-white canopy bed. One has a cranky rabbit
sitting on a bed. I have never seen so many stuffed rabbits, dolls,
and such, all so tastefully arranged. I was in Victoria's Chamber,
which has a king-sized bed and wonderful Victorian touches. The
Magees have come up with a beauty of an idea. Each room has a
cassette player and a tape that explains what you would have seen
from your window more than a century ago. The hats that Maureen has had made are worth the trip alone. A diary is in each room
for people to write in during their stay. They are fun to read. The

suites are in the tavern building. One of the six first-floor rooms equipped for the handicapped has wheelchair access, a special bathroom, and features designed for blind or deaf guests.

The porch on the second floor faces the Presidential Range. It's a special place to just sit and rock with Jake, the inn dog, or Zeke, the cat.

The Snooty Fox Pub, modeled after eighteenth-century Irish pubs, has an old crane in the fireplace for doing hearth cooking. The doors of the two intimate dining rooms remain closed until six o'clock. They are then opened to reveal highly polished 1850s Windsor chairs and pine tables set with antique silver and lit by candlelight. It takes two hours to dine here; it is all done right. The menu changes seasonally, and no processed foods are used in any of the meals. Try the pork and venison pâté or the smoked salmon and seafood sausage to start. Then sample the Vermont turkey and okra chili, the grilled twelve-spice duck breast, rack of lamb, swordfish, vegetarian plate, or beef tenderloin. Be sure to savor the homemade sauces, mustards, and salsas prepared with the vegetables, herbs, and edible flowers from the inn's garden. Save room for dessert. Whiskey toddy cake sounds divine. So does white chocolate tart. These are only a sampling of what you might find at this AAA four-diamond restaurant.

The inn is glorious. So is the whole area. You will not be disappointed with this one.

How to get there: Take Route 2 east from St. Johnsbury and turn right onto Route 18. Or coming from Route 5, take Route 135 east to Lower Waterford.

E: *In the evening while you're dining, your bed is turned down, your radio is turned on to soft music, your candle is lit, and a fabric heart is placed on your pillow. You are invited to use it as your do-not-disturb sign and then to take it home with you.*

Olive Metcalf

Wilburton Inn
Manchester Village, Vermont
05254

Innkeeper: Stanley Holton; owners, Georgette and Albert Levis
Address/Telephone: River Road (mailing address: P.O. Box 458); (802)
    362–2500 or (800) 648–4944
Rooms: 10 in main house, 24 in other 5 houses; all with private bath.
Rates: $85 to $155, double occupancy, MAP (includes full breakfast mid-
    May through October and holidays).
Open: All year.
Facilities and activities: Breakfast, dinner. Tennis, heated pool. Nearby: skiing,
    shopping, art gallery, theater, music festivals, swimming, canoeing,
    trout fishing, golf.

As you start up the winding driveway that surrounds the
estate you know you have found a romantic treasure. This inn was
built in 1902 for a friend of Robert Todd Lincoln. In 1906 James
Wilbur purchased the estate and lived here until his death in 1929.
Later, during World War II, it was a boarding school for daughters
of European diplomats. In 1946 the estate became a very elegant
inn, and in 1987 Georgette and Albert became the new owners.
The inn is set on a twenty-acre knoll that rises above the lush Bat-
tenkill River Valley.

The living room is huge with nice, comfortable couches and
chairs conducive to private conversation, a cocktail, or whatever
you have in mind. A huge table for serving tea, and a wonderful

fireplace with a wood-burning stove will keep you in the room to enjoy its wondrous view. A library and a porch where breakfast is served are also on the ground floor, along with the very well-appointed dining rooms.

The food here is glorious. For starters I was able to try the vegetarian ravioli with a tomato-sage cream sauce. Another night the gravlax was ambrosia, as were the rack of lamb and the salmon. Salads are excellent, and the desserts—well, you'd better come up here and see for yourself. Breakfast? Usually I could turn it down, but not when it's this grand. Fresh blueberry muffins and, of course, much, much more. The menus change twice yearly and specials abound. The pink and white napery add to the pretty ambience.

Accommodations in the main inn are luxurious. Most beds are queen- or king-sized with lovely bedspreads. Wonderful large windows provide a view of the surrounding mountains. Five other houses on the estate are just as nicely appointed.

After a day of whatever you do, return to the inn for tea or cocktails in the living room by the fireplace. This is a grand inn watched over by Chauncy, the inn's beautiful English setter.

How to get there: From the blinking light in Manchester, go 1½ miles south on Route 7A to River Road. Go left for 1 mile—the driveway is on the left.

The Four Chimneys
Old Bennington, Vermont
05201

Innkeepers: Alex Koks and Andra Erickson
Address/Telephone: 21 West Road; (802) 447–3500
Rooms: 12; all with private bath; some with Jacuzzi or fireplace; 2 specially
   equipped for handicapped.
Rates: $100 to $175, double occupancy, continental breakfast.
Open: All year.
Facilities and activities: Lunch, dinner, bar and lounge. Full license.
   Wheelchair access to dining room. Nearby: facilities at Mount Anthony
   Country Club.

The inn is a magnificent Georgian Revival built in 1912. As
you approach it, you can see its spectacular four chimneys. The
grounds surrounding the inn are glorious.

Master chef Alex Koks was the former owner of the Village
Auberge, and his reputation follows him. Educated at the presti-
gious Hotel Management School in the Hague, Netherlands, Alex
brings a distinct European touch to the inn. His cooking is basically
French. Roast stuffed quail, a turnover with hearty cheese, and a
galantine of goose liver mousse are just a few starters. These are followed by good soups and salads. There are entrees like sautéed
monkfish and grilled shrimp, supreme of Cornish hen Normande
flambée au calvados, rack of lamb, and breast of duck with cherries.
Save room for desserts like crème caramel (my husband's favorite),

fresh sorbet, and ice creams. Or you can just enjoy fresh fruit in season. All this superb food is served on tables covered with pink and white napery in a lovely dining room with three fireplaces. In summer the porch overlooking the gardens is ambrosia.

There are twelve guest rooms, and they are beauties. They have queen- or king-sized beds, quilts, and color-coordinated sheets and towels. The inn and restaurant together are a wonderful setting for weddings or anniversary celebrations.

How to get there: From Boston take I–90 to Lee. Go up Route 7 to the center of Bennington, and then take Route 9 west to the inn. From Lee, take Route 20, which becomes Route 7.

E: *Cut-glass lamps in the bedrooms are pretty and so romantic.*

The Inn at Weathersfield
Weathersfield, Vermont
05151

Innkeepers: Mary Louise and Ron Thorburn
Address/Telephone: Route 106, Box 165; (802) 263–9217 or (800) 477–4828;
FAX (802) 263–9219
Rooms: 9, plus 3 suites; all with private bath, 8 with fireplace.
Rates: $87.50 per person, double occupancy, MAP plus afternoon tea.
Open: All year.
Facilities and activities: Tavern, recreation room with aerobics equipment,
tennis, sauna, pool table, TV and VCR with movies, large library. Out-
side amphitheatre, gardens and recreation area suitable for weddings
or small conference groups, horse box stalls for rent, horse-drawn
sleigh and carriage rides.

This beautiful old inn was built circa 1795 and has a wonderful
history. Prior to the Civil War, it was an important stop on the
Underground Railroad, sheltering slaves en route to Canada. The
inn is set well back from the road on twenty-one acres of property.
Your rest is assured.

Everything that Mary Louise and Ron do to improve this lovely inn is done with class and lots of care. In the reconstructed barn
attached to the inn are five beamed-ceiling rooms with sensational
old bathtubs. These are real honest-to-goodness Victorian bathrooms. There are twelve fireplaces in the inn, and each of these
rooms has one. All the rooms are beautiful with fresh flowers, fresh
fruit, canopy beds, and feather pillows.

Over the years Ron has built an extensive and well-balanced wine cellar. The tavern is modeled after eighteenth-century Massachusetts taverns. The non-smoking greenhouse dining room is a handsome complement to the other rooms. Stencils copied from those used in the early 1800s decorate many of the rooms, as do many of Mary Louise's beautiful antique quilts.

Excellent food is served here. Game consomme with chantarelle and leek and roasted quail with Tokay grapes and chèvre might begin your meal. Six or more entrees like rack of Vermont lamb or their own farm-raised pheasant with roasted corn, red peppers, and spring onion are offered each night. The menu changes daily, taking advantage of what is in season. They grow their own herbs in a special space in the garden. Be sure to save room for desserts, as they are glorious. Mary Louise and her culinary staff are an extraordinary chefing team.

Daughter Heather and husband, Jack, are potters. Their fine work is used in the inn and is sold in the inn's gift shop.

There is a horse named Dick, who will take you on a winter sleigh ride or a summer ride on old country roads in an 1890 restored carriage. All of this and a beautiful country inn and, of course, a nice inn dog named Bonnie Lassie.

How to get there: Take I–91 North to exit 7 (Springfield, VT). Take Route 11 to Springfield, and then take Route 106 in town to the inn on your left, set well back from the road.

◆

E: *A wassail cup is served from a cauldron in the keeping room fireplace. High tea, served each afternoon, is special.*

Mid-Atlantic and Chesapeake Region

by Brenda Boelts Chapin

Sweet Caesuras in the Mid-Atlantic.

Love often happens overnight—what better way to remember that coinage than retiring to an inn for the night?

From the Blue Ridge Mountains to the Adirondacks, Mid-Atlantic inns represent a kaleidoscope of fine tastes, desirable comforts, and endearing experiences. Whether you choose a Victorian village inn along the ocean, sequester yourselves away in a lodge amidst the Pennsylvania woods, or select a historic mansion in the Finger Lakes countryside, these country inns have one element in common: They naturally kindle romance. They are haven to honeymooners of all ages, to those sharing anniversaries, and for holiday and birthday celebrations.

Reviewing the love stories told me during my travels, I believe the surprise occasions are among my favorites: taking him or her for an affectionate interlude that has been secretly planned. Even the day's pre-arrival events conspire to intensify the mystery-inn destination and make an impression that's never forgotten. I've also met those who would sooner travel without a map than without their velvet-boxed champagne glasses and their preferred beverage for a lovesome toast before the crackling fire or in the summer garden.

Seeking out a pleasure-bound setting results in the most rewarding experiences. In some European countries taking time away for retreats from work is referred to as "health-leave." Not counted as vacation, it is considered as necessary for a balanced existence as breathing the air. Perhaps Americans should have "love-leave," for I believe it would benefit the employer tenfold and nourish the lovers for a lifetime.

Mid-Atlantic and Chesapeake Region

Numbers on map refers to towns numbered below.

olive Metcalf

The Corner Cupboard Inn
Rehoboth Beach, Delaware
19971

Innkeeper: Elizabeth G. Hooper
Address/Telephone: 50 Park Avenue; (302) 227–8553
Rooms: 18; all with private bath, some with air conditioning. Pets allowed, charge.
Rates: Memorial Day weekend to mid-September: $140 to $225, double occupancy, MAP. Rest of year: $70 to $110, double occupancy, EPB.
Open: All year.
Facilities and activities: Reservations for breakfast and dinner a must. Dinner price range: from $12.50. BYOB. Nearby: beach, tennis, bicycling, golf, historic town of Lewes (15 minutes away).

The summer lighting filters through the tall, old shade trees onto the inn's maze of patios where we are sitting together. It's not the least bit formal, and at the moment we are deliciously exhausted after a long jog on the beach.

Around dinnertime our waiter chills and opens a fine wine, the select vintage we brought in a discreet brown bag. The ceiling fans turn. Dinner begins: crab imperial with just a touch of green pepper, or beautifully fried soft-shell crab, homemade bread, and more. After dinner, we go for a moonlit stroll hand in hand on the beach.

This is a year-round inn in a residential neighborhood. You find comfortable parlors and sun porches. We preferred the former attic room with an appealing private patio nestled in the treetops. "Eastwind" is a small cottage with a private brick patio. Each room is simple and different. Two queen-sized beds are available.

The rooms change according to the season. During summer, the inn is floored with grass mats; in the living room these are exchanged for oriental carpets in winter.

Elizabeth's decorating is a tasteful, homey blend of family heirloom and eclectic furnishings. An antique corner cupboard sits in the living room. A good selection of magazines and newspapers lines the parlor tables.

In the winter, couples return from a brisk walk on the beach, nestle around the fireplace, sip brandies, and share intimacies. Here, the cares of the world are washed away and cares for each other reconfirmed.

How to get there: From Route 1, exit into Rehoboth, cross canal bridge, take first left onto Columbia Avenue, and continue to Second Street, turn right. Go 1 block to Park and turn left; inn is located in the middle of Park.

ollve metcalf

Celie's Waterfront
Bed & Breakfast
Baltimore, Maryland
21231

Innkeeper: Celie Ives
Address/Telephone: 1714 Thames Street; (410) 522–2323
Rooms: 7, including 2 suites; all with private bath, air conditioning, small
  refrigerator, and telephone, 2 with balcony, suites with fireplace and
  whirlpool bath. Wheelchair access. No smoking inn.
Rates: $85 to $140, double occupancy, continental breakfast.
Open: All year.
Facilities and activities: Small conference room, off-street parking, boat dock-
  ing. Nearby: restaurants, Harborplace, museums, theater, shopping;
  Fort McHenry, historic Federal Hill, Maryland Science Center, USS
  Constellation, and Johns Hopkins Hospital.

Ringing the bell and peering down a long hallway, I wondered
if we had the right place. Quickly, a response came, and in we
walked; the light at the end of the shadowed hallway opened onto
a sunny brick patio. We turned into the guest parlor where we met
Celie, who doesn't look like her great-great-great-grandmother,
whose portrait in oil hangs above the fireplace.

Celie's bed and breakfast inn within the historic Fell's Point
District is beautifully designed in a warm contemporary style. Most
couples can barely keep up with her as she bounds up the stairs to
her rooftop deck view of Baltimore.

The night before we arrived, everyone had gathered here to watch the July Fourth fireworks over the harbor. You might consider planning in advance for New Year's Eve, when Baltimore puts on the annual winter fireworks display. It's also lovely at twilight, when just the two of you can watch the boats travel through the Baltimore harbor, and then again after dark, when the stars are out and you're sharing a split of champagne at midnight.

You might sleep in because Celie provides coffee makers and freshly ground coffees in every room. You can get up whenever you wish. You'll find thick terry-cloth robes in the closet, and if you were out late the night before at the theater, dancing, or at a jazz club, you can be indulgent for a change.

Each room has merits, but I recommend a spacious suite for two with fireplace and water view for an anniversary or any significant occasion.

You enter the small guest parlor to reach the breakfast room, where freshly baked breads are arrayed along the pine hutch. You might find apricot, cinnamon raisin, peach, or oat bran bread, which you slice thickly and toast, then spread with a choice of jams. You can have breakfast on the patio, in the dining room around a central table with other guests, or carry everything back upstairs to your lover.

Planning ahead has a way of enhancing romance. First book the room and a show. Select a pair of gift-wrapped, velvet-cased champagne glasses (these will travel well now and forever), a fine champagne, and a taste of chocolate—they make a lovely surprise before the fireplace. Then let the magic happen.

How to get there: From Pratt Street and downtown Harbor Place proceed east, turn right on President Street, turn left on Fleet Street, turn right on Anne Street, turn right on Thames Street. Inn is in middle of block on right, opposite the harbor.

olive Metcalf

The Inn at Buckeystown
Buckeystown, Maryland
21717

Innkeepers: Chase Barnett, Betty Farley, Rebecca Shipman-Smith; Dan Pelz, innkeeper/chef

Address/Telephone: Main Street (General Delivery, Buckeystown); (301) 874–5755

Rooms: 7, plus 2 cottages, 1 suite; all with private bath, 2 with fireplace. No smoking inn.

Rates: $209 to $230 per couple weekend, MAP; $167 to $188 per couple midweek, MAP; cottage $230. Checks preferred. Two-night minimum some weekends. Corporate rates.

Open: All year.

Facilities and activities: Dinner, public invited by reservation: $30 weeknights, $36 weekends. Two acres of land with pre–Civil War graveyard. Nearby: shops, antiquing, canoeing, bicycling, Antietam Battlefield, Harper's Ferry.

It's the young lovers who you'd expect to come, and certainly mid-aged ones, but who would have imagined one of Dan's favorites—the 80-year-old honeymooners. "They were wonderful," he said, "and as lovers will, they requested St. John's Cottage."

Enter an old-fashioned setting that emits aromatic scents and tender feelings from the moment you step inside. Dan Pelz's general good-naturedness influences the romantic ambience while his cuisine influences the palate.

Here's the weekly scenario: Saturday, expect to find a savory steak or beef dish; Monday, either pork or poultry is served; Tuesday means lamb or veal; Wednesday, it's a perfectly baked duck prepared in German style; Thursday is for beef as in London broil; and Friday, it's fresh fish. Each night of the week a multicourse dinner appears upon antique china around candlelit oak tables. Dinner is a single entree usually served at one shared seating, and it's a bundle of fun.

We brought two sweethearts with us—my parents—and joined everyone for an evening that became a memorable occasion with stories shared of how the couples had met. Romance can be very funny with the right crowd. Or you may request a private table for two.

On Sunday, imagine driving out to the country from Washington, D.C., or Baltimore, spending the day antiquing, and then coming here for an early dinner of stuffed chicken. It reminds me of going to Grandma's, and it's a nice way to surprise your lover.

Buckeystown is a nationally registered historic village on the Monocacy River. In the spring pink and purple azaleas, lilacs, and forsythia accent the lawn. The eighteen-room inn is an Italianate Victorian with two parlors and a wraparound front porch for cuddling; the woodwork is chestnut and oak, and the floors are heart-of-pine. Sitting on a bureau in your room is Dan and Chase's guide, "'Inn' Joying." It directs you to the best in Civil War sites, antiquing, golf, walking and cycling tours, orchards, and restaurants.

The inn is filled with collections that reflect Dan and Chase's appreciation for art. The parlors are softly lit with Art Nouveau and Tiffany lamps.

The attractive rooms are furnished with antiques, and the antique beds have been rebuilt to accept larger mattresses. You find everything from cozy pillows, dolls, and finely carved jade to handmade quilts and rockers. The honeymoon suite, St. John's Cottage (formerly a chapel), is a gentle walk down the hill. Outside the door is a hot tub. The loft bedroom, which overlooks the parlor and fireplace, makes you feel positively sybaritic.

This inn weaves a rich tapestry of romance, food, and wine. The four innkeepers make your journey through life a bit sweeter. In the world of country inns, this one is a classic. The only choice you have is the choice to come and that's the best one of all.

How to get there: From I–270 north of Washington, D.C., exit Route 85 South to Buckeystown. The inn is on the left in town.

Back Creek Inn
Solomons, Maryland
20688

Innkeepers: Carol Szkotnicki and Lin Cochran
Address/Telephone: Calvert and A streets; (410) 326–2022
Rooms: 7, including 3 suites; 4 with private bath, all with air conditioning, 1
   with fireplace and porch, suites with television. No smoking in rooms.
Rates: $65 to $100, double occupancy; full or continental breakfast. No
   credit cards. Package rates available. Two-night minimum most week-
   ends and holidays.
Open: March 1 to end of November.
Facilities and activities: Jacuzzi, dock. Nearby: restaurants, day-sailing excursions, museum, Sotterly Plantation, antiquing, bicycling, jogging, fishing.

   If I could have a Jacuzzi, I'd design and build it for two like the
one at Back Creek. Framed in wood with side areas for sitting or
placing a glass of champagne, it's surrounded by gardens—those
lucky enough to relax in it are lulled by the sounds of the fountain
trickling into the lily pond and entranced by the water view that
sweeps down to the sailor's haven, Back Creek, and out to the
Chesapeake Bay. The Jacuzzi is pleasant in the morning sun, in the
afternoon when you're lying about, or on a moonlit night when
you want an experience to remember.
   Lin and Carol's avocation is gardening. Besides the herb, vegetable, and strawberry gardens (the bounty of which flavors breakfast), an abundance of flowers grows. The small white garden is

modeled after Sissinghurst in England. Lin conceived the idea when touring English gardens with her mother. The rose garden is nurtured by Carol's husband, Mike. The setting is conducive to poetry. Why not memorize one of Shakespeare's love sonnets and deliver it casually while walking the garden?

The guest rooms are named for herbs. The "suite-rooms" are connected by a wooden deck to the inn, and one has a beautiful water view. My favorite bath-sharing room is the six-windowed Chamomile, and my favorite suite is Lavender with the water view. Carol's mother and grandmother have contributed to the decor with their quilts.

The oil and watercolor paintings you see throughout the inn were done by Carol, and they reveal a talent she never mentions. She also designed the stained glass in the hallway and decorates shells. In addition, Lin fashions pretty floral wreaths, a natural outgrowth of her garden.

The varieties of boat trips available from Solomons are wide ranging. You can board a large historic Chesapeake Bay bugeye from the Calvert Maritime Museum, join a tour boat to Hooper's Island, or take a small yacht cruise and romantically sail up the Patuxent River.

In the spring, summer, or fall, seated under the shade of the paper mulberry, a Colonial tree, you are served a delicious breakfast. It begins with the inn's secret blend of coffee. You might have buttermilk waffles with Vermont maple syrup and hot roasted almonds, or eggs Benedict (over pumpernickel) flavored with fresh tarragon. The view, the flowers, and the tastes conspire to create a most pleasurable experience.

How to get there: Take Route 4 to Solomon's Island (Routes 4 and 2 merge from the north). Before the bridge take Route 2 into Solomons; turn left on A Street. The inn is located at A and Calvert.

Clive Metcalf

Alexander's Inn
Cape May, New Jersey
08204

Innkeepers: Larry and Diane Muentz
Address/Telephone: 653 Washington Street; (609) 884–2555
Rooms: 4; all with private bath and air conditioning.
Rates: May to mid-June: Sunday–Thursday $100, 2-night weekend $275.
   Mid-June to October: Sunday–Thursday $100, 3-night weekend $375.
   Mid-October to May: Sunday–Thursday $75, 2-night weekend $250.
   Holiday weekends may require longer stay. EPB and afternoon tea;
   beach passes and parking included.
Open: All year.
Facilities and activities: Dinner. Nearby: beach (2 blocks away), Victorian
   House Tours, Victorian Week in October, Christmas Celebration,
   Emlen Physick Estate, carriage and trolley rides, bicycling, boating,
   summer band concerts.

Romance, elegant cuisine, sumptuous bedrooms, a flower-filled parlor, a wide wraparound porch filled with inviting furniture—the epitome of twentieth-century Victorian comfort—these are your surroundings at Alexander's Inn.

Be inquisitive. Larry and Diane are well-informed Victorian preservationists who harmonize authenticity with comfort. Every turn reveals a discovery. Come to dinner at Alexander's and you discover the fine touches. The silver wine carafes, the finger bowls floating with rose petals, the crystal, the china—but more than the accoutrements, it's the dining that sends you into un-Victorian excesses.

You might begin with the sausage-nut strudel—layers of pastry encasing sausage, cream cheese, almonds, walnuts, pecans, and herbs. And for an entree, perhaps grilled mako shark with a stuffing-filled pocket surrounded with a sauce, or classic filet mignon a la bourguignonne, grilled and served on Holland rusk with pâté and sauced with a heavenly dark burgundy wine sauce. You may go into ecstasy over desserts. The crème brûlée is a glimpse of heaven. It's almost torture to decide. If you've never had homemade white-licorice ice cream (created by Diane so it wouldn't stain the teeth), this is the moment.

Don't be surprised if a diner at the next table is taking notes. Culinary students and professional chefs come here to experience new tastes, textures, and ideas. Or else they're writing a love story.

Afterward you may want to walk 2 blocks down to the beach on a moonlit night, return and have a cordial on the porch, and finally retire satiated to one of four lavish rooms. One has French wallpaper and an ornate Victorian antique bedroom suite; across the bed is a gray-satin spread trimmed in frilly lace.

In the morning, breakfast is brought to your room. A tray is filled with a delicate carafe of hot coffee, fresh croissants, and a large bowl of fruit, and a single long-stemmed red rose lies across the white linen.

The King and Queen themselves would approve.

How to get there: From the ferry, take Route 9, then 109 to Cape May. Continue on Lafayette Street, turn left on Franklin Street, and turn right on Washington Street to the inn on the right. (Garden State Parkway leads into Lafayette Street.)

B: *Alexander's makes special occasions grand and any day a romantic occasion.*

Olive Metcalf

Chestnut Hill on the
Delaware
Milford, New Jersey
08848

Innkeepers: Linda and Rob Castagna
Address/Telephone: 63 Church Street (mailing address: P.O. Box N); (908)
995–9761
Rooms: 5, including 1 suite; 3 with private bath, all with air conditioning,
suite with fireplace. No smoking inn.
Rates: $75 to $100, double occupancy; $130 to $160, suite; EPB. Corporate
rates. No credit cards.
Open: All year.
Facilities and activities: Walking and hiking along Delaware. Nearby: restaurants, tubing, canoeing, tennis, New Hope and Flemington (30-minute
drive), Rice's Antique & Flea Market.

The Delaware River flows out front, the rare train travels
down the single riverside track, and a row of antique rockers lines
the front porch in anticipation of sunset on the river. Inside awaits a
resplendent Victorian inn with informal innkeepers who keep life
in good-humored perspective.

You might find a bevy of teddy bears clustered across the pillow or a pair of Raggedy Ann dolls hugging in a chair. In one bathroom a yellow rubber ducky shares the soap dish. You can let the
child in yourselves out while you're here. Be kids together again.

The rooms are prettily decorated according to themes that arose naturally. The sheets are crisply pressed—some were designed by Linda. In the Pineapple Room you enter on a platform and step down to the spacious room with fan, ferns, and warmth. In Peaches and Cream, a 1908 marriage certificate hangs above the bed alongside the marriage proverb, "I will love you and honor you all the days of my life."

Bayberry Room has a lovely bay window that looks out to the river. And upstairs in Teddy's Place sits a copy of a 1911 book Linda found one day, *The Diary of My Honeymoon*. Many a honeymooner has gotten off to a good start here.

In the Eastlake Parlor lined with apothecary shelves are an organ and piano and a very proper lady, a mannequin dressed in the clothes worn by the actual lady of the house around the turn of the century. It's a setting that draws you in to peruse and appreciate; to enjoy and relax.

Breakfasts differ depending on the time of your visit. They include fresh seasonal fruit, delicious sausage and baked German apple pancake, and a variety of omelets and pastries depending on the season.

Linda's antique wooden rockers line the front porch. This is where lovers of long ago would court; today it's a place to unwind and return to a slower pace of life. You could spend an entire quiet weekend here walking through the town, sitting on the front porch, biking the country roads, dining at the fine restaurants in town and nurturing your love.

How to get there: Direct bus service from New York City. Request driving instructions. Located in village.

Old Drovers Inn
Dover Plains, New York
12522

Innkeepers: Alice Pitcher and Kemper Peacock
Address/Telephone: Old Route 22; (914) 832–9311
Rooms: 4, all with private bath, 3 with fireplace.
Rates: $110 to $170, double occupancy, weekends, EPB. $90 to $150, double occupancy, midweek, continental breakfast. 20 percent service charge.
Open: All year. Closed Tuesday and Wednesday, except October.
Facilities and activities: Dinner Thursday through Monday; Saturdays begin serving at 3 P.M., Sunday and holidays from noon. Nearby: Hyde Park, golf courses, horseback riding, antiquing, country drives, fairs and festivals.

Do you have plans for Valentine's Day? Perhaps, like Alice and Kemper, you'll purchase your favorite inn on the most romantic day of the year. Before this venerable place became theirs, they used to appear on the doorstep when the need for R&R (repose and romance) touched them. Now they make Old Drovers glow with nurturing.

The Old Drovers is unique in the mid-Atlantic for its authentic character; you intuit a veritable sense of the past. The floors angle slightly and sometimes creak to the step as you descend to the romantic Old Tap Room. The "shell" cabinet in the parlor has its mate in the Metropolitan Museum of Art.

If this building, which dates from 1750, could talk, it would heave a pleasurable sigh of relief and thank its owners for restoring its beauty, for decorating its windows with colorful chintz, for placing down-filled couches in its parlors, and bringing lovers back to its hearth.

In the eighteenth century the drovers herding cattle into New York City would stop here with their herds for watering. "Only," explained Alice, pointing out the tavern sign that read DROVERS AND ANKLEBEATERS, "the drovers were actually gentry. They came ahead of the anklebeaters, who performed the cattle-driving work." The toughest animals you'll find are Alice's two Yorkies, Gordon Bennette and Jedediah, who greet everyone as if they were born to hospitality.

Before dinner we had a glass of wine in the library, then descended the stairway to dinner. In the candlelight of the star-patterned hurricane lamps we perused the chalkboard menu. Even before a drink arrived, the deviled eggs came with fresh condiments. Some traditions have remained the same here since 1937, like the double drinks. I ordered a potato-crusted salmon with vinaigrette and cilantro that was simultaneously moist and crispy; it got superior marks. For dessert we ate the naughty but divine Key lime pie.

Our room that night had a double barrel-vaulted ceiling and a fireplace where we nestled up in the cozy chintz chairs. There were robes in the closet, satin coverlets on the firm beds, and hooked rugs on the floors, and a fire on the hearth. What more could you wish for? It was perfect.

On weekends chef prepares a full breakfast; midweek there's a fine homemade granola and juice. The coffee is served in great oversized cups; we filled ours and meandered into the parlor, where the finches were chirping. We admired the rolltop desk and the wall mural painted by Edward Paine, and we found the couch convenient for dog-petting in the foyer.

By day you might explore the area's mansions, gardens, or villages or go for a horseback ride in the country. By night you're together before the fireside, sipping champagne and loving each moment of this sweet caesura.

How to get there: On Route 22 a sign for the inn is 3 miles south of Dover Plains. Turn east and drive a half mile. Inn is on the right; guests park on south side and enter through the porch.

❧

B: *Alice is a restaurateur from Nantucket and Kemper a film producer. They celebrate Valentine's at the inn.*

Olive Metcalf

Centennial House
East Hampton, New York
11937

Innkeepers: David Oxford and Harry Chancey
Address/Telephone: 13 Woods Lane; (516) 324–9414
Rooms: 6, including 1 housekeeping cottage; all with private bath, air conditioning, and telephone.
Rates: $165 to $250, double occupancy, EPB. $375, cottage, EP. Two-night minimum, more on holidays.
Open: All year.
Facilities and activities: Fax machine, swimming pool. Nearby: restaurants, ocean beach, shopping, antiquing, village touring, maritime and local history museums.

Let's confide a moment. Do you need pampering? Do you crave a gracious setting and a kind experience? And to amble down streets of privets to the beach catching the glint of the sun-struck leaves on a warm afternoon? Has the time come to step off life's carousel and return to tea in the parlor and a chat with kindly innkeepers?

David and Harry have completely restored the house in an irresistible manner. They saved the wide-plank pine flooring, added the appropriate amenities, then applied drapes of Scalamandre silks and selected antiques, which blend with furnishings of compatible ages and styles.

When we opened the door to our room, we found a queen-sized four-poster bed, a couch, and a coffee table upon which a tray containing sherry and scrumptious chocolate truffles was placed. In the bath was a lovely sesame-seed oil, which made oil-lovers out of us. Each room, you'll find, is unique. It's down-to-earth luxury.

If you could wrap the parlor up and take it home, you would. Two sitting areas create berths for conversing, for lounging, for reading. The innkeepers provide interesting reading materials—magazines, art, fiction, music, travel—that reveal a curiosity for the world and a love of beauty. A crystal carafe of sherry sits on a sideboard.

If you favor the small, discreet places in the world where plush comforts and good stories abound, then Centennial House will suit you.

Those who like to learn about the Hamptons can meet others and broaden their experience around the breakfast table. David specializes in buttermilk pancakes so rich you don't need to lace them with butter and in French toast that he learned to make from childhood family recipes. He's as quick to share his recipes as he is his ideas and insights on life in the Hamptons.

Were we at Centennial House at this moment, we'd be in either of two places: In summer—stretched alongside the swimming pool petting Earl and Edwinna (Lhasa apsos of a friendly disposition), admiring the clear skies and stark green of the trees and privet hedge; in winter, in the parlor near the gas fireplace drinking hot tea and reading, occasionally looking up to see who came and went and falling into conversation and mostly savoring the moment together.

How to get there: Easily reached by Jitney from New York. Driving, take Route 27 into East Hampton. As you enter the village, the inn is on the right before the left turn, marked by a small sign.

olive Metcalf

The White Inn
Fredonia, New York
14063

Innkeepers: David and Nancy Palmer and David Bryant
Address/Telephone: 52 East Main Street; (716) 672–2103
Rooms: 23; all with private bath, television, and telephone.
Rates: $59 to $179, double occupancy, EPB. Rollaway, $10. Two-night min-
    imum on college weekends.
Open: All year.
Facilities and activities: Lunch, dinner (dinner range: $10 to $20 with salad),
    tavern, craft shop. Nearby: Lake Erie, winery tours, antiquing, skiing,
    Chautauqua, Amish country, music and cultural events of university.

Chautauqua County's Fredonia was the mythical town in the
Marx brothers movie *Duck Soup,* and the Marx brothers played here
during their touring days. It's an all-American village, the first
Woman's Christian Temperance Union, the first Grange, and the
first gas well in the country. Keeping within the classic American
tradition, Duncan Hines visited here and gave The White Inn his
seal of approval. If there was a lover's seal of approval, they'd get
that too.

The inn was restored by David Palmer, a professor of business
ethics, and David Bryant, behind-the-scenes restorer; both have
Ph.D.s in philosophy. Nancy Palmer, who formerly taught medieval
art, translated her thirteenth-century talents into decorating. The
romantic panache in the rooms is impressive. In one, the white-

and-peach curtains have thirty yards of fabric at each window. You find rooms with elaborate antiques like the Eastlake or the rare queen-sized Victorian bed in the Lincoln Suite. The spacious Presidential Suite has a whirlpool bath. Two rooms have contemporary pine furniture and handsome plaid spreads for a modern country look. Many have love seats. Nancy's latest creation is a contemporary suite, so now you may select according to your lover's fantasy.

The area has a number of vineyards amidst gently rolling farmlands. The inn is 3 miles from the shore of Lake Erie, and thirty minutes from Chautauqua village for summer entertainment. In the early evening, you might take Nancy's map of Fredonia and take a walk along the tree-lined streets before dinner. It's a seductive place, an easy and graceful place to enjoy.

We dined on a perfect poached Norwegian salmon topped with sautéed julienne vegetables and beurre blanc sauce. We lingered knowing that upstairs every comfort awaited and we hadn't far to go.

Your days here might begin with no particular purpose, and sometimes those are the best of days together.

How to get there: Take Dunkirk-Fredonia exit 59 from I–90. Go left on Route 60 South. Turn right onto Route 20 West (Main Street). The inn is located on Route 20, Main Street, Fredonia.

olive Metcalf

Rose Inn
Ithaca, New York
14851

Innkeepers: Charles and Sherry Rosemann
Address/Telephone: P.O. Box 6576; (607) 533–7905
Rooms: 12, plus 3 suites; all with private bath and air conditioning, suites with whirlpool bath, 1 with fireplace. No smoking inn.
Rates: $100 to $160, double occupancy; $175 to $250, suites; EPB. Additional person, $25. Two-night minimum weekends, subject to 3-night holidays.
Open: All year.
Facilities and activities: Dinner Tuesday through Saturday (4-course dinner, prix fixe $50 per person). Conference center. Wine served. Twenty acres with pond, apple orchard. Nearby: winery tours, ski Greek Peak, lake mailboat tours, bicycling, cultural events, Cornell University.

What makes an inn linger in your memory like fine wine? What brings a smile to your lips every time the Rose Inn is mentioned? You could, of course, say it was the sunken whirlpool bath and the beautiful evening with the spring peepers calling away. Or the superb meal of artichoke-heart strudel and honey-almond duck enhanced by a Finger Lakes wine. Perhaps it was the myriad adventures you'd enjoyed throughout the day, thanks to Charles and Sherry's recommendations of wineries to visit and the Mackenzie-Childs' pottery shop down the road. But of course, a European-style inn is the culmination of all of the above and that's why you went to Rose Inn.

Sherry has an expert's eye for interior design. Charles trained in Europe and managed seven major hotels before he joined Cornell's School of Hotel Administration. Turning their full-time attention to the Rose Inn, they've created a small, elegant European-style hotel where your hosts speak eight languages fluently.

The Rose Inn has a mystique in the area. It was known as "the home with the circular stairway" because a museum-quality stairway was crafted from Honduran mahogany by a master craftsman who disappeared without a trace.

The luxury is overt and detailed. Never too much, never too little. Our room, Number 11, was contemporary in design with light and privacy as well as a romantic touch—a sunken whirlpool bath beneath triple Palladian windows and a white brocade love seat near the fireplace. One room, painted a deep forest green, was decorated with antiques and, at the windows, delicate French lace.

Dinner at the Rose Inn is served in small dining rooms. You make your selections in advance. Among the choices are smoked oysters in beurre blanc on puffed pastry, chateaubriand with sauce béarnaise served with a bouquetaire of vegetables, and scampi Mediterranean flambéed with brandy and a touch of tomato, curry, and cream. I chose the Chef's Surprise, a tender almond duck (and carried away the recipe). Dessert was a rich multiflavored chocolate-raspberry-hazelnut torte.

Behind the inn is the apple orchard, which is the source of Charles's delicious long-baked German apple pancakes. His recipe derives from his native Black Forest youth. His breakfasts begin with a tasty freshly squeezed blend of juice from imported oranges.

You enter unpretentiously through the kitchen, but be not deceived—romance lies beyond this unusual entrance. Later you'll say, "Do you remember that evening at the Rose?"

How to get there: From Rochester, take I-90, exit 40; follow Route 34S 36^1/$_5$ miles; the inn is on the left. From Ithaca Airport, turn right on Warren Road and go 1^3/$_{10}$ miles; turn left on Hillcrest Road for 1^1/$_2$ miles to the end. Make a right onto Triphammer Road (joins Route 34) and go north 4^2/$_5$ miles. The inn is 10 miles from Ithaca.

Olive Metcalf

The Interlaken Inn
and Restaurant
Lake Placid, New York
12946

Innkeepers: Roy and Carol Johnson
Address/Telephone: 15 Interlaken Avenue; (518) 523–3180
Rooms: 12, including 1 suite; all with private bath.
Rates: $100 to $160, double occupancy, MAP and afternoon tea. Plus 22
    percent tipping and state tax. EPB rate available for Sunday and Mon-
    day, $80 to $120. Two-night minimum on weekends.
Open: All year.
Facilities and activities: Dinner Tuesday through Saturday at 7:00 P.M. Public
    invited by reservation ($25). Pub, parlor with television. Nearby: lake
    and shops of Lake Placid, hiking, downhill and cross-country skiing,
    horseback riding, Olympic sites, year-round sporting events, golf.

      The Olympics forever changed Lake Placid. At times it looks
European, other times American, but what distinguishes it are three
things: the endless sporting competitions; the people who converge
here and their love of skiing, hiking, and sports; and the ski jump
complex on its eastern horizon.
      At the end of an athletic day, however, one likes to retreat to a
romantic little village inn. The Interlaken Inn is located outside the
fray, 2 blocks from Mirror Lake and the village center, on a residential street. We opened the big door and met Grandmother Fern.

Carol and Roy Johnson and clan were scattered about the inn preparing dinner with their guests in mind. Fern showed us up the stairs with alacrity (she could open a grandmother school, always smiling or saying the right things at the right time). We passed a family of teddy bears tucked along the stairway.

We'd arrived just in time for afternoon tea. Fern or one of the Johnsons oversees afternoon tea and takes that opportunity to visit. It was while munching on Key lime tarts and lovely petits fours that I discovered Carol (the master chef) and Roy (an architect) came east from California to establish their Adirondacks inn. "You need an architectural background," Roy explained, "to restore and repair a 1906 country inn."

Dinner happened like this: Around 6:00 P.M. guests began arriving in the parlor for a drink. My companion headed for the pub, where he immediately found Roy and Carol's golf-ball collection and discovered that they shared his love of golf.

Soon we were seated in the posh dining room and a young man recited the dinner menu: "Mushroom strudel, salad with Caesar dressing, scallops in puff pastry, filet mignon with mustard cognac cream sauce, poached salmon with fresh dill sauce, chicken Normandy with a sauce of Granny Smith apples and calvados." Happily, decisions were concluded and gastronomic directions taken. Finally the evening tapered; coffee came with individual chocolate pots and Chantilly cream; couples moved to the living room or small bar; some lingered; some went for an evening walk down to the lake.

Upstairs, the pretty rooms are softly furnished, some with lace curtains and thick carpeting; you'll find several antiques from the Johnsons' California home.

On each bedroom door hangs a straw hat garlanded with flowers. There's also one on the front door near the doll carriage filled with antique dolls. The hats are Carol's touch. She's reminding us we're on a carefree romantic holiday, and that's, indeed, the mood that Interlaken induces.

How to get there: From the intersection of Main Street and Saranac Avenue, continue north (a left turn from Saranac, a right hand turn from Main) on Main Street along the lake. The second street on the left is Interlaken. Climb the steep hill and you'll see the inn on the left. (Note: There might be no street sign for Interlaken Avenue.)

olive Metcalf

Gateway Lodge
Cooksburg, Pennsylvania
16217

Innkeepers: Joseph and Linda Burney
Address/Telephone: Route 36 (mailing address: P.O. Box 125); (814) 744–8017; Pennsylvania only (800) 843–6862
Rooms: 22, plus 8 cabins; 17 rooms and all cabins with private bath.
Rates: $95 to $125, double occupancy, EPB. $145 to $175, per couple, MAP. $120 to $140 for cabins that sleep 6 to 8, EP. For cabins bring linens, towels, and utensils; blankets, pillows, and firewood provided.
Open: All year except Thanksgiving and Christmas.
Facilities and activities: Dinner daily, reservations required; tea served daily. Tavern, indoor swimming pool for lodge guests (not for cabin residents), cross-country skiing from inn, skis available. Nearby: fishing, hunting, golf, bicycling, theater, Clarion River for canoeing and tubing, horseback riding, carriage and sleigh rides. 2,500-acre Cook Forest State Park, hiking.

Gateway Lodge is a log cabin jewel in the forest. Step a foot inside the door and the charisma of the front room allures you the rest of the way. Massive hemlock timbers compose the walls; the ceiling is pine, hemlock, and chestnut. The flooring is oak, and the trim is chestnut. It is lovely. We enjoy telling everyone about Gateway; we feel as though we're giving them a present.

Summer, winter, spring, and fall, the stone fireplace often has a blazing fire. Even in summer it can get cool at night. Around twilight, the lanterns are lit, and the wood gleams from the flame's reflections. The mood is one of pure contentment and romance.

A circle of couches and chairs surrounds the fireplace, a guitar sits casually to one side, and there's an ornately refinished piano. Jars of lemon candies sit within easy reach. Outside, the front porch beckons with cushion-tucked seatings.

We like coming here for many reasons: the beauty of the lodge, the outdoors, and the casual relaxed style of the innkeepers. You feel as if they did away with all the pressures of the world. You also feel as if you're entering the forest primeval when you walk into the nearby 60,000 acres of virgin woods granted to William Penn in 1681. These are encompassed within the state forest.

Joseph and Linda decorated the inn together. The petite and cozy country inn rooms have beige ruffled curtains, print wallpapers, little chests, and bookshelves. Linda keeps thick quilts on the beds all summer long and exchanges them for "haps," or much heavier quilts, for ski season. They are the real thing, handmade from old woolen clothes. They'd keep you warm through a blizzard should you be so lucky as to get "trapped" here.

In the dining room, you eat from tables gifted and inherited, which shine from their daily polishings. From the walls hang tools, hats, toys, jars, a great assortment of antiques.

Everything is homemade, from the creamy mashed potatoes to the relishes, jams, breads, and the sweets. Three entrees are served nightly from a weekly selection of thirteen. Request the brochure, which includes the menu. The entrees are family recipes of Linda's and include plump, stuffed chicken breast, moist and crisp; stuffed pork chop; savory sauced barbecued spareribs; sirloin steak with stuffing; trout; and prime rib. Among the desserts is a chocolate lover's delight. I'd order with abandon; you'll not have regrets afterward.

How to get there: From I–80, take Route 36 North. The inn is on the right just before the park. Fly-in, Clarion County Airport.

❀

B: *Steps from your room are the sauna and enclosed pool beautifully designed by Joe and heated by a wood-burning stove.*

olive Metcalf

Glasbern
Fogelsville, Pennsylvania
18051-9743

Innkeepers: Al and Beth Granger
Address/Telephone: Pack House Road, R.D. 1; (215) 285–4723 or (800) 654–9296
Rooms: 10, plus 13 suites; all with private bath, air conditioning, television, VCR, and telephone; 9 with fireplace and whirlpool bath.
Rates: $95 to $100, double occupancy; $125 to $200, suite; EPB. Two-night minimum on certain weekends.
Open: All year.
Facilities and activities: Dinner Tuesday through Saturday ($18 to $25), service bar. Outdoor swimming pool, pond, hot-air balloon rides, 16 acres farmland. Nearby: Hawk Mountain Sanctuary, antiquing in Kutztown and Adamstown, ski Blue and Doe mountains, visit wineries, and tour Historic Bethlehem.

Had we passed by chance, we'd have stopped and driven down the cobblestone lane, intent on discovering what purpose this visually compelling structure held.

Beth Granger gave the inn its name, Glasbern, meaning "glass barn." It's a Pennsylvania German barn architecturally transformed in 1985 by the Grangers to create a unique contemporary inn amidst the serenity of a stream, a pond, and the green hills of the countryside.

You enter the Great Room, the heart of the inn. Intact are the original haymow ladders. The beams in the vaulted ceiling are exposed, and the stone walls were cut open with a diamond-edged saw to let in the sunlight. The lighting reminded me of a cathedral designed by Le Corbusier I once visited in France. The Great Room is an elegant setting within a former hand-hewn "bank" barn.

The inn is a good place to commune with one another. On a clear fall day, you can board a hot-air balloon that departs from the inn. Walk the inn's country paths. Or perhaps on a winter's eve after a day of skiing ease into the whirlpool with the warmth of the nearby fireplace for total bliss. You may never leave the place.

The carriage-house suites have fireplaces framed either in stone or barn-wood siding. In the corner suites, two-person whirlpools are surrounded by windows opening out to the country-side. The rooms are a blend of today's comforts, good lighting, and quality-built furnishings tastefully selected by Beth.

By evening, guests gather in the Great Room, where you must reserve in advance, since the chef has a following. First you have a drink around the great stone fireplace. Once you're seated, hot fresh breads are served with crispy salads. You might have ordered a New York strip brushed with olive oil and rosemary, then broiled; perhaps you selected a range chicken or Dover sole sautéed with French country-style vegetables, tomatoes, herbs, and a reduced sweet cream and served with lemon angel-hair pasta. Later comes a light cheesecake soufflé coated with raspberry sauce. Some guests enjoy a liqueur upon returning to the stone fireplace or go for a walk around the pond.

Breakfast is served, in leisurely style, in the sun room. That morning we ate whole-wheat pecan pancakes coated with maple syrup and thick slices of bacon. We felt recharged. We noticed others looked that way, too. Was it the fresh air, the country walks, the fine meal, the whirlpool, and the fireplace? Or had someone anointed us with newfound energy during the night?

How to get there: From I–78, take Route 100 North a short distance to Tilghman Street and turn left. Go 1/3 mile and turn right on North Church Street; go 7/10 mile and turn right on Pack House Road. The inn is 8/10 mile on the right.

Olive Metcalf

The King's Cottage
Lancaster, Pennsylvania
17602

Innkeepers: Karen and Jim Owens
Address/Telephone: 1049 East King Street; (717) 397–1017
Rooms: 7; all with private bath and air conditioning. Some with telephone.
Rates: $75 to $115, double occupancy, EPB and afternoon tea. Two-night minimum most weekends. Checks and cash preferred.
Open: All year.
Facilities and activities: Television in parlor. Nearby: restaurants, Lancaster sites, Visitor's Center, antiquing, Landis Farm Museum, biking, golf, tennis, factory outlets.

The sun was well up. We had slept soundly but the aroma of a magnificent sausage compelled us to rise from the canopy bed and look from comforting quilt to windows veiled in curtain.

We had gone the night before to a little neighborhood restaurant, where the food was good, the atmosphere unassuming but pretty, and the conversation delightful. Karen and Jim have a knack for getting their guests to the right local restaurant.

Afternoon tea and cookies, served daily from 4:00 to 7:00 P.M., provides an opportunity to acquire a richer feeling for the area from your hosts. Between bits of lemon squares and cottage cookies, Karen produced a thick packet of bike tours, which range from 11 to 72 miles and carry you through the countryside from various beginnings. The quilt people are sent to the Amish quilt-maker's house, the art lovers to the Artworks, and shoppers to the markets. If you plan ahead, you could have dinner with a "plain sect" family. Advance reservations are necessary and it's a perspective on life that will add to your understanding of the area.

From King's Cottage, you travel on a spider web of roads together through the Amish countryside to villages distinctive to Lancaster County. A few blocks away is Lancaster's 200-year-old Farmers' Market, where cheeses, sausages, vegetables, fruits, breads, and pastries fill the individual stands. You can take a buggy ride if you wish to get the feel of the roads when pulled along at a horse's pace.

Everything at the inn contributes to the royal experience— from the king- and queen-sized beds to the eighteenth-century antiques and reproductions. Three spacious areas, the library, the formal parlor, and the Florida sun room, are entirely for couples. In the fall and winter, a fire is going; in the summer, you can read and sip tea in the King Street sun room, which is fan-cooled. The neighborhood around the inn is pleasant for walking.

Breakfast begins with freshly squeezed orange juice and coffee and is served in the formal dining room. Over compotes of fruits from the Farmers' Market, you can compare experiences. Take a bite of the heavenly peaches-and-cream French toast while you discover why King's Cottage is on the National Register of Historic Places.

"It's not for one particular style," said Karen. "It's because the house is the culmination of several styles that existed at the time." There's a Georgian fireplace, an Art Deco fireplace and stained-glass windows, Spanish Mission stucco and red tile on the exterior, and heavy oak beams and a carved stairway. The inn has earned historic-preservation awards and has a sparkling and tasteful decor, with teas in the parlor and breakfasts on white linens and fine china. These are the details that turn one's thoughts to pleasure.

How to get there: From Route 30, take Greenfield Road exit; at the end of the ramp, turn left onto Greenfield Road. Go under the one-lane bridge and turn right at first light onto Route 340 West. Go through two lights (first one bears you right onto Route 462, or East King Street); after second light, go ⁴/₁₀ of a mile and turn right onto Cottage Avenue. Turn left into the inn parking area.

Olive Metcalf

The Whitehall Inn
New Hope, Pennsylvania
18938

Innkeepers: Mike and Suella Wass
Address/Telephone: Pineville Road (mailing address: R.D. 2, Box 250); (215)
598–7945
Rooms: 6; 4 with private bath, all with air conditioning, most with fireplace.
No smoking inn.
Rates: $130 to $180, double occupancy, EPB and afternoon tea. Two-night
minimum on weekends, 3-night minimum on holiday weekends.
Open: All year.
Facilities and activities: Swimming pool, tennis court. Nearby: restaurants,
walking or biking country roads, James A. Michener Arts Center, art
galleries of New Hope, Mercer Mansion in Doylestown, antiquing, historic sites.

Chocolate, you say, your not-so-secret addiction?
Every April Suella and Mike host the chamber group from the
Philadelphia Orchestra, who perform for Chocolate Lover's Getaway (to some, it's lovers' chocolate getaway). A tea follows the
music and every delicious morsel (even the tea itself) is chocolate.
While those scents and sounds linger in your recent memory, the
following morning consists of an entire chocolate breakfast. It's a
weekend of tasetful excess.
"We are told by musicians," said Mike, "that the acoustics of
our living room are like the small European chamber halls." The

harpist plays on New Year's Eve and the Rondeau Players come with their baroque music in May.

While some come for the gala events of Candlelight Champagne New Year's Evening Concert, the Baroque Tea Concert, or Picnic Weekends, others prefer the quiet times. They enjoy the inviting waters of the swimming pool, play a game of tennis, have a look at the thoroughbred horses, and are seen heading out the lane toward the country roads together. You can also follow "inn-side" tips to mansions, art galleries, and covered bridges. You might also linger beside the fire in the great room, which is lined with bookshelves and musical instruments.

Rarely, I feel, should one arrive precisely on time—but never, ever arrive at Whitehall late. Tea is served at 4:00 P.M., and a relaxed 3:30 P.M. arrival is suitable. Later, you'll congratulate yourselves.

Breakfast is served at 9:00 A.M. It begins with a secret blend of coffee and freshly squeezed orange juice. Two baskets soon appear: In the first is an artistic, prize-winning ribbon cinnamon bread; another bears an immaculately light sourdough biscuit. Now taste the baked pear stuffed with golden raisins, walnuts, and lemon rind and coated with caramel sauce. You think you'll never eat another bite, but at the appearance of a gravity-defying soufflé with aromatic Buck's County sausage, your appetite sharpens anew. Handmade Whitehall chocolates are the vivacious finale. You feel like applauding.

The sunny rooms are attractively furnished with antiques and are expertly wallpapered. Everywhere you turn are thoughtful details. Reading lights, robes, a bottle of good local wine, and other amenities contribute to the quality of the romantic experience.

How to get there: From New York City, take New Jersey Turnpike south to exit 10, Route 287 North for 15 miles to U.S. 22 West and U.S. 202 South. Take U.S. 202 South to Delaware River Bridge. Continue on U.S. 202 South toward Doylestown for 4³/₅ miles to Lahaska. Turn left on Street Road (past Jenny's Restaurant). Go to the third intersection and turn right on Stoney Hill. Turn left on Pineville Road. The inn is on the right, 500 yards.

B: *You're coddled in all the right ways.*

The Bailiwick Inn
Fairfax, Virginia
22030

Innkeepers: Anne and Ray Smith
Address/Telephone: 4023 Chain Bridge Road; (703) 691–2266 or (800) 366–7666
Rooms: 14, including 1 suite; all with private bath, air conditioning, and telephone jack, 4 with fireplace, 2 with whirlpool bath. Wheelchair access. No smoking inn.
Rates: $105 to $165, double occupancy; $225, suites; EPB and afternoon tea.
Open: All year.
Facilities and activities: Nearby: restaurants (within walking distance), Washington, D.C. (17 miles), Manassas Civil War Park, George Mason University, Mount Vernon, swimming, golf, tennis, historic sites.

Waking up in bed at The Bailiwick, one lies beneath the satiny comforter and luxuriates in the sumptuous surroundings. You think back to your arrival.

You drove up to the Colonial brick mansion opposite the historic courthouse and entered through the great *faux bois* door. You were welcomed into the double parlor, and without coaxing you took a seat before the fire. Amid the furnishings of Chippendale, Sheraton, and Duncan Phyfe styles, you saw the raspberry glazed ceiling and absorbed the civilized impression.

But you hadn't told him where you were taking him: to a secret destination. The expression when he walked in was amused surprise. He liked this game and all its implications.

78

Anne and Ray Smith, romantics themselves, visited country inns for several years before they purchased the Federal-style brick building (circa 1812). Ray, who once built a house in three days for a charity event, applied his talents to the impeccably inviting restoration.

The Smiths selected seven decorators and gave each decorator two rooms to express their artful talents. Each room has special charms; most are named for former presidents. And in each is some memento of that person—it might be a favorite book, a portrait, or their favorite color expressed in the fabrics and paintings.

The Thomas Jefferson room with its private fireplace has a desk-chair similar to the one he used at Monticello. A huge satiny mound of feather comforter tops each bed along with a bounty of pillows. The Lord Fairfax room is furnished in English pieces styled after the family castle in Leeds with the family coat of arms on the wall. In the George Washington room, you find a four-poster bed. Two rooms are named for women. One is for Nellie Custis, the granddaughter of Martha Washington.

Afternoon tea is served in the elegant double parlors, where portraits of Anne and Ray hang above the fireplace. These were gifts from the decorators who knew that in Colonial times paintings of the owners were traditionally hung above the mantels.

Bailiwick, a historical word meaning "around the courthouse," implies egalitarianism, so at daily tea everyone happily serves themselves hot cups of raspberry tea with abundant slices of homemade fruit breads and cookies.

For breakfast you might have Robert E. Lee Eggs—an English muffin served with poached egg, Virginia ham, and a mushroom sauce. On another morning, it could be a sausage-and-egg casserole or a crabmeat omelet made from recipes Ray and Anne have researched in historic Virginia cookbooks.

Dinner focuses on the food and wine of Virginia. Since the menu changes weekly, depending on the season, you might find Shenandoah trout, rockfish, blue crabs, or partridge. Gold medal–winning wines from the state competitions are served. The setting is elegant and arranged for private, romantic dining.

How to get there: From I–66, take Route 123 East toward George Mason University. It's 1½ miles to the inn, which is opposite the old courthouse. Off-street parking behind the inn.

Olive Metcalf

High Meadows
Scottsville, Virginia
24590

Innkeepers: Peter and Mary Jae Abbitt Sushka
Address/Telephone: Scottsville (mailing address: Route 4, Box 6); (804)
    286–2218
Rooms: 10, including suite and private cottage; all with private bath, 3 with
    whirlpool, 1 with soaking tub, some with air conditioning, 5 with fireplace.
Rates: $110 to $145, double occupancy; $110, suite; EPB. No credit cards.
Open: All year.
Facilities and activities: Dinner served by reservation (about $30 per person,
    including wine; European supper baskets, $40 per couple; French
    bistro dinners for 2, Monday–Friday, $35 per couple). Located on 48
    acres, pond, vineyard. Nearby: James River for canoeing and tubing,
    bicycling, walking, 5 wineries within 20-mile radius, Monticello, Ash
    Lawn, Charlottesville.

A rose-scented gazebo, poetry, and an English supper basket
are the circumstances of love's idleness that flourish at High Meadows. Weather permitting, you'll have supper beneath the gazebo
surrounded by Jae's roses of antiquity. You open the basket lid to
find Cornish game hen or curried meat loaf with salad, fruits, and a
lovely dessert beside a bottle of wine. A book of love poetry is
always placed atop the tasteful contents.

We, my lover and I, chose to dine publicly that night with candlelight and music. As a misty rain fell on the vineyard, we gathered in the parlor tasting Virginia vintages, which is the delicious

custom here. Soon the aromatic scent of dinner led everyone to tables for two in the English basement.

Warmed by the wood-burning stove, we savored the freshly baked braided honey loaves served with a Virginia sherried peanut soup. There was an appetizer of *tyropeta duo*, a remarkable rosemary-and-prosciutto-filled phyllo affair. Then lovely Mediterranean poached stuffed chicken breast medallions in a white wine and tomato sauce. The dessert, a Bailey's Cream chocolate chip cheesecake, was delicious.

Peter and Jae began restoring the inn in 1984. It's composed of two houses dating from 1832 and 1882 connected by a longitudinal hall called the breezeway. Using original photographs of the home, they laid brick walks, landscaped, added a white picket fence—and earned a listing on the National Register of Historic Places.

Since those beginnings, the inn has grown: a new contemporary private cottage overlooks the pond, and the Mountain Sunset property is located a short walk down a country lane. Romantics with old-fashioned tastes or new-fashioned desires find appropriate love nests. Choose the Victorian room with canopy bed located opposite the music parlor, or the state-of-the-art whirlpool view of sunset across the Blue Ridge Mountains, or the fireplace suite with the meadow view from the Victorian steeping tub.

The common areas are diverse: a Federal fireplace-parlor, a long breezeway, and the Victorian music room, where an exquisite dulcimer sat. "It was left by a guest," explained Peter.

Breakfast debuts with fresh-squeezed orange juice and special blends of coffees and teas. Hot, scrumptiously fresh breads might accompany a lovely casserole with ham, egg, and tomato and a light sauce.

Peter and Jae conceived of their inn in England, where they acquired both their romantic ideas and many of the inn's antiques. Peter was a submarine captain who learned that if he didn't oversee what was happening in the galley he'd face a mutinous crew. Now inn aficionados come here for ambience, to visit in the music room or the parlor, to dine on delicious foods, and for the twilight ritual of Virginia wine tasting. Virginia's classic country inn is on an even keel.

How to get there: From Charlottesville, take Route 20 South (exit 24 off I–64) past Monticello for 17³/₅ miles. At Scottsville, turn left at High Meadows Drive.

Olive Metcalf

The Manor at Taylor's Store
Smith Mountain Lake, Virginia
24184

Innkeepers: Mary Lynn and Lee Tucker
Address/Telephone: Route 122 (mailing address: Route 1, Box 533); (703) 721–3951
Rooms: 6, including 1 suite; 4 with private bath, all with air conditioning, suite with whirlpool bath. Separate 3-bedroom cottage.
Rates: $65 to $90, double occupancy, EPB.
Open: All year.
Facilities and activities: Game room, exercise room, hot tub, guest kitchen, walking paths, ponds for swimming and canoeing. Nearby: restaurants and Smith Mountain Lake (5 miles), antiquing, country roads, state park, plane rides.

Mary Lynn and Lee, whose romance began when they met in a gourmet cooking class, have a talent for putting you together. They will arrange for a hot-air balloon ride from their meadow that takes you for champagne over the beautiful Virginia countryside and Smith Mountain Lake. You return for an elaborate brunch in their inn. (They, too, have taken the balloon ride.)

We spent the pleasantest of days here. Cheerfully, Mary Lynn had suggested a walk. We passed the paddock—home to two New-foundland dogs—and traveled down a shady lane. In the pasture a horse grazed. We came to the first of six ponds and met a gaggle of geese, which had been ordered as goslings from the Sears catalog.

Next, we came to a larger pond, a sunning deck, and, beyond that, two more ponds and a trail that led into the woods. We couldn't decide for a time which romantic spot to call our own for the afternoon.

Within the Colonial mansion dating from 1820 is a full range of opportunities for relaxing. There's the formal Victorian parlor with a double fireplace in the corner; through the dining room is the sun room, where you can step out onto the brick patio overlooking fields and trees. Downstairs, there are a pool table, a 55-inch television (with large video collection), the exercise room, and the outdoor hot tub.

Mary Lynn and Lee have made each bedroom as romantic as the next. The rooms were draped and canopied with the assistance of her aunt, a professional decorator. There's a sunken whirlpool bath for two in the Castle Suite. The Toy Room is filled with antique toys.

Mary Lynn's breakfasts are healthful and stimulating. She loves cooking, and creates masterpieces—individual fruit tarts in summer, whole-wheat waffles raised with yeast, and whole-grain dill breads. Her French toast has the delicate taste of Grand Marnier and is covered with Virginia maple syrup. Supporting these feasts is a handsome Queen Anne table handmade by Lee.

One of the directions couples go for dinner is toward Smith Mountain Lake for candlelight dining at waterfront restaurants. Lakeside is an airport that offers biplane rides, and several marinas offering boat rides. If you fly into the Roanoke Airport, Lee will provide limousine service in his 1960 Jaguar. He's a surgical pathologist who finds that the scientific side of his life balances with innkeeping.

The inn was a trading post as early as 1799, later an ordinary, and then a post office in 1818. Now it's a romantic destination for two.

How to get there: From Roanoke, take 220 South to 122/40 East and follow signs for Booker T. Washington Monument. The inn is 1³/₅ miles past the Burnt Chimney intersection on the right.

olive Metcalf

Trillium House
Wintergreen, Virginia
22958

Innkeepers: Ed and Betty Dinwiddie
Address/Telephone: Wintergreen (mailing address: P.O. Box 280, Nellysford,
    VA 22958); (804) 325–9126; for reservations (800) 325–9126 (9:00
    A.M. to 6:00 P.M.)
Rooms: 12, including 2 suites; all with private bath. Wheelchair access.
Rates: $80 to $95, double occupancy; $120 to $150, suite for 4; EPB. Lower
    rate applies midweek. Two-night minimum on busy weekends.
Open: All year.
Facilities and activities: Dinner by reservation Friday and Saturday ($22–$24),
    full beverage license. Privileges of Wintergreen Resort (additional
    charge). Skiing, nature trails, enclosed swimming pool, outdoor pool,
    whirlpool spa, golf, tennis, horseback riding, picnicking, 16-acre lake
    for boating and fishing, 11,000 acres of mountains and valleys. Nearby:
    restaurants, Monticello, Ash Lawn, Woodrow Wilson Birthplace,
    antiquing, universities, factory outlets.

The flag swayed gently in the summer breeze, the rhododendrons were in bloom, and on the porch a pottery cask of iced tea
looked inviting. Trillium House is an architecturally designed four-
season inn built by Ed and Betty Dinwiddie in 1983. They named
their mountain inn for the spring trillium flowers that blossom in
the woods around the inn, and from the beginning the place has
flourished with warm ambience.

In winter, the forest is frosted with snow, and a short distance downhill are the ski slopes. A walk up the hill and you're golfing. Cross the road and you slip into the clear waters of an indoor or outdoor pool. There are 20 miles of trails here and more along nearby Blue Ridge Parkway. Any direction takes you into the natural beauty of rolling hills, mountains, and valleys.

Above the inn's entrance is an exquisite Jefferson Palladian window. You enter a spacious living room, where three golden organ pipes are mounted on the soaring chimney. You circle the wood-burning stove on oriental carpets near stacks of magazines and upstairs the balcony houses a 6,000-volume library.

You can sit before the fire, pet the chocolate Lab Jemimah, and be at ease. Or go horseback riding, take a guided walk in the woods with a naturalist, or amble over to the spa for massages.

At breakfast, we watched birds from the windowed dining room and ate scrumptious French toast plump with a cheese filling. Chef Ellen English is a very talented chef whose creations have become deliciously synonymous with Trillium. She serves a four-course meal (single entree) on Friday and Saturday evenings. You happily enjoy dinner together here. You might have shrimp-phyllo purses with hot peanut sauce, spinach and orange salad with curry vinaigrette, lemon-grass beef tenderloin with rice stuffing and soy-scallion beurre blanc, a vegetable medley, and homemade pineapple ice cream. Make a reservation and go expecting pleasurable, interesting tastes. Betty and Ed give knowledgeable recommendations for restaurant choices on other weeknights.

Weddings are held here and honeymoons are remembered by couples celebrating their anniversaries. It's a new-fashioned inn that's contemporary in look but old-fashioned in hospitality. The balance of nature, comforts, and delicious foods conspire to give the two of you a mountaintop interlude that lives forever in your memory.

How to get there: Directions sent with gate pass.

Olive Metcalf

Hillbrook Inn
on Bullskin Run
Charles Town, West Virginia
25414

Innkeeper: Gretchen Carroll
Address/Telephone: Route 13 (mailing address: Route 2, Box 152); (304) 725–4223
Rooms: 5; all with private bath and air conditioning, 2 with fireplace.
Rates: $270 to $380 per couple, MAP (includes 7-course dinner with wine). Room tax is 3 percent.
Open: Thursday through Sunday, all year.
Facilities and activities: Dinner for guests not spending the night: $60 per person Thursday and Sunday by reservation, $70 per person Friday and Saturday; add 15 percent service charge and 6 percent sales tax to everything. Mention any special evenings coming up, especially January through March. Nearby: antiquing, tour Shepherdstown or Harper's Ferry, Summit Point Raceway, bicycling, and hiking along C & O Canal.

Hillbrook is a romantic European hideaway in the lush gentle countryside of West Virginia where you're smitten by the peace and solitude. After traveling and working around the world and staying in inns, Gretchen Carroll arrived by happenstance one rainy afternoon; the rest is champagne and candlelight.

Hillbrook was built during the roaring twenties of stone, timber, and stucco and was terraced with these materials to form a grand country house. Entry is into the living room, with fireplace burning, oriental rugs, and artworks to be appreciated; an atmosphere of casual elegance reigns. You notice the theme of people's faces in Gretchen's artwork and find interesting books on foreign travels adjacent to carvings, pottery, and prints.

Two bedrooms are off the living room; one is reached by climbing a stairway where a private balcony gives you a superior view. The downstairs room has a small private porch and fireplace. A third room is near the library. The rooms are uniquely furnished with antique or brass beds, down comforters, and Gretchen's worldly treasures, including an antique Vuitton trunk.

Dinner is an absolute affair with flavors. It's served by reservation at a fixed price and set menu; it is a seven-course palatable event. We began with a tasty tapenade artfully arranged, then came a creamy tangy carrot-and-orange soup, after that an absolutely delicious hot pasta. The entree was veal served with tastefully seasoned broccoli and squash; then a salad arrived followed by a superb cheese plate with English crackers; last came a perfect chocolate cake. Each table in the room was set differently; ours had black candles that burned exuberantly until after midnight, when we finished our brandies and congratulated the chef for a fine meal.

For daytime excursions, Gretchen suggests a route that takes you past several wonderful antiques shops and an excellent winery where you can have a picnic lunch (conveniently prepared by the first antiques shop). You might prefer to remain at the inn, walk through the garden, rock in the hammock down by the stream, sip a glass of wine on the patio, or simply lie back and catch up on your daydreams.

How to get there: From Charles Town take 51 West to Route 13 (Summit Point Road), which bears off to left at west end of town. Go 4⁴/₅ miles on Route 13 to the inn on your left (past elementary school on right). Watch for stone wall. Or from I–270 take 70 West to 340 West past Harper's Ferry to 51 West in Charles Town. Follow previous directions.

B: *Hillbrook is the inn for celebrating birthdays, anniversaries, or promotions; lacking these traditional excuses you might make a date for the season's solstice.*

The South

by Sara Pitzer

What's more romantic—a starry evening watching boats on the Mississippi River or a night in an elegant suite in Georgia with real gold fixtures in the bath? You can't really answer for anyone but yourselves because places aren't romantic—people are. It's what you bring to an inn that makes it romantic: your personal taste, your ideas of pleasure. A romantic getaway is to share the pleasures you enjoy most with someone special in a way that lets you be together at your best.

My parents made a two-week camping-canoe trip down the Delaware River on their honeymoon. It was, they've always assured me, truly romantic. (And that's before insect repellent was invented!) My own memorable romantic time was a vacation my husband and I took years ago, staying in an inexpensive room with shared bath, getting dressed to the nines, and eating outrageously expensive dinners in a gourmet restaurant every night. At the end of each meal we'd sip our liqueurs and sigh with pleasure.

If romance means being in special places, you almost can't go wrong in good Southern inns. Each one offers pleasures you just don't find everywhere. To choose well, all you need do is reflect on what appeals to you. Seclusion? How about Little St. Simons Island? Opulence? Maybe the Gastonian. Casual accommodations, a gorgeous view, warm people? The Lodge on Lake Lure. Gourmet food, lots of privacy, museum-quality art and antiques, unspoiled nature—you can find it all in Southern inns.

Each of the twenty inns I've described differs conspicuously from the others. I've explained what's special about each place. Those that sound like they'd make *you* feel good will make you feel romantic, too. I promise.

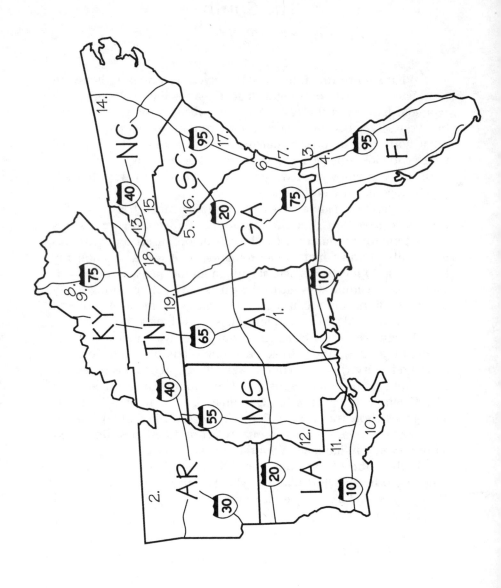

The South

Numbers on map refer to towns numbered below.

Red Bluff Cottage
Montgomery, Alabama
36101

Innkeepers: Anne and Mark Waldo
Address/Telephone: 551 Clay Street (mailing address: P.O. Box 1026); (205)
264–0056
Rooms: 4, plus 1 children's room; all but children's room with private bath,
television on request. No smoking inn.
Rates: $55 to $65, double, full breakfast. No credit cards.
Open: Year-round.
Facilities and activities: Guest refrigerator and coffee maker, children's
fenced-in play yard, gazebo. Nearby: restaurants, Alabama State Capi-
tol, historic sites, Jasmine Hill Gardens, Montgomery Museum of Fine
Arts, Alabama Shakespeare Festival Theatre.

You enjoy a wonderfully romantic sense of privacy at Red
Bluff Cottage without giving up the opportunity to spend time with
other guests when you feel like it. The guest rooms are all on the
ground floor, with the kitchen, dining room, living room, den, and
music room on the second floor, which makes the guest rooms
quiet and the public rooms exceptionally light and airy, looking out
over the yard and gardens.

The flower gardens are an important part of Red Bluff Cottage;
guest rooms are filled with fresh flowers, and seasonal blooms
adorn the breakfast table. Anne has been a passionate gardener for
years, an especially rewarding activity in Montgomery's climate

where it's moist and warm most of the year. When I visited, her border, full of intertwined patches of pink, white, yellow, and blue, looked like Monet's garden.

The Waldos' personal passions influence the look of the rooms inside the inn as well. In the music room, a harpsichord, a piano, and a recorder testify to the talent in the family—no guarantee that you'll hear a little concert during your stay, but it does happen.

In the guest rooms, you see furniture that's been in the family for years: the bed Anne slept in as a child, an antique sleigh bed that was her great-great-grandmother's, a spread crocheted by Mark's grandmother, and an old leather trunk from his great-aunt in Wisconsin, which contained invitations to fireman's balls dated 1850.

But artifacts of family past don't mean much unless you enjoy the present family. I enjoyed these people and the sense of old-fashioned love they communicate tremendously. Mark was the rector of an Episcopal parish in Montgomery for almost thirty years. During these years, the Waldos raised six children, all of whom keep in touch regularly. They tell funny tales of those tumultuous times.

After Mark's retirement, the Waldos became innkeepers because they wanted to keep new people coming into their lives. Where better to discover romance than under the roof of people who love flowers and books and music and can raise six kids and still be enthusiastic about taking in more of the human race?

How to get there: Take exit 172 off I–65. Go toward downtown (east) on Herron Street 1 block. Turn left on Hanrick Street. Parking is on the right off Hanrick by the inn's rear entrance.

Dairy Hollow House:
Century Inn and Restaurant
Eureka Springs, Arkansas
72632

Innkeepers: Crescent Dragonwagon and Ned Shank
Address/Telephone: 515 Spring Street; (501) 253–7444 or (800) 562–8650
Rooms: 3 in the Farmhouse, 3 suites in the Main House; all with private
   bath, 2 with Jacuzzi.
Rates: $115 to $175, double, full breakfast delivered to rooms in a basket.
   Two-day minimum stay on weekends. Children welcome in Main
   House.
Open: Year-round.
Facilities and activities: Dinner at the Restaurant at Dairy Hollow (seven
   nights a week in season; weekends only off-season) for guests and
   public. Reservations preferred, one seating nightly at 7:00 P.M., brown
   bagging permitted. Wheelchair access to restaurant. Fireplaces, 700-
   gallon outdoor hot tub. Nearby: restaurants; within walking distance of
   most Eureka Springs tourist attractions and historic sites.

We use the word "unique" sparingly, because so few things
really are. But Dairy Hollow House *is* a uniquely romantic experience and has been since the moment Crescent and Ned (who've
maintained an obvious longtime romance of their own) set their
hands to creating this inn.

Dairy Hollow House started as a restored Ozark farmhouse
painted a creamy peach and trimmed in deep teal. It has grown to

include a second building that is now the main house, where three suites, the restaurant, and a central, front-desk check-in area are housed.

I slept in the Iris Room, which got its name from the predominant color of its decor. The blue quilts on the beds are handmade. The window blinds are woven in shades of blue from fabrics Crescent chose to coordinate with the quilt.

Every room and suite has a fireplace trimmed in local "Eureka limestone." The recently renovated Main House is decorated as the original Farmhouse is, with antiques, fresh flowers, and eye-catching colors, including a turquoise that sounds unlikely until you see how well it works.

You haven't had the full Dairy Hollow experience unless you have dinner in the restaurant. The food is fresh and regional, but regional with a contemporary twist. Crescent and Ned call it Nouveau 'Zarks. They received an Inn of Distinction award from Uncle Ben's Rice for being named a Top Ten Country Inn three years running.

So many people asked for Crescent's unusual recipes that she and a cooking colleague wrote the *Dairy Hollow House Cookbook*, with more than four hundred recipes and a lot of commentary about Eureka Springs. And the *Dairy Hollow House Soup and Bread Cookbook* has just come out. What better way to bring back some romantic moments later than by re-creating some of the Dairy Hollow House specialties at home?

How to get there: Starting from the historic downtown area of Eureka Springs, take the old historic loop (old 62B, Spring Street) past the post office and all the other houses. Go just over 1 mile to where Spring Street curves sharply toward the original inn. The main house, where guests check in, is at the intersection of Spring Street and Dairy Hollow Road.

Heartstone Inn and Cottages
Eureka Springs, Arkansas
72632

Innkeepers: Iris and Bill Simantel
Address/Telephone: 35 Kingshighway; (501) 253–8916
Rooms: 10, plus 2 cottages; all with private bath.
Rates: $58 to $105, full breakfast. Inquire about winter discounts.
Open: Year-round except from mid-December through mid-January.
Facilities and activities: Massage/Reflexology therapist available by appointment. Located in the historic district, within walking distance of downtown Eureka Springs tourist activities. Nearby: restaurants.

I know this is going for the obvious, but—The Heartstone Inn gets its name from a large, flat, vaguely heart-shaped stone that the Simantels found on the property. They play with the heart theme, using the phrase "Lose your heart in the Ozarks" and a heart-shaped logo in their brochure. The doors have heart-shaped welcome signs. The stone that justifies it all rests in the front garden, surrounded by flowers. As far as I'm concerned, the Simantels have such heart they could use the theme even without the stone.

They came to the Ozarks from Chicago to become innkeepers. They love Eureka Springs. They love their inn. They love their guests. The inn is pretty. It's an Edwardian house, painted pink, with a white picket fence and lots of bright pink geraniums and roses all around.

Most of the rooms are furnished with elegant antiques, though a couple are done in country style. By the time you read this, there will be a new luxury Jacuzzi suite of special elegance, too. The fairly steady addition of such outdoor niceties as decks and a gazebo means there are always glorious places for special gatherings such as weddings.

But I think the attractiveness of the inn comes not so much from its pretty artifacts as from what those things reflect of Iris and Bill. For example, in the dining room I admired a Pennsylvania Dutch hex sign in which tulips and hearts make up the pattern. Iris said that the sign stands for everything they believe in and explained the symbols for faith, hope, charity, love of God, and smooth sailing. Then she kept the moment from getting too solemn by pointing to a print of yellow irises on the other wall. She said, "That's so I remember who I am in the morning."

The Simantels have been enjoying a good bit of "discovery," applause from magazines and newspapers and other innkeepers for doing such a good job. The praise, Iris says, has not gone to their heads. They are still keeping their prices moderate, because they don't want to attract snobs who go to places only because they are expensive. Not that Bill and Iris could be snobs if they wanted to. That Simantel humor bubbles too close to the surface. So, if you enjoy your romance with a bit of humor, this is your place.

When Iris was talking about the elaborate breakfasts they serve, she said that guests feel pampered by breakfasts including strawberry blintzes, coffeecake, and several kinds of fruit. As part of making breakfast special, she said that they dress up in long prairie dresses to serve it. "Well, Bill doesn't wear a prairie dress," she said. "That would be too special."

How to get there: From the west, take the first 62B exit off Route 62. From the east, take the second 62B exit. Follow 62B through town until it becomes Kingshighway.

The 1735 House
Amelia Island, Florida
32034

Innkeepers: Gary and Emily Grable
Address/Telephone: 584 South Fletcher; (904) 261–5878 or (800) 872–8531
Rooms: 6 suites; all with private bath and television.
Rates: $55 to $125, double, continental breakfast.
Open: Year-round.
Facilities and activities: Cooking and laundry facilities, beachfront. Nearby: restaurants, downtown historic Fernandina Beach shopping and sightseeing, boating from the marina.

So you'd like to sail away to a desert isle but you can't quite pull it off. Here's something almost as good. The 1735 House is a Cape Cod-style inn directly facing the ocean, furnished with antiques, wicker, and neat old trunks.

Maybe there will be no room at the inn, and you'll stay instead in the lighthouse. Its walls are covered with navigation maps. As you enter, you can either step down into a shower-and-bath area or take the spiral stairs up to the kitchen. A galley table and director's chairs make a good spot for playing cards, chatting, or ocean gazing, as well as eating. The stairs keep spiraling up to a bedroom with another bath, and finally up to an enclosed observation deck, which is the ultimate spot for romantic ocean gazing.

Wherever you stay, in the evening all you have to do is tell the staff what time you want breakfast and they'll deliver it right to your room in a wicker basket, along with a morning paper.

The physical setup is uncommon, but the staff have the true inn spirit. They'll give you ice, towels for the beach, bags for your shell collection or wet bathing suit, and just about anything else you need. All you have to do is ask.

The staff are full of helpful recommendations about good eating places, of which there are many on Amelia Island, too. The Down Under Seafood Restaurant, under the Shave bridge on A1A, is in keeping with the nautical mood of the inn and the lighthouse. The seafood is all fresh from the Intracoastal Waterway. There's a boat ramp with a dock, and the atmosphere is correspondingly quaint. You can enjoy cocktails and dinner.

If staying at The 1735 House gets you in the mood for more inns, you're welcome to browse through a large, well-used collection of books about inns in the office.

How to get there: Amelia Island is near the Florida/Georgia border. Take the Yulee exit from I-95 onto Route A1A and follow the signs toward Fernandina Beach. The inn is on A1A.

Casa de la Paz
St. Augustine, Florida
32084

Innkeepers: Sandy and Kramer Upchurch
Address/Telephone: 22 Avenida Menendez; (904) 829–2915
Rooms: 4, plus 2 suites; all with private bath and television. No smoking inn.
Rates: $65 to $115, double, continental breakfast. Two-night minimum stay
    on weekends.
Open: Year-round.
Facilities and activities: Nearby: walk to most St. Augustine historic sites;
    restaurants, tour carriages and trolleys, beaches.

At Casa de la Paz you're surrounded with the romance of history, beauty, and luxury. The Upchurches have created a beautiful inn. They started with a fine building, the only remaining example of pure Mediterranean Revival architecture from the turn of the century in St. Augustine. It has ornate iron molding and barrel-tile roofing.

Inside, the sun porch with huge arched windows, black-and-white tile flooring, white walls, and white wicker furniture, accented with lush green hanging baskets and foliage plants, feels so bright and airy and spacious that you scarcely distinguish between the outside and the inside. "That's the feeling we're trying to create all through the house," Sandy said, "cool, uncluttered, and clean."

Part of that effect in the guest rooms comes from handmade piqué blanket covers in geometric, scroll, or lace patterns, used

100

instead of heavy comforters. "After all, this is the South," Sandy said. The beds are made up with 100 percent cotton sheets, and six feather and down pillows to a bed!

In the dining room, the spacious effect comes partly from a Federal bulls-eye mirror hanging at the far end of the room. It's been in Kramer's family for years and has thirty-five balls, indicating the number of states in the Union at the time the mirror was made. It faces French doors at the opposite end of the room, reflecting the view overlooking Matanzas Bay.

You'll probably eat your breakfast in this room. The designation "continental" doesn't really do breakfast justice. Although the inn doesn't always serve eggs, when they do appear, a delectable version is a casserole of eggs whipped with cream cheese and baked with spinach, mushrooms, green onions, and Swiss cheese. All the inn's breads are homemade and baked in such variety that even if you stay for a week, you won't get the same breakfast twice.

How to get there: From I–95, take State Road 16 to A1A into the city, where A1A becomes Avenida Menendez The inn is just past Hypolita Street.

✳

S: *During their visits, many guests find the presence of the Upchurches' young daughter, Sydney, a bit of lagniappe.*

Glen-Ella Springs
Clarksville, Georgia
30523

Innkeepers: Barrie and Bobby Aycock

Address/Telephone: Bear Gap Road, Route 3 (mailing address: Box 3304); (404) 754–7295 or (800) 552–3479

Rooms: 16 rooms and suites; all with private bath, some with fireplace and television, some with wheelchair access.

Rates: $75 to $135, double, continental breakfast and full breakfast Saturday. Inquire about discounts for weeknights and stays of more than 3 nights.

Open: Year-round.

Facilities and activities: Dining room, with wheelchair access, open to guests and public most days; reservations requested; available for private parties; brown bagging permitted. Gift shop. Swimming pool, 17 acres with nature trails along Panther Creek, herb and flower gardens, mineral springs, conference room. Located in northeast Georgia mountains near historic sites. Nearby: restaurants, golf, horseback riding, boating, rafting, tennis, hiking.

I think I'm in love!

Usually country inns are elegant or they are rustic. This one-hundred-year-old place is both. The suites are beautifully finished and furnished with fireplaces; refinished pine floors, walls, and ceilings; local mountain-made rugs on the floors; whirlpool baths; and such niceties as fresh-cut pansies floating in crystal bowls. Some of the less-expensive rooms are simpler, though perfectly comfortable, with painted walls and showers in the bathrooms, but for a romantic interlude I can't think of anything more appealing than one of the suites in this old hotel in the country. Everything about the place invites pleasure.

The fireplace in the lobby is made of local stone, flanked with chintz-covered chairs.

An especially nice swimming pool, surrounded by an extra-wide sun deck that seems posh enough for any Hyatt hotel, overlooks a huge expanse of lawn that ends in woods.

The dining room is what I would call "subdued country," but there is nothing subdued about the food. It is simply spectacular—some of the best I've had anywhere in the South.

Because I sat with a large group for dinner, I had an opportunity to taste many more entrees and appetizers than ordinary. I remember scallops wrapped in bacon served in a light wine sauce; chicken livers in burgundy wine; fresh trout sautéed and then dressed with lime juice, fresh herbs, and toasted pecans; and halibut with Jamaican spices. I sampled desserts the same way and gave my vote to the homemade cheesecake.

The story here is that Barrie, a wonderful cook, had wanted a restaurant for a long time. But the Aycocks also wanted to work and live away from the city. They bought Glen-Ella even though the old hotel needed a tremendous amount of renovating.

They figured that here Barrie could have her restaurant, and since the inn was so far out in the country, lots of guests would spend the night. They do. And lots of other guests, who come for longer stays just to be in the country, enjoy the added pleasure of five-star quality food.

And now one more bragging point for Barrie and Bobby. The hotel has been added to the National Register of Historic Places.

How to get there: Go 8⁷/₁₀ miles north of Clarksville through Turnerville on U.S. Route 23/441. Turn left at the GLEN-ELLA sign on to New Liberty–Turnerville Road and continue for 1 mile to the next GLEN-ELLA sign at Bear Gap Road, which is a gravel road. Turn right. The inn is about 1¹/₂ miles on the left.

The Gastonian
Savannah, Georgia
31401

Innkeepers: Hugh and Roberta Lineberger
Address/Telephone: 220 East Gaston Street; (912) 232–2869 or (800) 322–6603
Rooms: 11, plus 2 2-room suites; all with private bath, fireplace, television, and telephone, rooms with wheelchair access.
Rates: $98 to $225, double, full sit-down Southern breakfast or silver-service continental breakfast in your room, afternoon tea, and wine and fresh fruit on arrival.
Open: Year-round.
Facilities and activities: Sun deck, hot tub, off-street lighted parking, garden courtyard. Nearby: restaurants, carriage tours of historic district, Savannah Riverfront shops.

If you equate romance with opulence, have I got a place for you—The Gastonian! Often an inn of this opulence turns out to belong to absentee owners, or to a group of owners who hire a staff to run the place. A staff may be perfectly competent, but it's not the same as being in an inn with innkeepers who've poured their passion into the property. And that sure describes Hugh and Roberta.

It's not just passion they've poured in, but also money—a million and a half of their own and $900,000 of the bank's, Hugh says, calling it a poor investment but a "hell of a love affair."

How could you not love it? The inn comprises two 1868 historic buildings sitting side by side and a two-story carriage house, joined by a garden courtyard and an elevated walkway.

The guest rooms are filled with English antiques, exotic baths, Persian rugs, and fresh flowers. The most outrageous bath is in the Caracalla Suite (named for a Roman emperor); it has an 8-foot Jacuzzi, sitting on a parquet platform draped with filmy curtains, next to a working fireplace. The fixtures here are of solid brass. In another room, they are of sculptured 24-karat gold. Each bath is unique and styled to complement the theme of its room—French, Oriental, Victorian, Italianate, Colonial American, or Country. All the inn's water runs through a purification system, which means, Hugh says, that you have to go easy on the bubble bath.

The public rooms are equally lavish, furnished with English antiques, satin damask drapes, and Sheffield silver. This kind of thing can easily be intimidating, but not when you're under the same roof with the Linebergers, who figure that having raised five daughters, a history-laden inn is a retirement pushover and jolly good fun at that. And darned convincing romance, too.

How to get there: From I-95, take I-16 to Savannah. Take the Martin Luther King exit and go straight onto West Gaston Street. The inn is at the corner of East Gaston and Lincoln streets.

Little St. Simons Island
St. Simons Island, Georgia
31522

Innkeeper: Debbie McIntyre

Address/Telephone: St. Simons Island (mailing address: P.O. Box 1078); (912) 638–7472

Rooms: 2 in main lodge with private bath; 4 in River Lodge, all with private bath; 4 in Cedar House, all with private bath; 2 in Michael Cottage share bath.

Rates: $350, double, all meals, wine with dinner, island activities, and ferry service. Minimum two-night stay. Inquire about longer-stay and off-season discounts.

Open: March through May and October through November for individuals; June through September for groups only.

Facilities and activities: Bar in lodge; collection of books about native birds, plants, animals, and marine life; swimming pool, stables, horseshoes, ocean swimming, birding, naturalist-led explorations, beachcombing, shelling, fishing, canoeing, hiking.

This is truly a special place. It is a 10,000-acre barrier island still in its natural state except for the few buildings needed to house and feed guests. You can get there only by boat.

When my husband and I visited, we felt welcomed as though we'd been visiting there for years. For us, the romance was in the sense of adventure and discovery of activities so different from our daily lives.

I still marvel at how much we did in a short time. The permanent staff includes three naturalists. One of the naturalists loaded us into a pickup truck and drove us around the island to help us get oriented. We walked through woods and open areas and along untouched ocean beaches. I saw my first armadillo. I gathered more sand dollars than I've ever seen in one place before. We saw deer, raccoons, opossums, and more birds than I could identify. Serious bird-watchers plan special trips to Little St. Simons to observe the spring and fall migrations.

We rode horseback with one of the naturalists. I was scared to death because I'd never been on a horse before, but they got me up on a mild-mannered old mare, and she plugged along slowly. By the end of the ride, I almost felt as though I knew what I was doing.

We canoed out through the creeks. When a big wind came up, I had a notion to be scared again, but the naturalist directed us into a sheltered spot where we could hold onto the rushes until the weather settled; then we paddled on.

When we weren't out exploring the island, we sat in front of the fire in the lodge, chatting with the other two guests and inspecting the photographs on the walls. They're standard hunting-camp pictures; rows of men grinning like idiots and holding up strings of fish, hunters with rifles grinning like idiots, and people climbing in and out of boats grinning like idiots.

One of the best meals we had while we were there was roast quail, served with rice pilaf and little yellow biscuits. As I polished off an unladylike-sized meal and finished my wine, I realized that *I* was grinning like an idiot.

How to get there: When you make your reservations, you will receive instructions on where to meet the boat that takes you to the island.

S: *The inn has added such creature comforts as nice bathrooms and handy ice machines, but these all rest lightly and inoffensively in the natural scene.*

Scottwood
Midway, Kentucky
40347

Innkeepers: Dale and Ann Knight Gutman
Address/Telephone: 2004 East Leestown Pike; (606) 846–5037
Rooms: 3, plus guest cottage; 2 upstairs rooms share 1 bath, all others with
    private bath, 2 with fireplace, all with television and VCR. No smoking
    inn.
Rates: $80 to $90, double, full breakfast.
Open: Year-round.
Facilities and activities: Formal rose garden, nature path, bird-watching. Near-
    by: Kentucky Horse Park Race Course, historic sites, Shakertown.

Scottwood is an early (about 1795) Federal-style Kentucky
brick house set among green fields, near a creek, across from a
horse farm. Dale and Ann want guests to think of it as a place to
which they can escape for periods of retreat and rest. It's a place
that invites a romantic interlude with time for introspection and
quiet talk.

Just being inside takes you from your ordinary life. Dale has
painted a fanciful mural of local houses and farms (in the Rufus
Porter style, he says) that sweeps up the stairwell and into the hall.
It serves as a lighthearted introduction to outstanding antiques
throughout the house. The Gutmans have been collecting antiques
for fifteen years and came to the inn business well prepared to furnish their rooms. Their folk art collection especially pleases guests.

The common room, done in period antiques, reminds you of a New England keeping room. Dale painted the ash floors in this room like a red-and-beige checkerboard, "the way it *should* be in New England," he said.

In the living room the focal point is a large red English architectural cupboard that houses an outstanding china collection.

In addition to whatever time you spend here admiring the antiques collections, reading, and walking outside, consider experimenting with photography. The flowers, the nature trail, the creek, and the nearby horses represent enough possible subjects to keep a photographer busy for a lifetime. Dale says some guests come for just that.

Since you're staying in a Kentucky house, you can reasonably expect a Kentucky breakfast. Dale's the cook. He prepares varied menus, trying to include some healthful choices, and he says, "something not so healthful" every day. Traditional favorites include country ham, spoon bread, fruits, and pancakes.

My discerning friend Howard Wells discovered this place and convinced me it was worth writing about. He liked everything about Scottwood, especially Dale and Ann. Their involvement is what makes everything work, he says, because "they're enjoying themselves." It has the sound of blessing.

How to get there: From I-64 take the Midway exit. The inn is 1½ miles east of I-64.

Shepherd Place
Versailles, Kentucky
40383

Innkeepers: Marlin and Sylvia Yawn
Address/Telephone: 31 Heritage Road; (606) 873–7843
Rooms: 2; both with private bath, television available on request. No smoking inside.
Rates: $56, double, full breakfast.
Open: Year-round.
Facilities and activities: Pond with ducks and geese. Nearby: restaurants, Lexington, Shakertown.

On five rural acres in the middle of Bluegrass Country, the Yawns keep fifteen sheep. Don't go thinking lamb chops, though; you'd have it all wrong. These sheep are for guests to enjoy watching and petting, for shearing, and for loving. Their wool, as far as Sylvia is concerned, is for spinning and knitting. She shears the sheep only once a year, even though twice a year is possible, so that the wool will be longer and more suited to her handcrafts.

Imagine an interlude in a rural inn with only two guest rooms, where the innkeepers indulge their love of crafts and color and caring by lavishing it on their guests. If romance is caring, this is it.

In busy times you might have to wait to book a night at the inn, too, but the experience is worth the wait.

To give you an idea, an old-fashioned swing sways on the porch. The downstairs parlor once had French doors. These have been converted to floor-to-ceiling windows that let in a glorious amount of light. The light is picked up by 12-inch-high baseboards painted white. Spice brown walls keep the overall effect from being glaring. Queen Anne–style chairs are set off by formal English sofa lamps, and a red-and-blue oriental rug unifies all the room's elements.

The guest rooms are uncommonly large, 20 feet by 20 feet, with bathroom facilities fitted into alcove rooms in their corners.

As pleasing as all this is, the real kick comes from Sylvia's pleasure with it all. In every way she's thrilled with being an innkeeper in her old Kentucky home. She's proud of the smooth gleam of interior paint Marlin (who used to be a professional painter) has accomplished. She enjoys cooking huge breakfasts, which often include Kentucky ham and such delicacies as whole wheat pancakes with walnuts. She loves the sheep and working with their wool. And, most significant of all, she enjoys the guests. "We get such *good* guests. We have a bulletin board full of cards and letters they send after they've been here," she said, "This is all even neater than I thought it would be. It's a real blessing."

How to get there: Coming from Knoxville on I–75, take exit 104 onto the Lexington Circle; from Cincinnati, take exit 115. From the Lexington Circle take exit 5B onto U.S. 60. Drive 6 miles to Heritage Road and turn left. The inn is at the corner of U.S. 60 and Heritage Road.

Madewood
Napoleonville, Louisiana
70390

Innkeepers: Keith and Millie Marshall
Address/Telephone: 4250 Highway 308; (504) 369–7151; for reservations, call
  10:00 A.M. to 5:00 P.M. weekdays
Rooms: 5 in mansion, 1 cabin and 3 suites in the Charlet House; all with pri-
  vate bath, some with wheelchair access. Inquire about pets.
Rates: $90 to $159, double. Charlet House and cabin accommodations
  include continental breakfast and wine and cheese on arrival. Mansion
  rooms include full breakfast and dinner. No personal checks.
Open: Year-round except Christmas Eve, New Year's Eve and Day, and
  Thanksgiving Eve and Day.
Facilities and activities: Dinner. Nearby: Mississippi River tour boats and tours
  of plantation homes.

Well, fiddle-de-dee, Scarlett would love it here. I know, she
was from Atlanta, but she would have loved it here. This is a Rhett-
and-Scarlett kind of place, a Greek Revival mansion with six white
columns. Irises grow around the sides of the porches; you can see
fields in each direction; pear trees on the property produce fruit for
the inn, and the parking area is shaded by established old trees.

The mansion itself is filled with antiques, oriental rugs, and
crystal chandeliers, and it has recently been painted and completely
refurbished, but Madewood still feels like a home rather than a
museum.

Upstairs, one room has been preserved as a dressing room–

bathroom, complete with an old scoop-shaped metal bathtub that would have had to be filled and emptied with a bucket. It makes you appreciate the modern bathrooms now available to guests.

And old clothes are displayed in some of the tour bedrooms, laid out and hanging as though someone were just about to put them on.

Be sure you arrange to have Thelma cook dinner for you. She's one of those cooks who can tell you exactly what's in a dish—she just can't give you exact amounts. She stirs things until they "feel right" and cooks them until they "look right." Her menu includes chicken pies and shrimp pies, gumbos, corn bread, green beans, bread pudding, and Pumpkin Lafourche. Pumpkin Lafourche is a casserole of apples, raisins, pumpkin, sugar, butter, nutmeg, cinnamon, and vanilla, and don't ask in what proportions or for how long or at what temperature Thelma bakes it. Just enjoy.

As for all that richness and all those calories—fiddle-de-dee, think about it tomorrow!

How to get there: From I–10, take exit 182, cross Sunshine Bridge, and follow Bayou Plantation signs to Highway 70, Spur 70, and Highway 308. The inn faces the highway.

S: *At the rear of the house, the original open-hearth kitchen for the plantation home is still intact, set up with odd tables and chairs, an antique washing machine, and assorted pieces of cooking equipment so that you can imagine what it must have been like when meals for the family and guests were prepared there.*

Barrow House
St. Francisville, Louisiana
70775

Innkeepers: Shirley and Lyle Dittloff
Address/Telephone: 524 Royal Street (mailing address: P.O. Box 1461); (504) 635–4791
Rooms: 3, plus 1 suite; all with private bath and television, telephone on request.
Rates: $75 to $85, double; $95, suite; continental breakfast, wine, and cassette walking tour of Historic District. Full breakfast available at $5 extra per person. Cash and personal checks only.
Open: Year-round except December 22–25.
Facilities and activities: Dinner for guests by advance reservation. Located in St. Francisville Historic District. Nearby: tour plantations and historic sites.

When you have an urge to get away with someone special to enjoy some really spectacular food without having to drive to a hotel after dinner, The Barrow House calls. Listen to this: crawfish salad, Chicken Bayou La Fourche (stuffed with crabmeat), Jambalaya Rice, Pecan Praline Parfait. Served on good china with sterling silver flatware by candlelight on a flower-decorated table in the formal dining room, under the old punkah "shoo fly" fan. Oh, be still my heart!

I can tell you lots more about Barrow House, and I'll get to it, but how can Louisiana food like that, served with such style, come anywhere but first? You have to arrange for such dinners ahead of time, and you select from a number of different possibilities for each course.

"We want people to have a good time here," Shirley said. And they do. Beyond the food there's the house, an 1809 saltbox with a Greek Revival wing added in the 1860s, that's listed on the National Register of Historic Places and furnished with 1860s antiques.

The gorgeous antiques include a rosewood armoire by Prudent Mallard and a queen-sized Mallard bed with a *Spanish moss* mattress. You don't have to sleep in that bed unless you want to, but one man, a doctor with a bad back, said it was the most comfortable bed he'd ever had.

Spanish moss was the traditional mattress filler used in Louisiana for two hundred years. The Dittloffs' informal tour of the house gives you a chance to learn how the mattress was made and to see all the fine antiques.

Similarly, the professionally recorded Historic District walking tour (with Mozart between stops) the Dittloffs wrote guides you from Barrow House to twenty-three historic stops.

The Dittloffs' inn came to my attention partly through a magazine article on inns in the magazine *Louisiana Life*. Barrow House was included in the article because when a magazine staffer was married in St. Francisville, she dressed for the wedding at Barrow House. By the time she drove off, everybody who should have was crying properly, and Shirley was carrying the bride's train. Shirley was crying, too.

Some people don't want too much personal fuss. Shirley says that she and Lyle have learned to know when guests would rather be left alone. You'll get whatever amount of attention you want— no more.

How to get there: Barrow House is behind the courthouse in the St. Francisville Historic District. You will receive a map after you make reservations.

Weymouth Hall
Natchez, Mississippi
39120

Innkeeper: Gene Weber

Address/Telephone: 1 Cemetery Road (mailing address: P.O. Box 1091); (601) 445–2304

Rooms: 5; all with private bath, some with wheelchair access. No smoking inn.

Rates: $75 to $80, double, full plantation breakfast, house tour, and beverage on arrival.

Open: Year-round.

Facilities and activities: Nearby: restaurants, Mississippi riverboat tours, tours of many historic Natchez homes.

Remember the old notion of lovers' lane? You sit on a hill overlooking the river, head-to-head, holding hands and whispering secrets as the sun sets and the stars come out a few at a time. If the river happens to be the Mississippi and you stay at Weymouth Hall, which happens to sit atop the hill, you have not just romance, but Romance.

Gene calls Weymouth Hall a "gem of Natchez" because of its unique architecture and fine millwork and bridge work, and, most of all, because of its spectacular view of the Mississippi River. Even before we had looked around inside, Gene showed me the backyard of the inn, where guests can sit in the evening to watch the sun set and the lights come on along the river. "When you've got a view like this, who cares about the house?" he said.

That's a deceptive line. I've never met an innkeeper more involved with the restoration and furnishing of a building than Gene. His collection of antiques by John Belter, Charles Baudoine, and Prudent Mallard is so impressive that even other innkeepers talk about it. The rococo furniture in the double parlor looks as though it had been bought new as a set and kept intact ever since, but Gene spent a lot of time assembling it from wherever he could find it, a piece at a time.

It's worth mentioning that at Weymouth Hall all the guest rooms (which have showers in the private baths) are in the house, not in adjacent buildings or added wings as is the case with some of the larger tour homes. And breakfast is served at a Mississippi plantation table in the main dining room. Gene says that in conversations many guests have said that "living" in the house is important to them.

On a more frivolous note, Gene keeps a player piano from the 1920s, partly to reflect his sense that the inn should be fun, not a museum.

Nor does Gene's involvement stop with the inn and its furnishings. He knows how to entertain guests. He knows the area well and likes to take guests on little personal tours of outstanding old homes in the area. Some guests find these tours more interesting and less expensive than the larger commercial ones available.

You may decide not to leave the property for any kind of tour, however, once you take in the view of the Mississippi River from Weymouth Hall's backyard. It's unquestionably one of the best vistas in Natchez. And the grounds keep getting more pleasing as the shrubbery and gardens mature. Sitting high on the hill catching the breezes and enjoying the view here can be entertainment aplenty, especially if you're with good company.

How to get there: From Highway 65 and 84 (John R. Junkin Drive) on the south side of Natchez, go north on Canal Street as far as you can. Make a left and a quick right onto Linton Avenue and follow Linton Avenue to Cemetery Road. The inn is directly across from the cemetery, on a small hill.

Windsong
Clyde, North Carolina
28721

Innkeepers: Donna and Gale Livengood
Address/Telephone: 120 Ferguson Ridge; (704) 627–6111
Rooms: 5; all with private bath, separate vanity and soaking tub, deck or patio, and fireplace. No air conditioning (elevation 3,000 feet). No smoking inn. One cottage.
Rates: $90 to $95, double; weekly rates 10 percent less; full breakfast. Inquire about cottage rates.
Open: Year-round.
Facilities and activities: VCRs and extensive videocassette library, guest lounge with refrigerator and wet bar (brown bagging), piano, pool table; washer and dryer on request; swimming pool, tennis court, hiking trails, llama treks. Nearby: restaurants, Great Smoky Mountain National Park, Asheville and historic sites, Biltmore House, craft and antiques shops, horseback riding.

At Windsong, you'll find romance in the spectacular mountain-top view, in the beauty of the contemporary lodge, and in the whimsy of the theme-decorated rooms. Donna and Gale built the rustic log building specifically to be a small inn and their own home. It has light pine-log walls and floors of Mexican saltillo tile. The rooms are large, with high, beamed ceilings. Skylights and huge windows let in light on all sides. The building perches on the side of a mountain at 3,000 feet so that looking out the front windows in the direction the guest rooms face, you get a panoramic view of woods and rolling fields below; looking out the back from the kitchen and entry, you see more wilderness higher up and, closer to the house, the perennial gardens, terraces, and recreational facilities.

In addition to sliding glass doors to let you look down the mountain, each guest room has either a deck or a ground-level patio where you can sit to watch the llamas that the Livengoods keep in some of the lower pastures.

Donna decorated the guest rooms in witty, sophisticated styles, using mostly items her family has gathered living in distant places: hence the Alaska Room with Eskimo carvings and art and a dogsled in the corner; hence the Santa Fe Room with Mexican furniture and a steerhide rug. The Safari Room is especially romantic in the style of African Queen. Mosquito netting is draped over the head of the bed, and the room is decorated with primitive artifacts, vines, and bamboo. Dieffenbachia and other junglelike plants flank the big soaking tub in the corner. A little sculptured giraffe with extra-long legs peers out at you from the greenery.

Two new developments may catch your fancy. The Livengoods' daughter Sara manages the beautiful herd of llamas, which not only adorn the surrounding hills but also are the focus of gourmet picnic and overnight hikes they call "llama treks," a romantic novelty. This is a delightful way to backpack without using your own back.

And higher on the hill a small cabin with kitchen, loft bedroom, and wood stove has great possibilities for two couples who would like to travel together and still have privacy.

How to get there: From I–40, take exit 24. Go north on U.S. 209 for 2¹/₂ miles. Turn left on Riverside Drive and go 2 miles. Turn right on Ferguson Cove Loop and go 1 mile, keeping to the left. you'll be driving straight up some narrow, unpaved roads. The distance will seem longer than it is.

S: *It seems to be the custom on these mountain roads for local drivers to pull to the side and give strangers right-of-way.*

La Grange Plantation Inn
Henderson, North Carolina
27536

Innkeepers: Dick and Jean Cornell
Address/Telephone: State Route 1308 (mailing address: Route 3, Box 610); (919) 438–2421
Rooms: 5; all with private bath, 1 with wheelchair access. No smoking inn.
Rates: $85, double, full gourmet breakfast in the dining room or continental breakfast in your room. Inquire about discounts for consecutive night stays.
Open: Year-round.
Facilities and activities: Swimming pool, lakeside fishing, walking trails, croquet, horseshoes. Nearby: restaurants, golf, boat ramps, swimming beaches, picnic grounds on several state recreation areas; water skiing, sailing, fishing on Kerr Lake.

"We wanted pampering and that's what we got," my friend said. I recommended this place to my friends the Jacobys and then waited nervously to hear whether they enjoyed it as much as I had. When Jay Jacoby began his report, it didn't sound good. "Everything was so empty as we drove up from Raleigh; I wondered if we were making a mistake."

I started wondering how mad at me he was.

"But then we rang the bell and Jean Cornell opened the door, and the instant we were across the threshold I knew everything was perfect."

What Jay saw as "empty" I consider "rural," which pleases me. Being more of a city boy, Jay probably had to adjust. But there's nothing rural inside La Grange Plantation Inn. The Cornells are sophisticated innkeepers (Jean is English) with exquisite taste. The place is furnished with American and English antiques in what Jean calls "relaxed English country style."

The front parlor has a wonderful fireplace, books ranging from current fiction to history and natural studies, and no television to break the mood. The Cornells, who are great readers, count among their enthusiastic guests the owners of a bookstore in Raleigh, so it's no surprise that one outstanding feature of all the guest rooms is a good bedside reading light.

To decorate the guest rooms, Jean made the window treatments and bed coverings herself, different in each room and elegant—made of rich fabrics, full of flowers, in muted colors.

The private baths are clustered in a central location just outside the rooms; Jean provides plush terry robes for guests to move from their rooms to their bathrooms but allows that you don't have to use a robe "if you'd rather streak!"

Turning La Grange into an inn was a major project. The Historic Preservation Foundation of North Carolina described the inn in an issue of its magazine, *North Carolina Preservation,* as a "two-story double-pile Greek Revival house with Italianate brackets." The oldest part was built in 1770. It took a lot of time and money as well as the expertise of an architect and an architectural conservator working with a contractor to restore the house to historic preservation standards and also make it comfortable. The Cornells did the interior painting and finished the floors themselves. Today the interior and the hospitality are, as my friends the Jacobys found them, pampering and "perfect."

How to get there: From I–85 take exit 214 to N.C. Route 39 North and proceed 4²/₅ miles to Harris Crossroads. There is a state sign pointing right to Nutbush Creek Recreation Area. Turn right and proceed ⁴/₅ mile to the inn, which is on the left.

The Lodge on Lake Lure
Lake Lure, North Carolina
28746

Innkeepers: Jack and Robin Stanier
Address/Telephone: Charlotte Drive (mailing address: Route One, Box 529A);
    (704) 625–2789
Rooms: 11; all with private bath.
Rates: $75 to $130, double, full gourmet breakfast. Inquire about discounts
    for week-long stays.
Open: February to January.
Facilities and activities: Lakefront, fishing, canoes, boathouse and boat rentals.
    Nearby: restaurants, 2 golf courses, hiking, tubing, tennis, horseback
    riding, antiques and crafts shops.

"The outside of the building doesn't tell the story; the view
tells the story," Robin said. The lodge is built in European hunting-
lodge style that sort of nestles into the lakeside. Inside, the high,
vaulted ceilings, hand-hewn beams, and huge stone fireplaces make
you think of a very *good* hunting lodge, but Robin is right—the
genius of the place is in the long row of windows and the porch facing the lake that take full advantage of the view that one suspects
could exist only here in the Blue Ridge Mountains.

The genius apart from the view is in the innkeepers, who've
patterned their operation on a famous inn in Mexico that they visited more than twenty-five years ago. The experience delighted them
so much that they've gone and done likewise—in their own style.

What Robin liked especially about the Mexican inn was that "it attracted great guests." So does the Lodge on Lake Lure.

It's a matter of kindred spirits. If you want Italian marble baths and gold fixtures, the lodge isn't for you. But if you like overstuffed chairs pulled around the fireplace, wormy-chestnut walls and four-poster beds, breakfasts ranging from banana-buckwheat pancakes to eggs Benedict, and straightforward innkeepers with more than a tad of humor, you'll love the lodge and, by definition, become one of the great guests.

The romance of this lodge is that you can come here and simply be yourself, no worries about fancy clothes or maintaining appearances or trying to seem more conversational than you feel at any given moment. However you are is how Jack and Robin welcome you.

My husband and I sneak away to the Lodge on Lake Lure fairly often. We're such old-timers, so grateful to get away, that we stay happily in any room in the place, but for a special experience you should really ask for the "Something Room." Dubbed so because the Stainers don't want its pleasures to seem limited to honeymooners, the "something" is whatever special reason you want a special room.

Although an inn's history isn't as important as its beds and food, it is fun, to know about the lodge's racy past. It was built as a getaway for the state highway patrol back in 1930, and *everybody* knows those guys didn't go up there to knit bonnets for their grandmothers! While you're in town, get the old-timers to tell you stories.

How to get there: From I–26, take Highway 64/74 to Lake Lure. The lodge is on Charlotte Drive, just off Highway 64/74. Turn at the Lake Lure fire station opposite the golf course. Ask for a map when you make reservations.

S: *The view from the porch dining room, across the lake to the mountains, changes beautifully minute by minute.*

The Belmont Inn
Abbeville, South Carolina
29620

Innkeeper: Janie Wiltshire
Address/Telephone: 106 East Pickens Street; (803) 459–9625
Rooms: 24; all with private bath. Pets allowed by arrangement in special circumstances.
Rates: $60 to $70, double, continental breakfast. Inquire about theater packages. Wheelchair access.
Open: Year-round.
Facilities and activities: Lunch, dinner, lounge, except Sunday. Nearby: theatrical productions at the restored Opera House next door; Russell Lake for fishing, boating, swimming, and water skiing; hunting; gift and antiques shopping in Abbeville.

If your idea of romance involves scenes reminiscent of a show like "The Music Man," with you and your significant other holding hands as you stroll along the streets nodding to folks, try the Belmont. After you walk the village, you can enjoy a romantic dinner-and-theater evening, all without ever having to step into an automobile (horseless carriage).

The old Spanish-style building was built as a modern hotel in 1902. For years, travelers associated with the railroad, the textile industry, and the Opera House stayed here. But it closed in 1972 and stood empty for eleven years, until Mr. and Mrs. Joseph C. Harden bought it. Restoration took almost a year and involved many people in Abbeville. Almost anyone at the inn can tell you stories about bringing The Belmont Inn back to life. Staying here, you feel like a guest not just of the inn, but of the entire community.

The relationship between the Opera House and The Belmont thrives again, too. You can make great package deals including theater tickets, dinner with wine, a drink in the Curtain Call Lounge after the show, your lodging, and continental breakfast the next morning. The package rates are always good, but they vary with the season and so does the show schedule. Activity peaks with summer theater at the Opera House.

Whether it precedes a show or not, dinner in the large dining room with its high ceilings and paddle fans is worth enjoying slowly. The menu tends toward continental cuisine without being self-conscious about it. The chef prepares veal a different way every day. After a nice meal of filleted chicken breasts Dijon with pecans, I let the waitress talk me into a slice of Irish Cream mousse cake.

How to get there: The inn is on the corner of the town square. From Greenwood, take Highway 72 west to Abbeville, turn right onto Highway 20 (Main Street), and go to the first traffic light. Turn right onto Pickens Street. The second building on the right is The Belmont. From I–85, take Highway 28 south into Abbeville where it joins Main Street.

≈

S: *When you walk around the town, everyone from merchants to workers in their vans wave as if they see you every day.*

Ansonborough Inn
Charleston, South Carolina
29401

Innkeeper: Allen B. Johnson; Eric A. Crapse, assistant innkeeper
Address/Telephone: 21 Hassel Street; (803) 723–1655 or (800) 522–2073
Rooms: 37 suites; all with private bath, telephone, television, and kitchen.
No-smoking rooms available.
Rates: Spring and fall, $89 to $138, double; summer and winter, $89 to
$114, double; continental breakfast and afternoon wine and cheese.
Open: Year-round.
Facilities and activities: Free off-street parking. In heart of waterfront historic
district. Nearby: historic sites, restaurants, shuttle transportation to visitor center. Walking distance to antiques shops and downtown
Charleston.

If I wanted to spend a few romantic days in perfect privacy in
Charleston, here's the place I'd choose. Like so many Charleston
inns, this one had a different function in its earlier time. It was a
three-story stationer's warehouse built about 1900. The building's
renovation not only kept the hart of pine beams and locally fired
red brick, which are typical of the period, but actually emphasized
them. The lobby soars three stories high, with skylights; the original
huge, rough beams are fully visible, an important part of the decor.

The original plan to use the renovated building as a condo
complex didn't work out, which probably was bad news for some
investors; but it's great for inn guests now, because the rooms,
which are really suites, are huge. At least one wall in each features

126

the exposed old brick. The ceilings are about 20 feet high. Because all the rooms were fit into an existing shell, no two rooms are exactly the same shape or size. Nothing is exactly predictable. The resulting little quirks, nooks, lofts, and alcoves add a lot of interest.

The living rooms are furnished in period reproductions with comfortable chairs and sofas. What's more, you really can cook in the kitchens. If you ask for place settings and basic kitchen utensils when you make your reservations, the kitchen will be ready when you arrive. The inn is just across the road from an excellent Harris Teeter supermarket housed in an old railroad station. I don't think it would be appropriate to whip up corned beef and cabbage or deep-fried chittlins in this environment, but the arrangement is great for preparing light meals—a good way to save your calories and your dollars for some sumptuous dinners in Charleston's excellent restaurants.

Clearly this isn't the kind of place where everyone sits around the breakfast table comparing notes about dinner the night before, but the continental breakfast (with sweet breads baked at a plantation in Walterboro) and the evening wine and cheese are set up in the lobby so that guests can sit in conversational clusters. But if you don't feel like talking to another single soul, you're entirely welcome to help yourself to wine and cheese and retreat to a private corner or back to your room.

How to get there: From I-25 East, take the Meeting Street/Visitor Center exit. Go 1¹/₅ miles to Hassel Street. Turn left and go through the next traffic signal. From Route 17 South, take the East Bay Street exit, go 1³/₁₀ miles to Hassel and turn left. From Route 17 North, after crossing the Ashley River, exit to the right and go through the first traffic signal onto Calhoun Street. Drive 1²/₅ miles to East Bay Street, turn right, and go to the second traffic signal (Hassel Street) and turn left. The inn is on your right.

Buckhorn Inn
Gatlinburg, Tennessee
37738

Innkeepers: John and Connie Burns
Address/Telephone: 2140 Tudor Mountain Road; (615) 436–4468
Rooms: 6, plus 4 cottages, 1 guest house; all with private bath, cottages and
  guest house with television, refrigerator or kitchenette, and fireplace.
Rates: $95 to $250, double, full breakfast. Only traveler's checks and personal checks accepted.
Open: Year-round, except Christmas.
Facilities and activities: Fixed-price, set-menu dinner for guests by reservation,
  $18 per person. Ice available. Small conference facilities. Spring-fed lake
  stocked with bream and bass. Located on 35 acres. Nearby: hiking,
  swimming, tennis, racquetball, basketball, skiing, golf, shopping, and
  tourist activities. Close to Gatlinburg.

People have been coming to Buckhorn Inn for romantic getaways for several generations now. The inn has been spiffed up, the
landscaping has certainly matured, and younger people have shoul-
dered the major innkeeping responsibilities, but the spirit of the
place remains the same.

The short drive up the hill from the glitz of Gatlinburg brings
you to a simple white building settled against a hill from where you
view the highest peaks of the Smokies. Inside, the living room and
dining room are divided from each other in one big, long room by a
large stone fireplace in the middle of the front wall. The chairs and
love seats are cool and summery looking in new upholstery.

From here, doors open out onto a narrow porch separated from a well-manicured lawn by a low hedge. From the lawn, stone steps lead to a footpath that wanders into the woods.

Once when I stopped here, I met an elderly woman who had first visited the inn when someone gave a trip here to her and her husband as an anniversary present. She has come back every year since, even though her husband has passed on. And I met a young couple entranced with the grand piano, the rockers, and the generous supply of books. I think they had come intending to follow a full-steam-ahead schedule of hiking, fishing, and fitness but had been lulled into rocking and reading instead.

The inn has always been known for its good food and that, too, is better than ever. Everything is home cooked daily, from breads to desserts. A professional chef on staff has been creating sophisticated menus. At breakfast, for instance, your choices, in addition to standards such as country ham and eggs, might include a strawberry or walnut waffle with bacon or Buckhorn's own version of müesli cereal. At dinner, they serve up meals such as Pesto Chicken with Basil Cream Sauce, preceded by Chablis Cheddar Soup, accompanied by rice pilaf, salad, and a fresh vegetable, and finished off with a dessert of fresh strawberries, honey, and cream. To quote an old television commercial, "It doesn't get any better than this."

How to get there: Take U.S. 441 to Gatlinburg and turn onto U.S. 321 north at Gatlinburg Chamber of Commerce corner. Follow U.S. 321 north about 5 miles. Turn left at Buckhorn Road and go ³/₄ mile. Turn right at Buckhorn Inn sign. The inn is ¹/₄ mile on the right.

Adams Edgeworth Inn
Monteagle, Tennessee
37356

Innkeepers: Wendy and David Adams
Address/Telephone: Monteagle Assembly; (615) 924-2559
Rooms: 10, plus 1 suite with kitchenette and fireplace; all with private bath,
some rooms with fireplace or wheelchair access. Smoking on verandas
only.
Rates: $55 to $125, double, continental breakfast. Two-night minimum on
special weekends.
Open: Year-round.
Facilities and activities: Dinner by reservation. Gift shop. On grounds of Monteagle Assembly. Nearby: golf, tennis, Tennessee State Park, wilderness
and developed hiking trails, Sewanee University of the South, Monteagle Wine Cellars.

This is romance in the most impeccable taste—museum-quality
art, fine antiques, shelves bulging with books, and seclusion on a
wooded bit of land in a historical community sometimes called "the
Chatauqua of the South."

David and Wendy Adams have a beautiful inn in a three-story
Victorian structure built as an inn nearly 100 years ago. You have a
couple of different possibilities for suites with private entrances and
such niceties as fireplaces, or you can enjoy a room on the second
floor.

Outside, if you prefer an active retreat to a sedentary one, the state park and wilderness areas offer lots of privacy and even, David says, some places you can skinny-dip.

Inside, they refurbished and brightened the interior without hiding the wood floors or changing the inn's warm character. They brought a large, eclectic collection of art, as well as antiques and interesting mementos they and their grown children have picked up in world travel. Also, they have some wonderful items from the years Wendy's father spent as a United States ambassador, including the gold-edge ambassadorial china upon which Wendy serves dinner.

Some of the guest rooms have been designed around quilts made by her mother and grandmother that Wendy uses as bedcovers. The library and guest rooms overflow with books. Classical music deepens the feeling of serenity in the sitting areas and floats out onto the shady porches.

Dinner deserves a write-up of its own. When Wendy dims the lights in the formal dining room, most of the illumination comes from candles, except for small lamps shining over each of the paintings in the room. Often a piano player or guitarist provides music.

We had an appetizer of smoked salmon with Russian black bread and Vidalia onions. Of the several choices of entrees, I especially enjoyed the chicken breast filled with fresh herbs. We had a variety of lightly cooked and sauced fresh vegetables, and a colorful salad of arugula and greens with Camembert. For dessert Wendy served fresh strawberries and kiwi in a custard sauce with a hint of either caramel or maple. Maybe both. The flavors were subtle enough to keep me wondering. If the gods get romantic, they must do it like this.

How to get there: From I–24 take exit 134. Turn right. In the center of the village you will see a steel archway with a Monteagle Assembly sign. Turn right through the arch, once on the grounds turn right at the mall sign and right immediately at Chestnut Hill.

The Midwest

by Bob Puhula

Many people consider the country's heartland nothing more than a tranquil region of family farms and wholesome values akin to something out of a Norman Rockwell painting. In the not too distant past, however, the Midwest was a dramatic theater of history filled with legend, lore, and romance.

On the outland border of the Old Northwest, frontiersmen braved both unbroken forests and oceans of tall prairie grasses standing as high as a horse's shoulder to conquer the wilderness and bring civilization to an untamed land. Some of those very log cabins and clapboard buildings that housed early settlers now welcome country inn guests for weekends dappled with history and romance.

Lumber barons hell-bent on clear-cutting virgin pine trees that blanketed North Woods terrain often built elegant mansions as a display of their wealth. Today, many of these same mansions have been converted into luxurious inns that pamper guests during whimsical overnight getaways.

Farmers built lonely homesteads in the midst of flat plains and rolling hills as they tilled the soil, transforming prairie into cropland. Many of these historic farmsteads have been transformed into country-tinged, out-of-the-way havens for privacy and romance.

Let's not forget Mark Twain's paddle wheelers, churning their way over the Midwest's mighty rivers like the Mississippi, Ohio, and Missouri. Historic inns that catered to riverboat passengers and elegant mansions owned by boat-company magnates have been restored to their former glory, opening their doors to couples looking for a special place to celebrate—whatever.

In fact, two of the most romantic retreats I've ever visited are located in the Midwest. They're included in the pages that follow, pages that offer you a passport to your own romantic fantasies.

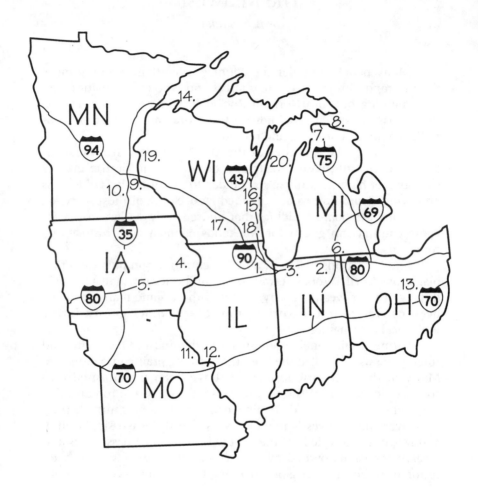

The Midwest

Numbers on map refers to towns numbered below.

The Wheaton Inn
Wheaton, Illinois
60187

Innkeepers: Ogden and Jackie Andrews
Address/Telephone: 301 West Roosevelt Road; (708) 690–2600
Rooms: 16; all with private bath and air conditioning, some with Jacuzzi. Wheelchair access.
Rates: $99 to $195, double, EPB. Weekend packages.
Open: All year.
Facilities and activities: Patio, lawn area with croquet course and gardens, sitting room, dining area. Near McCormick's Cantigny war museum, Prairie Path hike and biketrail; Herrick Lake paddle boating and fishing; Wheaton Water Park; Fox River and Geneva famous shopping districts; horseback riding; Morton Arboretum; Wheaton College's Billy Graham Center; golf courses; tennis courts; polo grounds. Also short drive to Drury Lane Theatres.

This splendid inn, located in Chicago's western suburbs, remains a glorious retreat in the Colonial Williamsburg tradition, possessing an unmistakable flair for romance.

As one of the most elegant Illinois inns around, the lavish getaway offers guest rooms that feature gas fireplaces, Jacuzzi whirlpools, and distinctive architectural touches. In fact, the innkeepers have even placed European towel warmers in bathrooms—a thoughtful touch, especially for romantics who venture out in frigid Chicago winters.

Rooms also boast oversized features often found in European

concierge hotels. I especially enjoy the Woodward Room, with a Jacuzzi situated in front of a large bay window that overlooks the inn gardens. Others might enjoy the McCormick Room's huge four-poster bed with vaulted ceilings. Another romantic charmer is the Morton Room; it boasts an alcoved ceiling, a cozy fireplace perfect for snuggling in front of, and a 4½-foot-deep Jacuzzi, a great spot for a relaxing soak—or whatever.

The only room that departs from the Colonial Williamsburg theme is the Ottoson Room, named for the inn architect. It features a sleek, brass-topped black iron-rail bed, with a cathedral ceiling skylight over the bed.

Then again, unabashed romantics like Debbie head straight to the Rice Room. Its Jacuzzi sits almost in the middle of the room, in front of a roaring fireplace, with *two* skylights above to gaze out at the stars.

Breakfasts include European-style buffets with imported coffees and teas, hot egg dishes, and delicious pastries and muffins. Personal services also include afternoon tea, 24-hour coffee, and bedtime service with chocolate treats left on your pillows.

How to get there: From Chicago, take I–294 to Roosevelt Road, then go west to inn.

The Checkerberry Inn
Goshen, Indiana
46526

Innkeepers: John and Susan Graff, owners; Shawna Koehler and Jane Erickson, assistant managers.
Address/Telephone: 62644 County Road 37; (219) 642–4445
Rooms: 13, including 3 suites; all with private bath and air conditioning. Wheelchair access.
Rates: $120 to $400, double, continental breakfast.
Open: May through December; limited time February through April; closed January.
Facilities and activities: Full-service dining room, swimming pool, arbor, croquet court, tennis court, hiking trails, cross-country ski area. In the midst of Amish farmlands; offers horse-drawn buggy tours of Amish surroundings, sleigh rides in winter. Near Shipshewana auctions, Middlebury festivals.

My wife, Debbie, and I especially like this inn's European ambience, certainly a surprise for a hostelry that's surrounded on all sides by hundreds of acres of Amish farmland. The romantic Continental feel begins the minute you walk into the Checkerberry. It's intimate and elegant, reminding us of small European hotels we've visited. Handsome photographs on the inn walls contribute to this texture; taken by John during his vacation journeys, they feature scenes from France's Bordeaux region.

Luxurious guest rooms boast their own European flair, featuring fine-arts prints and large windows that allow views of the rolling countryside just outside your room. Use your imagination, and you *could* be in the Bordeaux.

Whirlpool baths and sitting-room fireplaces make great spots for late-night romantic rendezvous, and amenities like Swiss goat-milk soaps in the bath add to the air of elegance. Still, regional touches, like Amish-style straw hats hanging on the walls over several beds, remind guests that they are indeed in Indiana.

The inn's restaurant is another European adventure, leaning toward country-French cuisine. Four-course meals might begin with a fresh garden salad, followed by a fresh fruit sorbet, entree, and dessert. An inn specialty is double duck breast sautéed and served over sweet onions, topped with orange and port wine sauce, accompanied by Pommes Anna and a bouquet of fresh vegetables. The vegetables, herbs, and spices are grown specially for the inn. Other favorites include chicken basil, veal medallions, and rack of lamb served off the bone with herb cream-and-garlic cheese.

In clement weather, take a quiet and romantic stroll over the inn's 100 acres, or have a swim together in the pool. In colder times, snuggle up in front of your guest room fireplace and reminisce about your own travels together.

Or just make some up!

How to get there: From Chicago, take the Indiana Toll Road (I–80/90) to the Middlebury exit (#107). Go south on Indiana 13, turn west on Indiana 4, then go south on County Road 37 to the inn. It's 14 miles from the toll-road exit to the inn.

B: The inn boasts Indiana's only professional croquet course. So now is the time to perfect your game.

Creekwood Inn
Michigan City, Indiana
46360

Innkeeper: Mary Lou Linnen
Address/Telephone: Route 20/35 at Interstate 94; (219) 872–8357
Rooms: 13, including 1 suite; all with private bath and air conditioning.
    Wheelchair access.
Rates: $99 to $120, double; $144 to $150, suite; continental breakfast.
Open: All year except two weeks in mid-March and Christmas Day.
Facilities and activities: Dinner served in parlor on weekends to guests only.
    Short drive to restaurants, southeastern shore of Lake Michigan, Indi-
    ana Dunes State Park, Warren Dunes State Park in Michigan. Charter
    fishing, swimming, boating. Antiquing in nearby lakeside communi-
    ties. Area winery tours. Old Lighthouse Museum. A short drive to
    heart of southwestern Michigan's "Fruit Belt" for U-pick fruit and veg-
    etable farms.

    The Creekwood Inn is one of our favorite romantic retreats in
winter months.

    A mantle of white snow cover acres of walnut, oak, and pine
trees, a private forest that the inn nestles upon. We don cross-country
skis, and in the silent landscape, broken only by an occasionally
chirping bird, we skim past tiny Walnut Creek, frozen in the winter
cold. Sometimes we even see a deer high-stepping through the drifts.

    When finished, we ski to the door of this charming English
cottage inn. First glance reveals that it is warm, cozy, and classically
gracious. Massive hand-hewn wooden ceiling beams lend a rugged

elegance. Wood planking covers the floors. A large bay window looks out over the snow-sprinkled grounds. The parlor's fireplace, surrounded by sofas and overstuffed chairs, is the perfect setting for intimate midnight conversation.

Guest rooms are equally gracious and especially roomy. We love those that have their own fireplaces and private terraces. All boast king-sized beds, overstuffed reading chairs, and mini-refrigerators to keep cold your late-night champagne.

Romantics can opt for intimate dinners served Fridays and Saturdays. Consider treats like orange roughy au gratin, beef medallions, and chicken tarragon. Then stretch your toes before the parlor fireplace, enjoying an evening cup of cocoa, or gaze out at the winter wonderland.

How to get there: Heading northeast to Michigan City on I–94, take exit 40B. Then take an immediate left turn onto 600W, and turn into the first drive on the left. The inn is at Route 20/35, just off the interstate.

B: *Mary Lou visited Oxford, England, and was inspired to plant an English perennial garden on the east side of the inn. Things just keep getting better.*

Squiers Manor
Maquoketa, Iowa
52060

Innkeepers: Cathy and Virg Banowetz
Address/Telephone: 418 West Pleasant Street; (319) 652–6961
Rooms: 6, with 1 suite; all with private baths and central air conditioning.
Rates: $65 to $95, double; suite $125; EPB.
Open: All year.
Facilities and activities: Library, parlor, porch. Short drive to Mississippi River
   towns; Dubuque, site of low-stakes riverboat casino gambling; and
   Galena, Illinois, a Civil War-era architectural wonderland.

We were not convinced that this marvelous 1882 inn was top
romantic material until we stepped into the Jennie Mitchell Bridal
Suite.

The glamorous room boasts a canopy brass bed more than 7
feet tall, with mother-of-pearl on its footboard. A Victorian Renaissance dresser with a marble top is yet another link to the romantic
past. But the clincher is a huge double whirlpool that, Debbie
assured me, would do any honeymoon suite proud.

In fact, every guest room and common room bespeaks luxury
and splendor. There's fine wood everywhere, including a walnut
parlor, cherrywood dining room, and butternut throughout the
house.

Antiques are museum quality. We were especially impressed
with the 1820s Federal four-poster mahogany bed in the Harriet

Squiers Room that would be a welcome addition to the Smithsonian.

Beyond the antiques, it's the guest rooms that add the crowning touch to this romantic retreat in Iowa's heartland.

Consider the J. E. Squiers Room, another romantic favorite with a Verde green marble floor that creates an alluring path to a cozy corner whirlpool for two. All kinds of possibilities await you here.

Later, you can sit in the formal parlor in front of a roaring fireplace with marble tiles depicting characters in Roman mythology. Or snuggle in the library, done entirely in butternut and boasting its original fireplace.

In the morning, enjoy Cathy's breakfasts in the elegant cherrywood dining room, a perfect spot for pumpkin pecan muffins, black walnut bread, eggs Katrina, pecan-stuffed French toast, seafood quiches, and more.

How to get there: From Dubuque, take U.S. 61 south to U.S. 64, then turn east into town. One block past the second stoplight, turn right, then go 1 block to the inn.

La Corsette Maison Inn
Newton, Iowa
50208

Innkeeper: Kay Owen
Address/Telephone: 629 1st Avenue; (515) 792–6833
Rooms: 5, with 2 suites; all with private bath and air conditioning. No smoking inn.
Rates: $55 to $75, double; $75 to $115, suites; EPB. Four-night minimum during Pella, Iowa, Tulip Festival and some other special events. Pets allowed by prearrangement.
Open: All year.
Facilities and activities: Gourmet six-course dinners. Two sitting rooms with fireplace; porch. Nearby: Maytag Company tours, tennis courts, golf courses, horseback riding, cross-country skiing. Short drive to Trainland, U.S.A.; Prairie Meadows Horse Track; Krumm Nature Preserve.

The most romantic breakfast Debbie and I ever experienced took place at this handsome Iowa inn.

We sat in front of a roaring fireplace in an elegant parlor, filled by only our table, in what amounted to a private room for two. Our gourmet-style morning meal started when Kay brought us fresh fruit compote that delighted with pink grapefruit, mandarin orange slices, grapes, and kiwi. Home-baked apple muffins with strudel were next; we could have eaten a half-dozen, easy, they were so delicious. We sipped on raspberry and orange juice, which washed down authentic English scones, another of Kay's specialties. Then came frittata with two cheeses, and some of the fabulous La Corsette French bread.

It was an ultimate bed and breakfast experience.

No wonder Kay's inn has received a 4¹/₂-star rating from the *Des Moines Register* and has been hailed as a "gleaming jewel in the crown of fine restaurants."

The mansion itself is a romantic masterpiece. The 1909 Mission-style home, built by an early Iowa state senator, is filled with gleaming mission oak woodwork, art nouveau stained-glass windows, and other turn-of-the-century architectural flourishes.

We stayed in the Windsor Hunt Suite, a massive bedchamber with a huge four-poster bed (reached by a stepstool) and a sitting room boasting its own fireplace—which we used for a romantic ending to a near-perfect day.

Another room for lovers is the Penthouse—bedchambers located in the home's tower and surrounded by beveled-glass windows that sparkle like jewels.

Kay's six-course gourmet dinners are part of the romantic mix. Imagine the likes of French veal in cream; broccoli-stuffed game hen with Mornay sauce; and roasted loin of pork with prune chutney.

Heavenly.

How to get there: From the Quad Cities, take I–80 to Newton (exit 164), and go north until the second light (Highway 6); then turn right and continue 7 blocks to the inn.

B: *Kay gives house tours before dinner each evening. One of her anecdotes reveals that Fred Maytag, of washing-machine fame, got his seed money from La Corsette's owner to start his company. Another tells that Fred personally used a "one-minute brand" washer made by another company in town. His own Maytag "chewed up" his clothes.*

Chicago Pike Inn
Coldwater, Michigan
49036

Innkeeper: Rebecca A. Schultz
Address/Telephone: 215 East Chicago Street; (517) 279–8744
Rooms: 6, with 1 suite; all with private bath, TV and phone on request.
Rates: $75 to $130, double, EPB. Two-night minimum on special weekends.
Open: All year.
Facilities and activities: Parlor, library, dining room, wraparound front porch,
gardens, gazebo. Walk to downtown shops. Nearby: antiquing, golf,
boating, fishing, swimming, cross-country skiing, orchards, nature
trails, lake activities, Turkeyville Dinner Theatre, museums, wineries,
historic architecture.

It's no wonder the Chicago Pike Inn lures lots of anniversary
couples and other romantic celebrants. One glance around this
beautiful retreat could send anybody's pulse racing—with or without your loved one at your side.

Built in 1903, Rebecca and her family have carefully restored
this spectacular house to its early grandeur. Step inside the formal
reception room and admire the double-mantled cherry wood fireplace adorned by Staffordshire dogs.

And that magnificent cherry staircase leading to upstairs guest
rooms might have been used by Rhett Butler to sweep Scarlett up
in his arms if their adventures had carried them north.

The inn is graced with all manner and styles of impeccable

146

antiques, reflecting fine taste and expensive fabric. Leaded Bradley and Hubbard lamps, Schumacher and Waverly wall coverings, fluted cherry wood columns, handcarved antique furniture, stained-glass windows, parquet floors—this seemingly endless list of outstanding features contributes mightily to the inn's romantic feel.

While all guest rooms are exquisite, I suggest you might choose Miss Sophia's Suite for an unforgettable night. Its two rooms are fully bursting with the accoutrements of a romantic encounter: hand-carved antique bed; oak-mantled fireplace that's a great backdrop for late-night goings-on; and even a private balcony.

Rebecca tends to even the smallest details. For example, rooms come with thick terry-cloth robes, and the handsome library, boasting its own fireplace, is always well-stocked with Victorian candies.

Breakfast is a formal affair, with Rebecca gussied up in Victorian lace and serving scrumptious, four-course delights that include crepes, soufflés, pastry puffs, and more. Put this all together, and you have the ingredients for one of the Midwest's most stylized romantic retreats.

How to get there: The inn is located on U.S. 12 (the old Chicago Pike), midway between Detroit and Chicago, just minutes south of I–94.

Kimberly Country Estate
Harbor Springs, Michigan
49740

Innkeepers: Ronn and Billie Serba
Address/Telephone: 2287 Bester Road; (616) 526–7646 or –9502
Rooms: 7, with 1 suite; all with private bath. Wheelchair access. No smoking inn.
Rates: $100 to $250, double, EPB. Two-night minimum on weekends.
Open: All year, except April.
Facilities and activities: Living room, library, lower-level entertainment room, terrace, swimming pool. Nearby: golf, biking, hiking, sailing and other water activities on Little Traverse Bay. Short drive to chic shops in Harbor Springs, downhill skiing at Boyne Highlands and Nubs Nob.

Imagine yourself luxuriating on an elegant plantation in the Old South. Now imagine yourself doing the same thing, but traveling north, to the peninsular coast of western Michigan, in order to get there.

That's the treat waiting for couples at Kimberly Country Estate, a Southern-plantation-style home that offers a rare romantic ambience one usually finds on the other side of the Mason-Dixon line.

Ronn and Billie's inn could be a showcase for *House Beautiful*. Chippendale furniture, Battenburg linens, Laura Ashley fabrics, and exquisite antiques collected by the innkeepers over 40 years are a definition of inn elegance.

The Lexington Suite is the epitome of romanticism with its four-poster bed, wood-burning fireplace, and swirling Jacuzzi.

Le Soleil is another of our favorites, especially for spring and summer visitors, with its walls of windows and sunny yellow colors that are as refreshing as morning dew. Four guest rooms open onto a shaded veranda overlooking the inn's huge swimming pool; the romantic possibilities here are seemingly unlimited.

Pampering is part of the inn's romanticism. We found a decanter of sherry in our guest room upon arrival, with an invitation to join Ronn and Billie for afternoon tea and hors d'oeuvres. At night, guests return to their rooms to discover beds turned down and chocolate truffles on the pillows. The rest is up to you.

Even breakfasts often offer Southern-tinged treats like scrambled eggs with smoked turkey sausage, home-baked muffins, and more. Afterward, you might retreat to the elegant library, just to revel in its atmosphere; it's entirely paneled with North Carolina black walnut, milled on the spot as the house was built, Billie told me.

If you can, walk the grounds hand in hand one more time before you leave.

How to get there: From Petoskey, take U.S. 31 north to Michigan 119. Continue north toward Harbor Springs. Turn right at Emmet Heights Road, then left on Bester Road, and continue to the inn.

Grand Hotel
Mackinac Island, Michigan
49757

Innkeeper: R. D. Musser, III, corporation president
Address/Telephone: Mackinac Island; (906) 847–3331
Rooms: 317; all with private bath.
Rates: $120 to $235, per person, early May through mid-June; add $15, mid-June through late October; MAP. Special packages available.
Open: Mid-May to late October.
Facilities and activities: Main dining room, Geranium Bar, Grand Stand (food and drink), Audubon Bar, Carleton's Tea Store, pool grill. Magnificent swimming pool, private golf course, bike rentals, saddle horses, tennis courts, exercise trail. Carriage tours, dancing, movies. Expansive grounds, spectacular veranda with wonderful lake vistas. Nearby: museums, historic fort, and other sites, guided tours; specialty shops. There are no motor vehicles allowed on historic Mackinac Island; visitors walk, or rent horses, horse-drawn carriages and taxis, and bicycles.

Let me just straight-out say it. There's almost nothing that can beat the extraordinary Grand Hotel if romance is your game.

Sitting on a high bluff overlooking the Straits of Mackinac at the juncture of lakes Huron and Superior, the Grand Hotel is an elegant reminder of the days of Great Lakes steamers, well-dressed ladies carrying colorful parasols, and gentlemen who'd lay their coats down on the ground so a lass could cross a puddle without getting her feet muddy.

A ride in a horse-drawn coach (with a driver wearing formal

pink hunting jacket) from the ferryboat docks, up the hill, to the hotel starts your return to the romantic, turn-of-the-century past.

Each time we step inside the elegant 1887 building, we immediately feel immersed in luxury. Hotel attendants are dressed in long red coats and black bow ties. High-back chairs and Victorian sofas are everywhere in numerous public common rooms. Special pampering services include complimentary morning coffee, concerts during afternoon tea, horse-drawn carriage island tours, live-music dinner dances, and more.

Exquisite guest rooms include many with spectacular lake views, some seemingly jutting out over the water defying gravity. The sound of crashing waves, the black of the night, and an occasional glimpse of the northern lights add to the hotel's romantic persona.

Make sure you take your loved one out on the famous veranda, 660 feet long and providing magnificent views of manicured hotel grounds and the straits. And to get into the mood at dinner time, share this dessert treat—the Grand pecan ball smothered with hot fudge. It can make you both melt.

How to get there: From either Mackinaw City from the Lower Peninsula or from St. Ignace on the Upper Peninsula, a 30-minute ferry ride brings you to Mackinac Island. Dock porters will greet your boat. There's an island airstrip for chartered flights and private planes.

B: *For a romantic getaway in the Grand-est style, this inn cannot be beat.*

Thorwood Inn
Hastings, Minnesota
55033

Innkeepers: Pam and Dick Thorsen
Address/Telephone: Fourth and Pine; (612) 437–3297
Rooms: 7; all with private bath and air conditioning. Wheelchair access. No smoking inn.
Rates: $75 to $150, double, EPB. Can arrange for pet sitters. Special package rates available.
Open: All year.
Facilities and activities: "Hat box" dinners in your room. Walking tour of historical area just blocks away. Quaint Mississippi River town with specialty and antiques shops, several good restaurants. Parks and nature trails nearby; also river, streams, lakes, and all sorts of summer and winter sports.

Innkeepers Pam and Dick have a romantic streak second to none among Midwest innkeepers. Just step inside their dreamy inns, called Rosewood and Thorwood, and you'll graphically see why.

The Rosewood Inn, a handsome Queen Anne house built in 1878, offers elegant romantic hideaways with inspired luxuries to pamper you. Consider Rebecca's Room, a stirring romantic retreat with an all-marble bath highlighted by a double whirlpool resting in front of its own fireplace; a second fireplace in the bedroom sits opposite an inviting four-poster antique bed.

Then there's the Vermillion Room, with its see-through fireplace that toasts both an ornate brass bed and a sunken double whirlpool. For sheer decadence, try the Mississippi Room, as large as an apartment with skylights over a French sleigh bed and a large copper tub, double whirlpool, and meditation room.

It's more of the same at their Thorwood Inn, also in Hastings. The 1880s Second Empire-style house includes perhaps the ultimate retreat—the Steeple Room. Complete with see-through fireplace and double whirlpool, it is built—you guessed it—right in the home's steeple. In fact, the 23-foot-tall steeple rises high above the tub and boasts a glitzy ball chandelier that shimmers from the pinnacle like stars in the sky.

To all this add complimentary bottles of wine, breakfast baskets delivered to the door of your room, and hat box suppers served in your romantic digs. You need look no farther for a special getaway retreat.

How to get there: From LaCrosse, take U.S. 61 north to Hastings; then turn left on Fourth Street and proceed to inn.

B: *Decadent suites strike a hotly romantic chord.*

Schumacher's
New Prague Hotel
New Prague, Minnesota
56071

Innkeepers: John and Kathleen Schumacher
Address/Telephone: 212 West Main Street; (612) 758–2133
Rooms: 11; all with private bath, double whirlpool, air conditioning, and
phone, some with gas fireplace and hairdryer.
Rates: $104 to $120, double, Sunday through Thursday; $130 to $150, double, Friday through Saturday; EP. Special packages and senior citizens'
rates available. Personal checks from Minnesota only.
Open: All year except Christmas Eve and Christmas Day.
Facilities and activities: Full-service restaurant with wheelchair access. Bavarian bar, European gift shop, travel agency. Drive to cross-country and
downhill skiing, swimming, golfing, boating, fishing, biking, hiking,
orchard, museums, racetrack, amusement park.

Come to this inn only if you're longing for a very romantic
European vacation celebrated in lavish style, along with some of the
best ethnic cooking this side of the Atlantic.

That's what you'll get at this handsome Old-World inn, a
showcase for Bavarian and Czech antiques and gourmet meals that
rival many European country hotels I've visited on my travels.

Built in 1898, the inn is imbued with a peaceful atmosphere,
rich craftsmanship, and some of the most unique, romantic bedchambers found in the Midwest.

Upstairs are eleven individually decorated rooms, named in German for the months of the year, and furnished with Old-World trunks, chairs, beds, and wardrobes. Several rooms boast their own fireplaces, and all offer double whirlpools. Authentic European touches include eiderdown pillows and comforters, bedding and other stylistic flairs purchased in Austria, Czechoslovakia, and West Germany by John and Kathleen themselves.

August is a favorite of Debbie's, with it's king-sized bed, primitive Bavarian folk art, and stenciled pine plank floor. An ornately decorated wardrobe graces one wall. In this room you'll feel like you've stepped into some charming German pensione.

I also like Mai, with its canopy bed reached by a small stepladder; the design inside the canopy features storybook-style figures from newlyweds to seniors. To help set the mood, John provides a complimentary bottle of imported German wine and two glasses in each room.

John is also a classically trained chef whose European concoctions are unusual and heavenly to American palates. Try the Central-European meal that includes romacka (cream of bean soup with dill) and Czech roast duck served with red cabbage, potato dumplings, and dressing—with apple strudel for dessert.

How to get there: From Minneapolis, take 35 W south; exit on County Road 2. Continue to Minnesota 13 and turn south; proceed directly into New Prague; the hotel is on the left.

B: *A romantic "European" retreat in the classical style.*

Garth Woodside Mansion
Hannibal, Missouri
63401

Innkeepers: Irv and Diane Feinberg
Address/Telephone: R.R. 1; (314) 221–2789
Rooms: 8; all with private bath and central air conditioning, phone on
request.
Rates: $58 to $90, double, EPB.
Open: All year.
Facilities and activities: BYOB. Sitting rooms, parlors, wraparound porch. Acres
of gardens, meadows, woodlands. Tours of the mansion given 11:30
A.M. to 3:00 P.M. daily. Short drive to restaurants, Mark Twain's boy-
hood house, Huckleberry Finn landmarks, Mississippi River paddle-
wheel rides, caves, sightseeing tours, Mark Twain Outdoor Theater,
specialty shops, and Great River Road that follows the Mississippi.

Staying at the Garth Woodside Mansion is like having your
own romantic country estate. Sprawling on 39 acres of meadows
and woodlands, complete with its own lake, the 1871 house was a
summer home for a prominent Hannibal businessman and a meeting place for passing-through notables—like Mark Twain.

I don't know if the hometown author thought of romance
while at the house, but guests should, given the elegant flourishes
of Victoriana that grace the historic inn.

Mostly original furnishings are exquisite, including 1840s
Empire furniture, walnut paneling, and even a marble fireplace
with gold inlay in the library. The dining room is another opulent

room and includes special chairs built extra-wide to accommodate the full petticoats that were the style of the day.

To reach guest rooms, we climbed a "flying staircase" that vaults three stories high with no visible means of support. It appears even more spectacular, hanging high in the air, because of the mansion's 14-foot-high ceilings.

Guest rooms are decorated in romantic Victorian splendor. Debbie especially likes the John Garth Room (the old master bedroom), decorated in grand Renaissance Revival style; its centerpiece is a walnut Victorian bed with a 10-foot-tall headboard.

The Rosewood Room is a guest favorite, with its great vistas of estate grounds, claw-footed bathtub (painted by the innkeeper's daughter), and the "most expensive bed in Missouri"—a walnut half-tester from the 1850s; it's museum quality.

Breakfasts feature goodies like quiches, home-baked muffins, and more. You can whisper sweet nothings on the expansive veranda in between sips of iced tea (served throughout the summer). Then take a walk on the grounds and simply enjoy.

How to get there: From St. Louis, take I–70 west to Missouri 79 and go north into Hannibal. Turn west on Broadway, then south on U.S. 61. Turn east at Warren Barrett Drive (the first road south of the Holiday Inn) and follow signs to the inn.

B: *A grand mansion, romantic grounds, and Mark Twain, too.*

St. Charles House
St. Charles, Missouri
63301

Innkeepers: Patricia and Lionel York
Address/Telephone: 338 South Main Street; (314) 946–6221, or (800) 366–2427
via town Tourism Center
Rooms: 1 suite with sitting room, porch overlooking Missouri River, and private bath. One 2-room guest cottage with 2 baths, dining room, small porch. No smoking inn.
Rates: $90 weekdays, $115 Friday and Saturday for suite; $75 weekdays, $90 weekends for each room in cottage; deluxe continental breakfast.
Open: All year.
Facilities and activities: Suite has sitting room, huge bath and porch overlooking Missouri River. Guest cottage has dining room, small porch. Both located on Main Street, in center of more than one hundred historic buildings dating to the 1800s, quaint shops, restaurants, riverboat cruises, first-state-capitol tours. Short drive to downtown St. Louis and the Arch, St. Louis Art Museum, restored Union Station, Opera House, Powell Symphony Hall, and Fox Theatre.

What could be more romantic than your own private "residence" in a historic building nestled within sight of the lazing Missouri River at the center of Missouri's old state capitol village? In fact, we're not sure anyone can be prepared for the opulence awaiting couples at the St. Charles House.

Old-World elegance reigns in the 1800s brick building that's been restored to an elegance that early pioneers could never imagine. For example, the one-room inn boasts antiques pre-dating the 1850s; especially noteworthy are a massive Austrian buffet with intricate handcarving and a 9-foot-tall French walnut armoire.

But these are only the barest indications of the luxury awaiting guests at the inn. The house's open floor plan features a four-columned foyer and bedchamber complete with oak hardwood floors, queen-sized canopy bed, elegant sitting room, and antiques galore.

An especially romantic feature is the downstairs bath. We descended a staircase and walked through handsome double doors to discover a claw-footed bathtub sitting beneath a crystal chandelier, with mirrors everywhere.

The enclosed porch out back allows you to sit contentedly and watch the Missouri River ramble by. Or you can walk hand in hand down Main Street, which is lined with historic brick buildings dating to the mid-1800s, now filled with specialty boutiques.

Then you can always come back to your private paradise and create your own memories.

How to get there: From St. Louis or Kansas City, exit I–70 at First Capitol Drive, and follow that north, then east to Main Street; turn right and continue to the inn.

The White Oak Inn
Danville, Ohio
43014

Innkeepers: Joyce and Jim Acton
Address/Telephone: 29683 Walhonding Road; (614) 599–6107
Rooms: 10; all with private bath and air conditioning. No smoking inn.
Rates: $60 to $90, double; $75 to $130 for fireplace rooms (3) on weekends;
    EPB. Two-night minimum on weekends in May and October, and all
    holiday weekends.
Open: All year.
Facilities and activities: Dinner available. BYOB. Expansive grounds, lawn
    games, screen house. Good antiques in area stores. Kokosing River
    offers some of best smallmouth-bass fishing in Ohio; also canoe livery.
    Thirty minutes from Millersburg, center of Amish culture in the United
    States; 35 minutes from Malabar Farm State Park; 25 minutes from
    Roscoe Village in Coshocton, restored canal-era town with own canal
    boat and towpath, specialty shops, and craft stores.

Romance can be defined many ways. Lavish appointments, double whirlpool tubs, turn-of-the-century opulence, and other tangibles make some inns obvious candidates for getaway retreats.

But quiet surroundings, fabulous scenery, a sense of place, and wonderful innkeepers also can imbue an inn with a kind of romantic ambience. That's why the White Oak Inn holds a special place in our memories.

We reached the inn after an adventurous drive down winding backroads through the rolling hills of Walhonding Valley. The forest

160

literally glowed in the setting sun. Debbie spotted a wild turkey off the side of the road. The journey was peaceful and lifted our spirits.

That same feeling came over us upon arrival at the White Oak Inn. The cozy house, completed in 1918, is a wonderful place to unwind, relax, and enjoy the one you love.

A huge brick fireplace in the parlor is a great spot to cuddle in front of with your partner late at night. Or you might prefer to retreat to your guest room, boasting all kinds of hardwoods like walnut, maple, cherry, oak, and poplar.

We especially liked the Cherry Room. Its four-poster bed looked inviting and was adorned with a handmade quilt. Debbie decided that its snuggling potential was unlimited.

Joyce and Jim's breakfast treats include French toast made from homemade breads, scrambled eggs, muffins, sausage, bacon, coffeecakes, and juices. Dinners might offer beef Wellington with Yorkshire pudding; braised pork loin, chicken breast stuffed with ricotta cheese, and much more.

Here's a country inn that's peaceful; whose innkeepers are among the most gracious hosts in the Midwest; and where you can listen to your heart without any distractions.

How to get there: The inn is closer to Millwood than Danville. From Columbus, take U.S. 62 northeast to the junction of U.S. 36 and U.S. 62. Go east on U.S. 36 for 1 mile to Ohio 715, then 3 miles east to the inn.

B: *Country inns can't get much better than this; neither can innkeepers.*

Old Rittenhouse Inn
Bayfield, Wisconsin
54814

Innkeepers: Jerry and Mary Phillips
Address/Telephone: 301 Rittenhouse Avenue (mailing address: Box 584); (715) 779–5765
Rooms: 10, including 1 suite; all with private bath, 9 with fireplace, 5 with whirlpool, some with wheelchair access.
Rates: $79 to $139, double; $179, suite; continental breakfast. Special off-season-rates packages.
Open: All year.
Facilities and activities: Champagne in rooms every night. Three romantic dining rooms. Recreational activities of all kinds available: fishing, sailing, Apostle Islands National Lakeshore; fur-trading museum and other attractions on Madeline Island; canoeing on Brule River; annual festivals; cross-country skiing (in season).

Victorian elegance often translates into high romanticism. That's certainly the case at the Old Rittenhouse Inn, an opulent, sprawling turn-of-the-century inn located in a historic fishing village on the shore of Lake Superior.

Jerry and Mary do everything possible to concoct an unforgettable atmosphere at their showcase hostelry. An elegant Victorian dining room boasting an undercurrent of classical music offers formal breakfasts next to a roaring fireplace, complete with the likes of brandied peaches, blueberries in sour cream, and New Orleans-style French toast.

At night candlelit tables cast a romantic glow over gourmands who enjoy multicourse meals created by Mary herself. They might include everything from steak Bercy stuffed with oysters to fresh trout poached in champagne. Incredible desserts like Jerry's white chocolate cheesecake are a scrumptious aphrodisiac.

Guest rooms are wonderfully inviting. In the original portion of the 1898 building, fine Victorian furnishings include four-poster beds, marble-topped dressers, and (in some) fireplaces to take the chill out of cold winter nights.

We especially enjoy the new inn rooms, all graced with cozy fireplaces, big brass iron-rail and walnut beds, and stained-glass windows depicting Bayfield lakeshore scenes.

If you venture outside, take a sunset walk along the water. Hop aboard a ferryboat to Madeline Island, a historic fur trading post. Or browse specialty shops in the sleepy fishing hamlet.

Wherever you go, romance is in the air.

How to get there: From Minneapolis–St. Paul, take I–94 east to U.S. 63. Take 63 north to State Route 2 and go east to Route 13. Take 13 north to Bayfield. The inn is on the corner of Rittenhouse and Third.

B: *A romantic inn along the spectacular shoreline of Lake Superior with historic islands nearby to explore —an almost perfect destination.*

The Washington House Inn
Cedarburg, Wisconsin
53012

Innkeeper: Wendy Porterfield, manager
Address/Telephone: W62 N573 Washington Avenue; (414) 375–3550 or
   (800) 369–4088
Rooms: 29, including 3 suites; all with private bath, air conditioning, TV and
   phone. Wheelchair access.
Rates: $59 to $139, double, continental breakfast. Special packages avail-
   able.
Open: All year.
Facilities and activities: Situated in heart of historic Cedarburg; walk to restau-
   rants and Cedar Creek Settlement: old Woolen Mill; Stone Mill Winery;
   antiques, craft, specialty shops. Short drive to Ozaukee Pioneer Village,
   Ozaukee Covered Bridge (last covered bridge in Wisconsin).

   This inn includes one of my favorite rooms in the Midwest,
perfect for romantic getaways with your most significant other.
   Imagine a lavishly deluxe bedchamber adorned with elegant
country-style antiques. Downy beds in sleeping lofts with fireplaces,
offering no better place to cuddle on cold winter nights before a
roaring blaze.
   But that's not all. In this lavish room a second loft awaits
adventurous inngoers; there a 200-gallon spa tub is warmed by yet
another fireplace. If these surroundings can't inspire lovey-dove
goings-on, nothing can.

It's all part of the charming ambience at the Washington House Inn, located in Cedarburg, a historic woolen mill town now crowded with antiques and specialty stores along its Main Street and mill buildings.

Most of the town's "cream city" brick and stone buildings date from the mid-1800s. In fact, the downtown area alone boasts more historic structures than any other city west of Philadelphia.

But this inn, completed in 1886, is special. Guest rooms are filled with country Victorian delights, including floral wallpapers, fancy armoires, cozy down quilts, fresh flowers, and more. Some even feature "pioneer style" architectural flourishes like exposed cream city brick and wooden timbers. Others might be more heavily Victorian, with feminine touches.

And then you find those special retreats like the double loft described above that is unlike anything else in the Midwest. Romantics shouldn't miss the chance to enjoy this one.

Breakfast, concocted from a turn-of-the-century Cedarburg cookbook, features home-baked breads, rolls, cakes, and more. Afternoon social hours are a good time to share town wanderings with other guests. Then you can return to your own private heaven.

How to get there: From Chicago, take I–94 to I–43, just north of Milwaukee, and get off at the Cedarburg exit. This road eventually changes to Wisconsin 57; follow it into town (where it becomes Washington Street). At Center Street, turn left and park in the lot behind the hotel.

B: *A historic hotel, elegant antiques—and whirlpool tubs, too.*

The American Club
Kohler, Wisconsin
53044

Innkeeper: Susan Porter Green, vice-president; Brian O'Day, general manager
Address/Telephone: Highland Drive; (414) 457–8000 or (800) 344–2838; fax (414) 457–0299
Rooms: 160; all with private Kohler whirlpool bath, air conditioning, TV, and phone. Wheelchair access.
Rates: May 1–October 31: $134 to $338, double, EP. November 1–April 30: $114 to $295, double, EP. Two-night minimum on weekends from Memorial Day through Labor Day and December 30 through January 2.
Open: All year.
Facilities and activities: Nine restaurants and full-service dining rooms. Renowned for extravagant buffets, special-event and holiday feasts; large Sunday brunch. Ballroom. Sports Core, a world-class health club. River Wildlife, 500 acres of private woods for hiking, horseback riding, hunting, fishing, trapshooting, canoeing. Cross-country skiing and ice skating. Also Kohler Design Center, shops at Woodlake, Kohler Arts Center, Waelderhaus. Nearby: antiquing, lake charter fishing, Kettle Moraine State Forest, Road America (auto racing).

Debbie's favorite romantic retreat, excepting our days and nights in Paris, might be The American Club.

On our last visit to this magnificent inn that more resembles a manicured baronial estate, we stayed in a luxurious two-room suite that could have hosted royalty. Gleaming brass, custom-crafted oak furniture, and quality antique furnishings are standard features of

166

the inn's elegant and romantic ambience.

But we also enjoyed the skylight over our head, a huge whirlpool, and the saunalike environmental chamber that features a pushbutton choice of weather—from bright sun with gentle breezes to misty rain showers.

(Though we did get a big laugh out of a mistake I made in the contraption—dialing up ice-cold sprinkles on an unsuspecting Debbie.)

The inn's decidedly European feel is added to by handmade Continental comforters and four fluffy pillows adorning each bed—authentic Euro-style.

It would be difficult to find a more romantic restaurant than the inn's signature dining room, The Immigrant. Featuring ethnic decors of different Wisconsin immigrant groups, candlelight dinners, and gourmet food that includes the likes of Irish smoked salmon and a very impressive wine list, it's more than enough to put anyone in the mood for amour.

For dessert, we walk hand in hand to the Greenhouse, located in an outside courtyard. This antique English solarium is a perfect spot for chocolate torte, other Viennese delights, and sweet whisperings.

Daytime pursuits include coed workouts at the inn's Sports Core or a round of golf at either of its two award-winning Pete Dye–designed courses at Blackwolf Run.

Then again, you might just desire a quiet hike through River Wildlife, a private 500-acre retreat teeming with deer and other woodsy creatures.

How to get there: From Chicago, take I–94 north and continue north on I–43, just outside of Milwaukee. Exit on Wisconsin 23 west (exit 53B). Take 23 to County Trunk Y and continue south into Kohler. The inn is on the right. From the west, take I–94 south to Wisconsin 21 and go east to U.S. 41. Go south on 41 to Wisconsin 23; then head east into Kohler.

B: Incomparable luxury, intimacy, elegance—the essence of romance.

Mansion Hill Inn
Madison, Wisconsin
53703

Innkeeper: Polly Elder
Address/Telephone: 424 North Pinckney Street; (608) 255–3999
Rooms: 11, including 3 suites; all with private bath, air conditioning, cable TV, stereo, VCR, and mini-bar.
Rates: $100 to $250, double, continental breakfast. Two-night minimum on holidays and football weekends.
Open: All year.
Facilities and activities: Victorian parlor, dining room (with catered dinners available), belvedere, private wine cellar, garden. Access to health spa, private dining club. Mansion Hill Historic District invites touring, especially Period Garden Park. Madison is state capital; many fine ethnic restaurants, specialty shops, art galleries, recitals, theaters, nightclubs. Also University of Wisconsin main campus nearby. Swimming, fishing, boating in surrounding lakes.

This extraordinary inn is an architectural showplace that can almost overwhelm first-time visitors. But after a few moments to adjust to your opulent surroundings, you'll realize that it would be difficult to find another Midwest inn so elegantly romantic.

Built in 1858, the inn has undergone a two-million-dollar restoration that includes white sandstone from the cliffs of the Mississippi, Carrera marble from Italy, and ornamental cast iron from Sweden. Handsome arched windows and French doors allow sunlight to pool into antiques-filled rooms. Fireplaces blaze with warmth and atmosphere. And a spiral staircase winds four floors up to the belvedere, offering panoramic views of Madison—and a great location for a late-night rendezvous.

We stayed in the McDonnell Room, feeling like royalty. Arched windows, French doors, a 10-foot-tall tester bed and oval whirlpool tub convinced us that there might be nothing better to do than spend the night inside our suite.

Deliciously romantic is the Turkish Nook, swathed in Victorian silks, strewn with pillows and ottomans, and boasting a tented sultan's bed—all evoking the sensual delights of the mysterious Middle East.

Yet another favorite is a room with floor-to-ceiling bookcases that possess a hidden door opening into a bathroom with arched windows, classical Greek columns, and a huge marble tub.

You can dine on gourmet meals arranged by the innkeeper. Or rent a limo and retreat to one of the city's most romantic restaurants—L'Etoile, perhaps. But the real adventure starts once you get back to your elegant surroundings.

How to get there: From Milwaukee, take I–94 west to Madison. Exit west on Wisconsin 30 to Wisconsin 113. Go south to Johnson; then west to Baldwin. Turn south on Baldwin to East Washington, and then turn west toward the capitol building. At Pinckney Street, turn north. The inn is on the corner of Pinckney and Gilman.

B: *"Too much is not enough" is the inn maxim.*

Inn at Pine Terrace
Oconomowoc, Wisconsin
53066

Innkeeper: Jill Lau, manager
Address/Telephone: 371 Lisbon Road; (414) 567–7463
Rooms: 13; all with private bath, air conditioning, phone and TV, 6 with
   double whirlpool. Wheelchair access. Well-behaved pets OK.
Rates: $69.50 to $131.46, double, continental breakfast.
Open: All year.
Facilities and activities: Sitting room, swimming pool on grounds, breakfast
   room, conference room. Short walk to Lac La Belle for swimming,
   fishing, boating, and 3 beaches. Restaurants and Olympia Ski Area,
   with downhill and cross-country skiing, a short drive away.

Imagine a romantic three-story Victorian mansion magnifi-
cently restored to its former grandeur—with more than $750,000
spent just in millwork alone to bring back the elaborate butternut
and walnut moldings that adorn every room.

Then imagine that all the antique-style Eastlake furniture was
custom made especially for the house. That its curving handrail cost
nearly $60,000 all by itself. That most guest rooms have double
marble whirlpools; that doors boast brass hinges and hand-carved
wooden doorknobs. That rooms feature brooding Victorian colors
and exquisite wall coverings.

And note that five U.S. presidents were guests here, along with
other notables like Mark Twain and retailer Montgomery Ward.

It's all part of the turn-of-the-century retreat that's otherwise called the Inn at Pine Terrace, an 1884 manse that's been transformed into a romantic paradise.

Eleven elegant guest rooms offer getaway havens for couples. My favorite, and perhaps one of the most romantic rooms in the Midwest, is the first-floor suite.

Of course, the massive bedchamber boasts Eastlake-inspired antiques, but its unique flavor is captured by marble steps leading to a marble platform—upon which rests a white enamel, brass-claw-footed bathtub. The tub sits in front of three ceiling-to-floor windows, which can be shuttered for privacy.

Lovers also can lounge at the inn's swimming pool or take a refreshing dip in the water while making plans for a romance-inspired evening.

How to get there: From Milwaukee, take I–94 west to U.S. 67. Exit north and continue through town to Lisbon Road. Turn right; the inn is just down the street.

St. Croix River Inn
Osceola, Wisconsin
54020

Innkeeper: Bev Johnson
Address/Telephone: 305 River Street; (715) 294–4248
Rooms: 7; all with private bath and air conditioning, 2 with TV.
Rates: Friday and Saturday, $100 to $200; Sunday through Thursday, $85 to $150, double; EPB. Gift certificates.
Open: All year.
Facilities and activities: Outdoor porch, sitting room overlooking St. Croix River. Nearby: several area antiques shops, canoeing, fishing, downhill and cross-country skiing at Wild Mountain or Trollhaugen. Short drive to restaurants and Taylors Falls, Minnesota—lovely little river town with historic-homes tours and cruises on old-fashioned paddlewheelers.

This eighty-year-old stone house is poised high on a bluff overlooking the scenic St. Croix River. It allows unsurpassed, breathtaking views while providing one of the most elegant lodgings in the entire Midwest.

I'm especially fond of a suite with a huge whirlpool set in front of windows, allowing you to float visually down the water while pampering yourself in a bubble bath.

"The house was built from limestone quarried near here," Bev said. "It belonged to the owner of the town's pharmacy and remained in his family until a few years ago."

Now let's get right to the rooms (suites, really), which are named for riverboats built in Osceola. Perhaps (and this is a *big* perhaps) Jennie Hays is my all-time favorite inn room. It is simply exquisite, with appointments that remind me of exclusive European hotels. I continue to boast about a magnificent four-poster canopy bed that feels as good as it looks and a decorative tile fireplace that soothes the psyche as well as chilly limbs on crackling-cool autumn or frigid winter nights.

Then there is the view! I'm almost at a loss for words. A huge Palladian window, stretching from floor to ceiling, overlooks the river from the inn's bluff-top perch. It provides a romantic and rewarding setting that would be hard to surpass anywhere in the Midwest. The room has a whirlpool, and there's also a private balcony with more great river views.

The G. B. Knapp Room is more of the same: a huge suite, with a four-poster canopy bed adorned with a floral quilt, tall armoire, its own working gas fireplace, and a whirlpool tub. Then walk through a door to the enclosed porch (more like a private sitting room), with windows overlooking the river. There are also exquisite stenciling, bull's-eye moldings, and private balconies.

Pampering continues at breakfast, which Bev serves in your room or in bed. It might include fresh fruit and juices, omelets, waffles, French toast, or puff pastries stuffed with ham and cheese, and home-baked French bread and pound cake.

Bev also delivers to your room a pot of steaming coffee and the morning paper a half hour before your morning meal. She can recommend a great place for dinner. But you simply may never want to leave your quarters.

How to get there: From downtown Osceola, turn west on Third Avenue and follow it past a hospital and historic Episcopal church (dating from 1854, with four turreted steeples). The inn is located on the river side of River Street.

◆

B: *One of the Midwest's most romantic retreats—pure grace and elegance.*

White Lace Inn
Sturgeon Bay, Wisconsin
54235

Innkeepers: Bonnie and Dennis Statz
Address/Telephone: 16 North Fifth Avenue; (414) 743–1105
Rooms: 15, in 3 historic houses; all with private bath and air conditioning, some with fireplace, whirlpool, TV, and wheelchair access.
Rates: $66 to $146, double, continental breakfast. Special winter or spring fireside packages available November through May.
Open: All year.
Facilities and activities: Five blocks to bay shore. Close to specialty and antiques shops, restaurants, Door County Museum, Miller Art Center. Swimming, tennis, and horseback riding nearby. Short drive to Whitefish Dunes and Potawatomi state parks, Peninsula Players Summer Theater, Birch Creek Music Festival. Cross-country skiing and ice skating in winter. Gateway to the peninsula.

The White Lace Inn might be Door County's most romantic retreat. At least that's what Debbie and I think about this lavish hostelry.

In fact, the inn is essentially your own private Victorian village, with three handsome historic buildings connected by a red-brick pathway that winds through landscaped grounds filled with stately trees and colorful wildflower gardens.

There's even a turn-of-the-century gazebo overlooking the inn's rose garden that features varieties dating from the 1700s. It's a great place to gaze into the eyes of your loved one and whisper sweet nothings.

Bonnie has put her degree in interior design to splendid use with some of the most romantic, intimate inn rooms found anywhere in the country. Laura Ashley fabrics, antique furnishings, canopy beds adorned with handmade comforters and fluffy down pillows, lacy curtains add to the dreamy ambience.

The Main House was built in 1903, and the 1880s Garden House boasts rooms with their own fireplaces. The decor varies from country elegant to the grand boldness of Empire stylings.

On our last visit, we stayed in the Washburn House. Debbie loved the room's huge brass canopy bed; I liked the crackling fireplace at the foot of our bedchamber; and we both enjoyed a two-person whirlpool, complete with heavenly Ralph Lauren towels.

Bonnie's delicious Scandinavian fruit soup or old-fashioned rice pudding are breakfast treats, along with homemade muffins and beverages—all served in front of yet another fireplace.

Bonnie and Dennis call their inn a "romantic fireside getaway." They're absolutely right, as Debbie and I have discovered again and again and . . .

How to get there: From Milwaukee, take U.S. 41 north to Wisconsin 42, toward Sturgeon Bay. Just outside the city, take Business 42/57 and follow it into town, cross the bridge, and you'll come to Michigan Street. Follow Michigan to Fifth Avenue and turn left. White Lace Inn is on the right side of the street.

Or you can take the 42/51 bypass across the new bridge to Michigan Street. Turn left on Michigan, go to Fifth Avenue, and take a right on Fifth to the inn.

♣

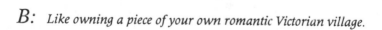

B: Like owning a piece of your own romantic Victorian village.

The Southwest
by Eleanor S. Morris

Ah, romance! Who can define it?

Dictionaries try. *Webster's* defines romance as "extraordinary life, not real or familiar," adding "colloquially, to make love." *Thorndike Barnhard* agrees; its definition reads, "a love affair, an interest in adventure and love." *Collins Gem* (of a French dictionary) declares it *"poesie,"* and *"idylle,"* and *Cassell's New Compact French Dictionary* says romance is not only *"amourette"* and *"aventure"* (love and adventure), it is also *"inventer a plaisir"*: to imagine a pleasure, a delight.

So, is it more of a feeling we bring to a place, or can the place itself be romantic, engendering romantic feelings in us? I think it's both; I like the way the French say that romance means to invent a delight. Imagination inspires us to look for surroundings that will complement and enhance romance.

Herein are twenty inns of the Southwest that provide a delightful ambience of *"idylle et poesie."* Although they help keep romance alive, part of their magic comes from what you bring along with you. Whether it's romance amid the opulence of a Victorian mansion, in an eagle's aerie in the mountains, or in the pampered Southern comfort of an antebellum plantation, these inns provide the perfect setting for a wonderful experience of romance.

The rest is up to you.

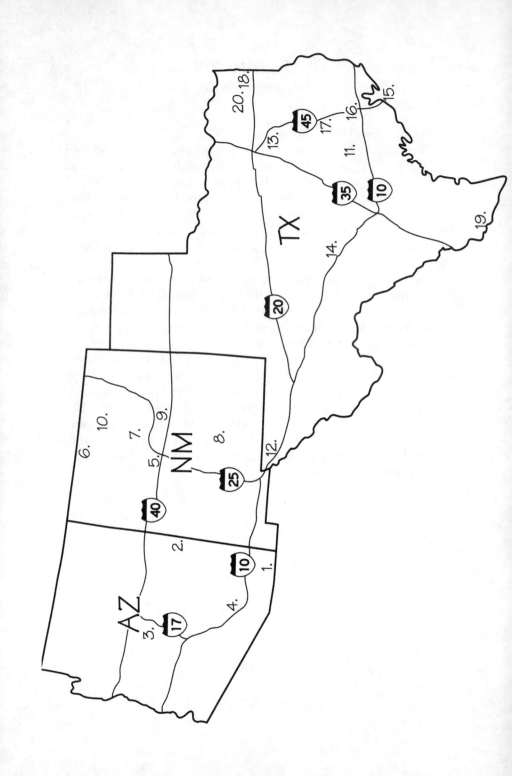

The Southwest

Numbers on map refer to towns numbered below.

Copper Queen Hotel
Bisbee, Arizona
85603

Innkeepers: Karen and Mark Carrera and Fran and Howard Schonwit
Address/Telephone: 11 Howell Avenue (mailing address: P.O. Drawer CQ);
(602) 432–2216
Rooms: 43; all with private bath, phone, and TV; wheelchair accessible.
Rates: $63 to $80, double, EP.
Open: All year.
Facilities and activities: Restaurant, lounge, outdoor cafe, swimming pool.
Nearby: Copper Queen Mine Tour, shops, Coronada Trail, hiking, and
rock hunting.

Copper fortunes built the beautiful old Copper Queen, and
Karen and Mark feel fortunate to be in charge of this historical treasure.

"She's an old love, a gracious old lady," everyone says of the
hotel, which was built shortly after the turn of the century. Both
the guest rooms and the halls, with red wall coverings, made us feel
like we'd turned back the clock and were here with Lily Langtry
and other Gay-Nineties folk.

Antiques furnish many of the rooms, and both Dining Room
and Saloon are restored to their original rustic form of Western
Mining Town ambience.

"It's a funky old bar, and people have a lot of fun here," Karen
told us, and we did. "This bar is like some of the locals' living

room—they come every evening to have a glass of beer or wine." Local musicians come to play the piano or their own instruments on nights the saloon doesn't offer entertainment.

We loved the huge oil painting in the bar, showing Lily Langtry and Eros reclining on a chaise lounge with a Cavalier on horseback in the background. When she came to Bisbee she sang at the Opera House, causing a sensation. Maybe the feeling we got was genuine and Lily still haunts the hotel!

The hotel's past also includes Teddy Roosevelt and "Black Jack" Pershing, who was sent to comb the nearby hills for Pancho Villa. (He didn't find him.) Other guests of note include John Wayne and Lee Marvin, and we hoped we would run into some more current ones. It was a distinct possibility since Karen told us that film people frequent the hotel.

When the hotel was built, Bisbee was the largest copper mining town in the world. Although the Copper Queen Mine is no longer in operation, we donned yellow slickers and miner's hats, complete with a light above the brim, and a battery pack around our waist. Then we rode the little mine train down there: VERY DARK, even when you're carrying your own light!

We took wonderful photos of the hills, a blazing rust-orange color from the ore, and oohed and aahed at the open pit mine nearby, a huge red circle in the earth.

Food is served outside on the veranda as well as in the restaurant. As the innkeepers say, "Our weather here is super." We especially enjoyed the breakfast special "Queen's Favorite," a savory mix of scrambled eggs, sautéed spinach, ground beef, and Parmesan cheese.

Gourmet dinner specials include roast duck a l'orange and prime rib, in addition to other specialty items. Bisbee may be a mining ghost town, but the Copper Queen Hotel is right up to the minute!

How to get there: From I–10 drive into Bisbee taking Howell (not Tombstone Canyon Road) and you'll see the hotel; you can't miss it. Streets are narrow, winding and one-way, so drive by the hotel and on up to the parking lot at the YWCA at the end of the street.

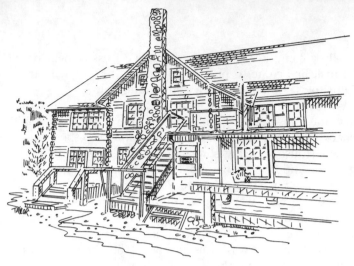

Greer Lodge
Greer, Arizona
85927

Innkeepers: Barb and Rich Allen
Address/Telephone: P.O. Box 244; (602) 735–7515
Rooms: 11; 7 with 7 baths in Main Lodge, 4 with 3 baths and kitchen in Little Lodge; no air conditioning (elevation 8,500 feet); wheelchair accessible. Smoking permitted except in dining room.
Rates: Main Lodge: $55, per person, double, EPB. Two-night minimum stay on weekends, three nights on holidays.
Open: All year.
Facilities and activities: Restaurant serving breakfast, lunch (May to September), and dinner; picnic lunches, cocktail bar, stocked trout pond, hiking, horseback riding, skiing, bobsledding; bird watching; canoeing.

Here's a great place for communing with nature. On the inn grounds we spotted a blue heron and got a real touch of the wild when an owl zoomed down and buzzed the pond, catching his dinner. If he doesn't get a fish, he'll get a duck, the innkeepers say; owls have been seen pulling a full-sized duck out of the water!

Such is the view, and the action, from Greer Lodge's magnificent two-story greenhouse lounge at the back of the inn, all glass with an indoor stream and waterfall and plants everywhere—a regular conservatory. The room overlooks the pond and the pine-covered mountains in the distance, to which we struck out for a hike, picnic lunch in hand, and later on, some horseback riding into the national forest.

We weren't far from nature even indoors: The inn's spacious, comfortable rooms have windows with views of the splendid sur-rounding wilderness. The color scheme is rust and white; rust car-pets, rust curtains and coverlets sprinkled with little white flowers, fresh comforters, linens, and towels. The air is exceptionally clear, and the whole atmosphere is bright; the inn sparkles, bright and shiny. Upstairs rooms are accessible from a walkway ringing the perimeter of the cathedral-ceilinged common room, where in the evening a roaring fire often crackles in the big fireplace. A lovely place for cuddling is the small lounge upstairs, facing the gorgeous views at the back of the inn.

Everything served in the restaurant is homemade, from the biscuits and gravy to the cinnamon rolls. For breakfast we had flaky just-baked croissants with our "eggs any way," but we could have had waffles or pancakes. Tasty were the homemade soups in the cool mountain air—soups like clam chowder or, my favorites, cream of cauliflower or broccoli soup. Fresh-baked kaiser rolls or whole wheat bread make the thick roast beef, turkey, or ham sand-wiches special.

After lunch we sat on the back porch and just threw our lines in the stream feeding the pond; it's stocked with two-pound rainbow and German brown trout; we could see fish jumping out of the water, just waiting for Greer Lodge guests to catch them. There are canloupes, too, but we had to ask what *they* were. They're fish from the Canadian lake of the same name—we forgot to ask how they got here!

Ah, Paradise. Horses grazed in the meadows in the distance. Elk and deer grazed in the sunny alpine meadows. The hurly-burly of the city is far, far away.

How to get there: Greer is at the end of Highway 373, a short road that runs south from Highway 260 between Eager and Indian Pine. The inn is at the end of the road on the left.

E: We agreed with assistant Bob Pollack when he said, "This is Ari-zona's most beautiful setting." And in case we didn't agree, he cinched it. "Even the governor thinks so!"

The Marks House Inn
Prescott, Arizona
86303

Innkeepers: Dottie and Harold Viehweg
Address/Telephone: 203 East Union Street; (602) 778–4632
Rooms: 4 suites; all with private bath; no air conditioning (elevation 5,300 feet). No smoking inn.
Rates: $75 to $110, double; $130, for 4; EPB.
Open: All year.
Facilities and activities: Nearby: Historic Prescott Courthouse Square, restaurants, shops, and museums; golf, boating, hiking, tennis, and swimming at area lakes Lynx, Walker, Goldwater, and Watson.

High on a hill overlooking Courthouse Square and Whiskey Row, the historic Marks House stands in regal splendor, a fine old dowager of a mansion built in 1894 by an early Arizonian who was reputed to be the wealthiest man in the area at the time he built the home for his bride, Josephine.

What was wonderful to us was the surprise of finding such lovely features in a house built so shortly after the first settlers arrived in Prescott. Barely thirty years later, here was this two-story Queen Anne Victorian with sunburst window designs, a romantic turret, and one of our favorite details, an ornately decorated wraparound front porch.

Jake Marks, trader, mine owner, and general merchandiser, evidently was quite an adventurer, and we felt adventurous staying

184

in his house. He joined General Crook in fighting the Pitt River Indian Wars, and when he wasn't off fighting the Indians, he was involved in both the liquor business and politics. "He and General Crook were great friends, and the general stayed at the house when he was in town," says Dottie as she served hors d'oeuvres to us in the late afternoon on the veranda.

The old house is on the National Register of Historic Places, and it took seven years to restore it. The spacious mansion certainly bears witness to wealth, with polished hardwood floors and beautiful wood moldings and doors. The dining room floor is inlaid with a pattern of walnut, oak, and mahogany, and its fireplace sits back to back with the parlor fireplace. The original wood floors creak even when lightly trod upon, and there seems to be a resident ghost—"who apparently is a prankster," says Dottie, "opening doors, turning on lights, and generally misplacing things." We didn't experience any of this, but maybe we were too busy enjoying the sensation of going back in time in a mighty posh way to notice the creaks, thumps, and bumps that add to the aura of this great old house!

Gorgeous sunsets are on view from the veranda and the curved windows in the circular corner turret of both the parlor and the Queen Anne Suite above; we preferred to watch the glorious sight from the Queen Anne Suite, a pretty cozy place to lie in bed and watch night fall. The two bedrooms of the Ivy Suite on the main floor are decorated in soft greens which complement the Victorian antiques, and the big 1890s copper tub in the Princess Victoria room, from a bathhouse in Syracuse, New York, is a treat.

In the morning, along with fresh or cooked fruit, homemade muffins, coffee, tea, cocoa, and juice, Dottie served us her Overnight French Toast Casserole because, she told us, "It's what most guests seem to like best." She generously gave me the recipe, so I could make it at home and remember the romantic Marks House Inn. Hint: It's so rich because there's cream cheese in it, too.

How to get there: From Courthouse Square go east up the hill of Union Street to Marina. The inn will be at the corner of Marina on the right.

El Presidio Inn
Tucson, Arizona
85701

Innkeepers: Patty and Jerry Toci
Address/Telephone: 297 North Main Avenue; (602) 623–6151
Rooms: 4; all with private bath, phone, and TV. No smoking inn.
Rates: $85 to $105, double, weekly and monthly rate; EPB; no credit cards
   accepted.
Open: All year.
Facilities and activities: Courtyard garden. Nearby: restaurants, historic dis-
   trict, Sonora Desert Museum, Old Town Artisans handicrafts.

   The delightful Territorial Victorian adobe building, looking
deceptively small, is on a corner, hiding a large back courtyard that
is the pride of Patty and Jerry's gardening talents. Centered with a
fountain Jerry found in Mexico, the courtyard is shaded with a
huge magnolia that provides greens for Christmas celebrations. The
most romantic rooms are those that open to the courtyard, partially
hidden by the greenery. The Victorian Suite, with a huge sitting
room furnished in cool white wicker, has a photograph of Patty's
grandmother setting the period mood. The Carriage Suite mixes an
Eastlake lady's desk with a collection of Southwest antiques, including a trunk that held a pioneer's goods. The Gatehouse Suite has
Bar Harbor-style wicker furniture, and with the garden, it's hard to
believe you're still in town.
   This is where Tucson began, at El Presidio, when Tucson was a

walled city to protect the settlers from renegade Apaches. But with Patty as innkeeper, you might feel like you're part of the Deep South even here. "I'm a good old Southern girl," she says. "We always had magnolia greens back home for Christmas, and when old friends visit us here, they can't believe our big magnolia, growing right here in Tucson, Arizona!"

Breakfasts on the bright glassed-in sun porch are leisurely feasts, so don't be in a hurry: take your ease and relax. Patty says she has so many repeat guests that she makes notes on what she fed them last. We found the long table is beautifully appointed, and we toasted each other with fresh orange juice, then progressed to a magnificent fruit cup of kiwi, strawberry, orange, pineapple, and cantaloupe.

Next came two kinds of French toast, one made of cinnamon-y raisin bread, the other stuffed with homemade peanut butter and bananas. Canadian bacon came with this, and we really could not resist having two of the lemon nut muffins topped with streusel. Like every good cook, Patty was pleased as punch to see us stuff ourselves!

"The recipe for the lemon muffins isn't original with me," she says. "But the streusel topping is." She puts her happy touch on everything. Guest rooms are provided with fruit, juice, coffee, teas, and snacks. There are bathrobes to wrap up in. The Zaugan Room, the lovely common room, has a tile fireplace, wreaths of fragrant dried flowers, books to read, and current magazines providing information on the best of Tucson. "We've been living here long enough to know the best things to do," the Tocis say, just in case you find you want to get out on the town some of the time.

How to get there: From I–10 take the St. Mary's exit and go right 4 blocks to Granada. Turn south, and after you cross the railroad tracks Granada changes to Main Avenue. Go 1 block past the traffic light and turn right into West Franklin. The inn is on the corner of Main and West Franklin. Curbside parking is permitted if you get a permit from Patty to put on your windshield.

Casas de Sueños
Albuquerque, New Mexico
87104

Innkeepers: Robert Hanna and Mari Penshurst-Gersten
Address/Telephone: 310 Rio Grande SW; (505) 247–4560 or (800) 242–8987
Rooms: 12 casitas; all with private bath, phone, and TV; 1 with wheelchair
access. No smoking inn.
Rates: $66 to $225, double, seasonal, EPB.
Open: All year.
Facilities and activities: Dinner by reservation. Nearby: Historic Old Town
Plaza with shops, galleries, and restaurants. Health club, museums,
zoo, festivals, golf, swimming, horseback riding, longest aerial tram in
North America.

What could be more romantic than an inn called "houses of
dreams" in Spanish? But the romance comes later: Be prepared for a
wild surprise when you drive up to this adobe inn! Above the
entrance gates looms a most unusual structure, added to the inn in
1976 by Albuquerque's famous artist Bart Prince. "I tried to call it the
Nautilus, but our neighbors call it 'the snail,'" Robert says. But it
doesn't matter what they call it, because, says Robert, "People become
different in that space." Robert, who left his law practice to become a
full-time innkeeper, ought to know. "When you're in it, there's no
contention, no divorce. People let go of their preconceptions."
Whatever you call it, it's a fascinating structure, and we
weren't surprised that people knock on the door to ask, "What *is*

that thing?" As fantastic inside as out, the "snail" is entered by a spiral staircase, and it serves as a lounge and television and meeting room. Built-in ledges on all of the structure's three levels provide perfect places for cuddling up and daydreaming as you gaze out the windows to the nearby mountains.

We thought it would be hard for the rest of the inn to live up to such an introduction, but not so. These "houses of dreams" were built in the 1930s by artist J. R. Willis, growing into a cluster of small casitas around a huge old elm in the flowery courtyard. "To support his painting expenses, Willis kept building these casitas to rent to friends," Robert says.

Today the innkeepers have turned them into a delightful collection of unique suites furnished with antiques, art, heirlooms, and oriental and Indian rugs. Imagine bathing with fancy bath amenities, wrapping yourselves in luxurious towels, and then snuggling into goose-down comforters. Some of the suites even have kitchens (if concocting your own special treats won't upset your romantic mood), and most have fireplaces, adjoining sitting rooms, and outdoor garden areas.

We loved Cascada with its own waterfall, so soothing to fall asleep to. The Cupid Suite has a skylight, so romantic with moonlight shining down. The Rose Room is sentimental, with a nice blend of yesterday's romance and today's comfort.

Though we preferred the romance of Cascade, it was fun to check out the Route 66 Suite, so named because it's just 1 block off the famous highway. (That's why the rate stays the same, too!)

The dining room used to be the artist's studio, and we ate facing the northern wall of windows, looking out at the pretty flowers and shady trees of the lovely gardens. Breakfast was a buffet of gourmet coffee and tea, fresh fruit, cereal, yogurt, and a specialty: decadent French toast with fresh fruit sauce. There's always coffee, tea, and cake on hand; we devoured a moist poppyseed cake crunchy with Brazil nuts.

How to get there: From I–40 west take Rio Grande exit south toward Old Town. Cross Mountain Road and Central Avenue and go 2 more blocks. The inn will be on your left, facing the Albuquerque Country Club Golf Course.

✳

E: *I guarantee you sweet dreams in this house of dreams!*

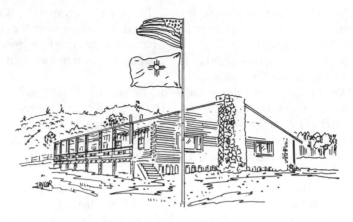

Oso Ranch and Lodge
Chama, New Mexico
87520

Innkeepers: Martha and Bruce Peck
Address/Telephone: P.O. Box 808; (505) 756–2954
Rooms: 6; all with private bath and TV; wheelchair accessible; no air conditioning (high elevation).
Rates: Summer and fall: $65 double, EP; $85 double, EPB; $300 AP.
Open: All year.
Facilities and activities: Outdoor Jacuzzi, hunting, fishing, horseback riding, hiking, sailing, cross-country skiing, snowmobiling, overnight pack trips. Nearby: Cumbres & Toltec Scenic Railroad.

Ah, wilderness. Where the deer come down and feed at night. Where coyotes and eagles can be sighted. Where the mountain air is crisp and clear, and the sky an incredible blue. Where snow-capped peaks and momentous sunsets are the norm. All can be enjoyed while soaking in the outdoor Jacuzzi either under the bright day sun or the romantic moonlit night.

"Right here you have the feeling of being isolated," say innkeepers Martha and Bruce Peck. "But we're only five minutes from town," they added, so we felt we had the best of two wonderful worlds! Oso Ranch, two miles south of the small town of Chama, is a perfect place for sports and nature lovers and other lovers, too, who want to get away from it all.

The large log lodge has a huge activities room with hunting

trophies not only over the mantel but hanging from the rafters, too. The biggest trophies personify the inn's name. *Oso* means "bear" in Spanish, and there are several big old stuffed ones in the room.

You'll find American West and Native American art, too, and a library stocked with histories of the American West. A widescreen television, a piano, and game and pool tables are here if you want to be sociable.

The six guest rooms are down a hall off the big room. Each door is completely covered with a scene made from colored leather; each is very unique and individual, so it was easy to find which room was ours. We opened the door on a large and comfortable room with a king-sized bed and a romantic mountain view from the window.

Some folks just liked to relax around the big fireplace, and we didn't blame them, particularly when they were waiting for a meal to begin. Tables were set at the far end of the room, and delicious hand-cooked food was served. We savored "good eats" like rich pecan rolls with fried potatoes and ham and eggs for breakfast, homemade chili for lunch (or a packed lunch if you want to go out to enjoy nature) and maybe roast beef, potato salad, carrots, corn, homemade bread, and banana pudding for a hearty dinner. Especially delicious was Martha's pull-apart Cinnamon Delight.

We didn't need a license to fish in the ranch lakes, personally stocked with rainbow trout. For a small fee we had a lesson in fly fishing, something we'd never done before. We also fished for trout in the nearby Chama River, but we didn't catch anything; never mind, it was fun anyway!

The village of Chama offers some special shopping opportunities. Nearby Tierra Wools raise their own sheep and shear, dye, and spin the wool; we watched, fascinated, as the weavers created unique woolen items. We were delighted to find an adventure of a different kind on the Cumbres & Toltec Scenic Railroad, a spectacular steam-powered train making a round trip to Osier, Colorado, from mid-June through October.

How to get there: From Highway 84 turn west on Seco Drive (about 2 miles south of Chama). Drive 1/2 mile to the end, over the river, and up to the lodge.

Hacienda Rancho de Chimayo
Chimayo, New Mexico 87522

Innkeepers: Florence and Laura Jaramillo
Address/Telephone: P.O. Box 11; (505) 351–2222
Rooms: 7; all with private bath.
Rates: $54 to $81, double, continental breakfast.
Open: All year except January.
Facilities and activities: Restaurant (closed in January). Nearby: 1850s Church of San Tuario, the "Lourdes of the U.S."; weavers' shops famous for rugs, jackets, cushions.

The rooms of this romantic inn open from a walled courtyard featuring a sparkling fountain and bursting with bright flowers. The view is toward the mountains and our room had the same view, with French doors opening onto a little balcony. That's where we had our simple continental breakfast, although it was tempting to join other guests in the courtyard when we heard their happy voices in the pretty courtyard.

We found the sense of history here intriguing: Chimayo is a very small town with its history bound up in Hacienda Rancho de Chimayo and in the Restaurante Rancho de Chimayo (where we had delicious native New Mexican cuisine just across the road). Both belong to a family that has lived in Chimayo since the 1700s, tracing its roots to the first Spanish settlers.

In the 1880s two brothers, Hermenegildo and Epifanio Jaramillo, built family homes facing each other across the road. Their descendants restored the homes, creating in 1965 the Restaurante Rancho de Chimayo in Hermenegildo's home and in 1984 the Hacienda Rancho de Chimayo in Epifanio and Adelaida's home.

Our very large room had twin mahogany beds forming a king-sized bed. In front of the French doors, so we could lounge and watch the lovely view, there was a taupe velvet sofa, a coffee table, and two wing chairs. We enjoyed details like the pink linens, rose lace shower curtain, and old prints on the walls. Each room is practically a suite, there's so much space, and the antique furniture is lovely. I particularly admired our room's mahogany dressing table and antique blanket stand holding a white woven afghan in case we got chilly in the evening, watching the sky turn from blue to pink to lavender to navy blue—New Mexico sunsets are lovely.

I asked Florence how they were lucky enough to have so many lovely antique pieces. "We searched all of San Antonio, Austin, and Denver for our antiques!" she said. They've done a wonderful job, recreating the distinctive charm of the Colonial New Mexico of their ancestors.

"We've traveled a lot in the States, and we always like to sit for a while in our room, perhaps have some wine and cheese and relax, before we go out to dinner," Florence says. We could have helped ourselves to wine from the kitchen of the office/lobby, kept there for whoever wants it. But we had our own bottle of wine in our room, placed there by Florence because we had notified her of our special occasion. Other evidences of thoughtfulness are the small cans of fruit juice placed in guest rooms—you never know when thirst will strike!

The restaurant is justly famous: Lunch was a small sopapilla (puffed slightly sweet Mexican roll) stuffed with chili and cheese, served with guacamole (avocado salad). For dinner we had *carne adovado* (pork marinated in chili), another specialty of the house. It was wonderful, just walking across the road in the cool mountain air to a delicious dinner, and then walking back to watch the moon over the mountains from our lovely room.

How to get there: From Highway 60 north of Santa Fe, take Highway 76 east 10 miles to Chimayo. The highway runs right between the inn and the restaurant.

The Lodge
Cloudcroft, New Mexico
88317

Innkeepers: Carole and Jerry Sanders
Address/Telephone: P.O. Box 497; (505) 682–2566 or (800) 842–4216
Rooms: 47 in main lodge, 11 in Bed and Breakfast Pavilion, including 2
   suites; all with private bath; no air conditioning (elevation 9,200 feet).
Rates: $65 to $165, double, seasonal, EP.
Open: All year.
Facilities and activities: Restaurant, lounge, saloon on weekends, swimming
   pool, Jacuzzi, sauna. Nearby: 9-hole golf course, skiing, village with
   shops and restaurants, Sacramento Peak Observatory at Sunspot.

With a name like The Lodge, we expected something pretty
rustic, so imagine our surprise at what we found in this mountain
wilderness. Set like an eagle's aerie high in the clouds 9,000 feet
overlooking the San Andres Mountains, the Black Range, and
White Sands National Monument below, The Lodge looks like the
mansion of a lucky prospector who finally struck gold. A porte-
cochere, glassed-in verandas, sprawling wings with gabled windows, and over it all a 5-story copper-clad tower, make a romantic
mixture of styles we couldn't quite put a name to.

Built in 1899, burned and rebuilt in 1911, the fanciful facade,
unchanged by numerous interior renovations, graces a hostelry that
has never closed its doors. We were thrilled to learn that stars such
as Judy Garland and Clark Gable had signed in, as well as presidents

194

and astronauts. Even Pancho Villa was a guest, when he was an escapee from Mexico in 1911.

The two-story lobby is surprisingly cozy, like a larger-than-life but wonderfully comfortable living room. A surprise was the huge stuffed bear guarding the lobby's great high fireplace. Fires here lessen the mountain chill present even in summer.

We stayed in the Honeymoon Suite, a sight for Victorian eyes as well as ours, all red velvet and gold, with a red satin four-poster topped by a gold and mirrored crown. Complimentary champagne and breakfast comes with all this!

Hallways and stairways branch off the lobby like a very elegant rabbit warren. Rooms, furnished with antiques, are all sizes and shapes, with different views. Imagine seeing from your windows the pine-studded mountain, or perhaps the glistening White Sands National Monument miles away, or even the golf course, highest and most scenic in the country.

Innkeepers Carole and Jerry have capitalized on the romantic story of the beautiful Rebecca, flame-haired ghost of a redheaded maid who disappeared when her lumberjack lover found her in the arms of another. They've named their haute cuisine restaurant after her. "We think she's a friendly spirit," says Carole. "She roams the corridors in search of a new lover, particularly haunting Room 101, the Governor's Suite."

It's also possible that Rebecca is not alone; another ghost may haunt The Lodge: the long wooden bar in the lounge once belonged to notorious Prohibition gangster Al Capone. Just think of the illegal libations served across its polished surface!

It was wonderful to dine by candlelight on such culinary delights as flaming peppercorn tournados or Chateaubriand brought flaming to our table, and we almost died for the house dessert, called DBC (for Death by Chocolate). The Lodge wins awards regularly at the New Mexico Culinary Arts show.

How to get there: Cloudcroft is approximately 8 miles east of Alamogordo on Highway 82. Signs point to The Lodge.

E: *What could be more romantic than the story of the fair Rebecca and her disappointed lover? You might be inspired to invent your own romantic story here.*

The Galisteo Inn
Galisteo, New Mexico
87540

Innkeepers: Joanna Kaufman and Wayne Aarniokoski
Address/Telephone: Box 4; (505) 982–1506
Rooms: 11; 8 with private bath; no air conditioning (elevation 6,500 feet); wheelchair accessible. No smoking inn.
Rates: $55 to $150, double, EPB; MasterCard and Visa accepted.
Open: All year.
Facilities and activities: Box lunches and dinner (Wednesday through Sunday) by reservation; horse boarding, swimming pool, hot tub, sauna, trail bicycles, hiking, horseback riding, skiing the Turquoise Trail. Nearby: old pueblo, old church, old Spanish graveyard, museum, petroglyphs (Indian paintings) three miles south of town, Old Turquoise Trail mines.

Talk about the romance of the Old West—originally, the Galisteo Inn, a fourteen-room hacienda owned by the Ortiz y Pino family, was the hub of a Spanish trading post centuries ago. When it was remodeled, it was done so carefully that it continued to fit with its surroundings, which include some of the oldest buildings in America. People seem to associate colonial architecture with the Northeast, but Spanish colonists were here long before the Pilgrims landed.

The inn is situated on eight acres of land under huge old cottonwood trees. It's a long low building hidden behind a long low adobe wall, and we almost missed it. Galisteo is not much more than a mark on the map, so don't go looking for it in the dark!

But what a wonderful place to discover, no matter if we had a little difficulty finding it! Staying here is like going on a restful retreat, a real getaway to rediscover yourselves. The simple rooms have whitewashed walls with wood vigas above. Handmade furniture and handwoven rugs are the decor; some rooms are angled, some have adobe fireplaces, all are clean, simple, and uncluttered. And we were simply entranced by the pink and blue mountains surrounding us.

"We fell in love with New Mexico," say the innkeepers, both fugitives from California. "The clean air, the serenity. . . ." We fell in love with it, too. Horseback riding by ourselves in what to us is wilderness, tying the horses up and picnicking; basking in the sun in the hot tub and then steaming in the sauna; splashing in the pool under deep blue New Mexican skies—it was wonderful.

Breakfast is a refreshing eye-opener with fruit smoothies, a fruit platter, waffles, breakfast breads, and quiche. "We use seasonal and local foods whenever possible," Wayne says. Dinners are superb, a heavenly feast in the wilderness (the inn is 23 miles south of Santa Fe). The food is a delicious combination of Southwest and New Mexican cuisine prepared with French techniques, a delicious mix. *Carne Adovada* and *Calabasitas* are specialties. The innkeepers tend their own garden, using fresh lettuce, peppers, squash, and herbs, as well as fruit from their apple, pear, and almond trees. Vegetarian meals can be requested. "A lot of health-conscious people come here," Joanna says.

Don't miss walking around the old Spanish village; we strolled hand in hand to the old church and the old Spanish graveyard. Or if you're feeling lazy, settle yourselves in hammocks down by the duck pond at the edge of the property and swing gently to and fro.

How to get there: From Albuquerque, take I–40 east to Moriarty, 41 north toward Santa Fe through Galisteo. Or from Santa Fe, take I–25 north to 285 south toward Lamy, 41 south to Galisteo.

Willows Inn
Taos, New Mexico
87571

Innkeepers: Estella Enrique and George de Kerckhove
Address/Telephone: Kit Carson Road at Dolan (mailing address: Box 4558); (505) 758–2558
Rooms: 5; all with private bath; limited wheelchair access. Pets boarded down the street. No smoking inn.
Rates: $110 to $125, EPB.
Open: All year.
Facilities and activities: Lunch and dinner by reservation. Nearby: Historic Taos Plaza with restaurants, shops, and art galleries; Taos Indian Pueblo; museums; hiking, horseback riding, skiing; tours.

This lovely inn is on a corner, hidden behind high pink adobe walls and guarded by two large willows in front, which innkeeper George told us are the oldest trees in Taos—we were instantly charmed. The pretty pink adobe building was once the home of Taos artist E. Martin Hemmings, famous enough to have one of his paintings hung in the White House. We wouldn't have missed seeing his studio for the world; it's at the back edge of the shady rear courtyard and George uses it for his work now. The pungent scent of turpentine and oil paint makes an artist's studio a magic place, and the paintings George creates here decorate the inn and several galleries in town.

Not only the studio, but the entire inn is a quiet retreat, hidden away from the noises of Kit Carson Road outside the walls. We sat in the courtyard and dreamily watched a fountain sparkling in the sunshine, and later on, in the moonlight. No ringing phones disturb the quiet, and even Bruno the cat is unobtrusive. "Our guests don't want to be bothered by telephones," Estella says decidedly.

The inn is decorated in Southwestern style highlighted by special antiques, like the dining room's hutch, dating from 1690. "We've tried to blend European and Southwest," the innkeepers say. Every room has a New Mexican kiva fireplace; don't miss the delight of lolling in front of the fire in the cool New Mexican evening, lulled by the flames.

Baths are of Mexican tile, sweet with fresh flowers as well as whatever amenities guests may need. Bottled water, mouth-watering chocolates from Italy, other complimentary refreshments, in fact "everything," says Estella, "is done with special thought in mind." Romantic thoughts, for sure.

In the morning, we sank into the living room's comfortable overstuffed sofas and chairs covered with Laura Ashley fabrics and lazily leafed through the books and magazines scattered about, relaxing utterly until we were called to the breakfast laid on the graceful Duncan Phyfe table. Estella is the chef, with George helping to serve, and we dove into the Belgian waffles (of course!) with a will. Another time there might be a German puffed pancake, or a special southwestern-seasoned dish of egg and cheese or sausage. Every day there are homemade breads and muffins and freshly ground coffee, too, all served on fine linen.

Estella, born and schooled in Las Cruces, was teaching in California, and George, brought up in Brussels and trained in the hotel industry, had already turned to painting when they decided to stop vacationing in Taos and make it their home instead. The main house was built in 1926 by Taos Indians for Hemmings; George and Estella added four rooms in a romantic courtyard setting. Everything had to be in keeping with the original house, fitting into the secluded, romantic hush that lays over the inn and the courtyard without disturbing the historical marker beside the front door.

How to get there: From U.S. Highway 68 turn east onto Kit Carson Road (the traffic light just east of the Plaza) to Dolan. The inn will be on the right.

The Browning Plantation
Chappell Hill, Texas
77426

Innkeepers: Mildred and Dick Ganchan
Address/Telephone: Route 1, Box 8; (409) 836–6144
Rooms: 6 in main house and Model Railroad Depot; 2 with private bath, 2 with TV. No smoking inn.
Rates: $85 to $110, double, EPB. No credit cards.
Open: All year.
Facilities and activities: Swimming pool, model train with 1½ miles of track, 220 acres of natural trails, fishing in lakes on property. Nearby: historic sites in Washington-on-the-Brazos and Independence; good restaurant in Brenham.

We felt like Scarlett O'Hara and Rhett Butler, driving up to this beautiful antebellum mansion hiding in the woods. It's so elegant you could be awed by its splendor, but with innkeepers like Dick and Mildred, the spirit of fun rules instead.

"We have a good time," Dick says. "We feel that people are here to watch Mildred make her biscuits in the kitchen while they have their coffee. People don't want to hear how the house was put together or how old Browning died. Mildred and I tell them all *our* troubles, and we have a good laugh instead."

Still, the Ganchans have made an entertaining story of the resurrection of the old Browning plantation, a completely ruined mansion left over from cotton-and-slavery days. Today it's one of the most romantic settings you could imagine. Just driving across the cattle guard and under the long arch of trees leading up to the house is an adventure—you can't see the house at all from the road.

Upstairs guest rooms in the big house, with 12-foot ceilings and massive windows, are furnished with nineteenth-century antiques, including plantation and tester beds for sweet dreams of what many might call "a more glorious time." And you can still be Scarlett and Rhett when you come down to breakfast around the huge dining room table, eating dishes like eggs Sardou, accompanied by a hot fruit compote. There's an "Orange Julius" eye opener, and often Southern-style hot biscuits, too. More Southern hospitality: There's a social hour with snacks before dinner.

If all this is not enough, there's the romance of the rails; One Ganchan son-in-law is such a train buff that he's built a model railroad on the property, and if he's in residence, you may be able to cajole him into a ride.

"He has more rolling stock than the Santa Fe," Dick brags as he proudly shows off the new two-room depot he designed, a replica of a Santa Fe original. Guest rooms inside the depot have an early-settlers-of-the-West feeling, with horizontal pine paneling and blue-striped ticking curtains and bedspreads.

Choosing a place to relax can be difficult: in the parlor? the library? or maybe the south veranda, with its beautiful view over the vast acres of green farmland? For a more breathtaking scene, climb three flights to the rooftop widow's walk that crowns the house—we looked over the property and pretended it was our own, pre-1861.

The two large bathrooms on the third floor are lots of fun. One is all decked out for Gents—very masculine, with bear rugs and trophies on the wall. The other is for Ladies, and oh la la! Shades of Belle Watling—wait until you see!

How to get there: From U.S. Highway 290 east of Brenham, take FM 1155 south until you come to a short jog to the left. Immediately to your right you'll see a dirt road. Turn right onto it; continue south across the cattle guard and under the arch of trees until you reach the plantation house.

Sunset Heights Inn
El Paso, Texas
79902

Innkeepers: Richard Barnett and Roni Martinez
Address/Telephone: 717 West Yandell; (919) 544–1743 or (800) 767–8513
Rooms: 6; all with private bath and TV, 3 with telephone jack. No smoking inn.
Rates: $70 to $165, double, EPB.
Open: All year.
Facilities and activities: Dinner for minimum of six people; pool and Jacuzzi. Nearby: many museums and historic fort, old Spanish missions, Tigua Indian Reservation, zoo, scenic drive, Ciudad Juarez in Mexico just across the Rio Grande.

The inn is a decorator's dream, with beautifully coordinated fabrics and wall coverings, mirrored doors, and sybaritic bathrooms. The Oriental Room with an antique Coromandel screen and a brass bed, has a bathroom with brass fixtures and a huge bathtub perfectly made to soak for hours in. Built on what was once a porch, the bath is surrounded by windows—but not to worry: All the windows are now one-way mirrors! For less-intimate soaking, the poolside Jacuzzi is also wonderful.

Built in 1905 up in the high and mighty area of El Paso overlooking downtown, this inn on the National Register of Historic Homes is a three-story corner house of dark yellow brick surrounded by an iron fence. Tall palm trees wave over it, and the large grounds of almost an acre are graced by roses blooming much of the year. "Twenty-nine bushes," Richard says, confessing that he doesn't take care of it all by himself.

Food, gourmet food, is his specialty, and you won't be able to predict what he'll feed you for breakfast because he doesn't know himself until the night before. "I don't decide what to serve until I look at my guests the evening before," he says, a comment that brought forth a contented groan from a guest who was recovering from the morning feast in a corner of the beautifully decorated parlor.

The five- to seven-course meal we had was more like a lunch or dinner buffet than a breakfast. We began with prunes in cream, went on to quiche served with kiwi and purple grapes. Then came chicken cordon bleu on rice with tomato and avocado, eggs Benedict with papaya and star fruit, and angel food cake with blueberry yogurt. We also groaned with pleasure, and this took us through the day until the champagne and late-night snacks before bedtime!

This old house is so large you can wander away by yourselves and never meet another guest unless you want to. The porches are quiet havens and so are the spacious grounds, which surprised us in such a city setting. The mountains to the north and Mexico just over the border to the south add a touch of mystery to this romantic place.

Most of the furnishings are antiques from Richard's family. The parlor has a Victrola dating from 1919, and it still plays. Although the old table radio is a replica, the kerosene lamp is one Richard studied by when he was a boy on a farm in Oklahoma. "We didn't have electricity," he says. "That old lamp got me through school." The piece we loved most was another wonderful Coromandel screen behind the old sewing machine in the parlor; don't go away without hearing Richard's romantic story of how he was able to get his screens out of China back in the days when U.S.-China relations weren't so great.

How to get there: From I-10 West take Porfiro Diaz exit and turn right; go 2 blocks to Yandell. Take a right and go 6 blocks (count the ones on the right, not the left) to Randolph. The inn is on the far corner to the left.

Raphael House
Ennis, Texas
75119

Innkeeper: Danna K. Cody
Address/Telephone: 500 West Ennis Avenue; (214) 875–1555
Rooms: 6; all with private bath and air conditioning; TV available. Smoking
   in sun room and porches.
Rates: $65 to $88, double; $10 less weekdays; corporate rate with light
   breakfast $52, otherwise EPB.
Open: All year.
Facilities and activities: Lunch, dinner, tea, receptions by reservation, cooking
   classes spring and fall. Nearby: Colonial Tennis Club, shopping area's
   twenty-five antiques shops, Landmark Commission driving tour,
   spring Bluebonnet Trail.

Ennis Avenue is a commercial street near the downtown, and
we weren't quite sure what to expect as we drove up to the
Raphael House, which has stood on the wide avenue since 1906. It
looked pretty imposing from the outside, with its wide lawn and
many steps leading to the fancy front door, but that still didn't prepare us for the space and elegance we found inside. Innkeeper
Danna Cody has done a magnificent job restoring the old home to
all its former glory, which evidently was very glorious indeed! Picture a huge entry, a magnificent parlor, baronial dining room, and
manorial library, all gleaming with richly polished old wood floors,
walls, and furniture.

Danna confesses to acquiring the house as a sort of lark. She'd come back to her hometown to visit her family after a buying trip to New York, and she wanted a sentimental last look at the mansion. "Once Ennis Avenue was lined with big houses like this, but this was the only one left," she says nostalgically. "I wanted to see it before it was torn down or burned."

She couldn't stay away. She returned three times and finally made an offer to buy the house from the last surviving member of the Raphael family. Almost before she knew it, she was the new owner of the wonderful old house.

We thought that was a pretty romantic story. "I feel like I've adopted a family," she says as she shows off the family photographs that stayed in the house. In fact, the walls are covered with Raphaels, one of the first families in Ennis back at the turn of the century, when they built the first department store, the Big Store. Rooms are named for the Raphael family members who lived in them. Julia's Room has its original set of white French furniture from 1918, bought by sister Wilhelmina, but kept by her parents. "They wouldn't let Wilhelmina take the set with her because they didn't like the man she married," Danna is delighted to explain

She was fortunate to be able to buy much of the home's original furniture. Ernest's Room has a beautiful Tiger Oak chest, which was hidden under a coat of nondescript paint when Danna acquired it.

The entry is so huge it holds a grand piano, which Danna encourages guests to play. It was wonderful to have a singalong with sentimental old tunes to fit the mood of the house. The library is stocked with old books as well as new ones, magazines, a television, and a VCR. We curled up there one evening to watch a romantic old film.

Breakfasts are as rich as the house, with French toast stuffed with strawberries and cream cheese or Danna's "Tex-Czech" breakfast with local kolabasse sausage and marvelous strudel stuffed to the rim with apples, pears, pecans, and coconut.

How to get there: Ennis is on Highway 287, which becomes Ennis Avenue. Raphael House is on the northwest corner of Ennis and Preston Street.

E: *If you can't be romantic in this romantic setting, romantic inns are not for you!*

Country Cottage Inn
Fredericksburg, Texas
78624

Innkeeper: Jeffery Webb
Address/Telephone: 405 East Main Street; (512) 997–8549
Rooms: 7 suites; all with private bath, phone, TV, refrigerator, microwave
   oven, coffee maker. No smoking inn.
Rates: $85 to $105, continental breakfast.
Open: All year.
Facilities and activities: Whirlpools, fully equipped kitchen available. Nearby:
   German restaurants, Admiral Nimitz Museum, Pioneer Museum,
   almost-monthly celebrations in historic Fredericksburg, antiques
   shops, small museums.

This romantic little cottage was built in 1850, just four years
after Fredericksburg was founded, and it was the only two-story
house in town. Its cool stone walls are more than 24 inches thick,
and the hardware throughout the house was forged in the owner's
smithy. The walls are whitewashed, and exposed rafters are hand
cut. Most of the antique furniture was made in town in the mid-
1800s.

The old inn building is beautifully restored and scrupulously
clean, and its simple structure enhanced by Laura Ashley fabrics
and bed linens. Soft terry robes and ice water in each room made
me feel like a fraudulent pioneer—it wasn't like this a little over a
hundred years ago, when hostile Indians were near and the living

was pretty tough! Still, we found it fun to pretend we were pioneers—especially when we could stop for a whirlpool bath, something those early settlers certainly couldn't do!

One of the rooms is furnished with antiques from the birthplace of Admiral Chester W. Nimitz, hero of the Pacific Theater during World War II. He was born just 2 blocks away from the cottage. His grandfather's old Steamboat Hotel is now a first-class museum. Behind the building there's a beautiful Japanese Garden, contributed by the people of Japan, and a block away you'll find the Walk of the Pacific War, lined with airplanes, tanks, landing craft, and other machines used in the Pacific during World War II. They're all out in the open in sunny Hill Country scenery for kids and adults alike to touch and wonder at.

Country Cottage has other Nimitz mementos. The Pecan Room has a Nimitz night table as well as a chuck-wagon pie safe, an Amish quilt on the wall, and an eighteenth-century mantrap over the sofa, and a coffee table made from an 1825 wooden bellows from France. So many interesting details make it difficult to look at everything at once, so take your time!

The Oak Suite has its original fireplace where guests are permitted to build a fire, but we took to heart Jeffery's admonition: "Please build only small fires!"

The Henke Suite is in the original front room of the historic house—Henke was Admiral Nimitz's maternal grandfather. Fredericksburg's Historical Society is really up on the town's genealogy, what with Chester Nimitz making such a name for himself! The Nimitz Suite is part of the house that was added on in 1873, and it too is full of family memorabilia.

The inn may be charmingly historic, but the bathrooms are beautifully modern—we were completely restored in our large whirlpool tub after a wonderful day taking in all the small town's historic sights.

Breakfast was hot chocolate, coffee, or tea and sweet rolls from one of Fredericksburg's famous bakeries. Two of them, Dietz's and the Fredericksburg Bakery, have been in business since the town began, and I really recommend a sweet visit!

How to get there: Highway 290 goes through town, becoming Main Street; the inn is right there in the 400 block.

The Gilded Thistle
Galveston, Texas
77550

Innkeepers: Helen and Pat Hanemann
Address/Telephone: 1805 Broadway; (409) 763–0194
Rooms: 3; 1 with private bath; half-bath downstairs; all rooms have TV. No smoking inn.
Rates: $135 to $145; EBP; snack tray in evening.
Open: Year-round.
Facilities and activities: Historic Ashton Villa and the Bishop's Palace are just down the street on Broadway. The historic Strand, with Galveston Art Center, Galveston County Historical Museum, Railroad Museum, and shops and restaurants is just five minutes away. The Seawall and Gulf Coast beaches are nearby.

We asked innkeeper Helen Hanemann to explain The Gilded Thistle's intriguing name. Helen, very much into the island's history, said that, like native thistle, sturdy Texas pioneer stock sank deep and lasting roots into the sandy island soil, building a Galveston that flowered into a gilded age of culture and wealth.

We thought that was pretty romantic. This home was built during the heydey {heyday?} of those stalwart people—in the late 1800s Galveston's Strand was known as "the Wall Street of the West." The Gilded Thistle is a lovely memorial to Galveston's glorious past.

The beautiful antiques throughout the house make it an

exceptionally elegant place to stay, yet the atmosphere is so welcoming that our awe melted away to pure admiration. We didn't find it difficult at all to get used to being served on fine china (it has a lovely design of purple thistles on it) or with coffee or tea poured from a family silver service.

Breakfast, Helen told us, is "whenever you want," so we could sleep late and then eat lazily on the L-shaped screened porch outside of the dining room, where there was such a lovely Gulf breeze we could hardly keep the tablecloth on the table!

We especially enjoyed Helen's special quiche casserole and potatoes seasoned with herbs, lemon, dill, and basil. Helen also makes wonderfully crispy waffles, and she's happiest when her guests like her food so much "they eat everything but the thistles off the plates!" For quick pick-ups, there's always a bowl filled with apples or other fruit on the sideboard. Tea and coffee are also available at all times, and a very special touch we loved was a pitcher of orange juice and a pot of boiling water for coffee or tea left at our bedroom door in the morning.

The evening snack tray could almost take the place of dinner, with strawberries and grapes and other fruit in season, at least four kinds of cheese, and wine. "It's my gift to you for coming," Helen says. She loves company and is in her element when two of Galveston's big hotels send her their overflow. She'll even trade her bedroom with those guests who prefer her twin beds to the guest rooms' doubles.

But we reveled in the master bedroom, with its four-poster bed facing the bay window, making a cozy setting for the antique sofa and chairs surrounding the mantelpiece.

The Gilded Thistle has been gilded horticulturally. The inn's landscaping won two prizes in 1986: the Springtime Broadway Beauty Contest and, in second place, the award for a business in a historic building.

How to get there: Stay on Highway 45 south, which becomes Broadway as soon as you cross the causeway onto Galveston Island. The inn will be just beyond 18th Street, at your right.

E: *The silk and paper garlands of roses Helen has made to drape around the mirrors and beds make romance very easy to kindle.*

La Colombe d'Or
Houston, Texas
77006

Innkeeper: Steve Zimmerman
Address/Telephone: 3410 Montrose Boulevard; (713) 524–7999
Rooms: 5 suites; all with private bath; wheelchair accessible.
Rates: $195 to $575, per suite, continental breakfast.
Open: All year.
Facilities and activities: Restaurant, bar. Nearby: within five minutes, Houston
central business district, Houston Museum of Fine Arts, Rice University, and Menil Art Foundation; the Astrodome.

Put away the guidebooks to France if you're looking for romance: Right here in Houston this very special inn is patterned after one of the same name in St. Paul de Vence, France, where many of France's famous painters traded their work for lodging. Although Houston's *Colombe d'Or* is not fortunate enough to have any of the original art of those masters, fine reproductions abound to set a very romantic French mood. We weren't surprised to find this exquisite inn close to two art collections, the Houston Museum of Fine Arts and the Menil Art Foundation.

La Colombe is French for "dove," and *Or* is "gold"; we had a golden time in Houston's version of the inn on the Riviera. Each suite has a name we readily recognized; ours was the Van Gogh Suite, one of our favorite Impressionist painters; others are named for Degas, Cezanne, Monet, and Renoir. The largest suite, up at the top, is called simply The Penthouse. Each suite is decorated with reproductions of its painter's work. We didn't miss the originals for a minute, especially since we were so swathed in the beauty and luxury of this prince of an inn. Owner Steve Zimmerman has succeeded in bringing to Houston's *Colombe d'Or* the casual elegance of the French Riviera. European and American antiques, as well as his own collection of prominent artists' works, are set in the luxurious house that was once the home of Exxon oil founder Walter Fondren and his family. The 21-room mansion, built in 1923, is divided into suites of huge bedrooms with sitting areas. Each suite has a lovely floral-covered king-sized bed, a soft cushioned sofa, fine tables, and comfy occasional chairs. On our coffee table we found a lovely bowl of fresh fruit, along with Perrier water and wine glasses waiting to be filled from our complimentary bottle of the inn's own imported French wine, which you can be sure is of a superior vintage.

The sitting area of each suite adjoins a private glass-enclosed dining room with Queen Anne furniture, china plates, and pretty linen napkins, all in readiness for breakfast. Just a minute after we rang in the morning, a waiter rolled in a tea cart from which he served a very French-style plate of sliced kiwi, raspberries, and strawberries, in addition to orange juice, coffee, and crusty croissants with butter and jam. You can imagine how romantic we felt, eating this artistic offering surrounded by the leafy boughs waving outside our glass room.

You may have luncheon or dinner served in your private dining room, too, but we elected to feast in the main dining room downstairs on meunière of shrimp and lobster, cream of potato and leek soup, the inn's Caesar salad, and capon Daniel. As if that weren't enough, we ended with crème brûlée!

The inn is a member of *Relais et Chateau,* a French organization that guarantees excellence. We absolutely soaked up the hospitality, tranquility, luxury, and romance!

How to get there: 3410 Montrose is between Westheimer and Alabama, both Houston thoroughfares.

E: *France is known for romance and La Colombe d'Or is pretty close to anything you'd find in Paris.*

The Whistler
Huntsville, Texas
77340

Innkeeper: Mary T. Clegg
Address/Telephone: 906 Avenue M; (409) 295–2834 or (713) 524–0011; or
    catch Mary on her digital pager (713) 788–8672
Rooms: 5; 4 with private bath. No smoking inn.
Rates: $85 to $100, double, EPB. No credit cards.
Open: All year.
Facilities and activities: Lunch and dinner by reservation, three acres of
    wooded land. Nearby: Sam Houston State Park, restaurants and shops
    on Town Square, Sam Houston's home, the Woodlands, and Steam-
    boat House, historic cemetery.

When Mary Clegg says she is inviting you into her ancestral
home, she's not fooling: This 130-year-old mansion has been in her
family for four generations. Mary's great-uncle built the home
around 1859. Mary's mother was born in the house and lived there
for most of her ninety years.

Mary delights in showing off the many family mementos, the
lovely old furniture, and the fascinating old photographs and portraits of her family. She is particularly proud of the framed procla-
mation from the Heritage Land Program, signed by Texas's past
governor Dolph Briscoe, attesting to the fact that the land was in
constant use for agricultural purposes in the same family for more
than one hundred years. The house's remarkable history goes back

almost to the founding of the Republic of Texas in 1836.

In view of its grandeur, we wondered about the rather whimsical name of the inn. Mary said she named it in honor of her mother's father. "My grandfather, he was happy, he whistled all the time, and we all loved to hear him." The name seemed apt—there was a happy feeling in the air as we wandered around the huge rooms, admiring the inn's wonderful furniture, much of it on a scale to match the heroic proportions of the house.

Our interest was piqued when Mary told us that a great deal of the furniture was made by inmates of Huntsville's penitentiary! The lovely dining room table has a different story. It's from the Deep South, Mary told us, and during the Civil War the owner went down on her knees to beg Union soldiers not to damage her rosewood piano. "Her rosewood piano?" we asked, wondering what that had to do with the table. Well, it must have been some piano, because what is left of it is now the inn's large dining table!

A surprising contrast, although on the same expansive scale, is the huge, modern cathedral-ceilinged common room and kitchen added to the rear of the house. When we said how much we'd love to have one just like it, Mary laughed. "All my guests love this room and say they're going home to build one just like it!"

Guest rooms are on the same generous scale, and Mary's downstairs bathroom claims the distinction of having the first indoor plumbing in Huntsville.

Mary's breakfast specialty, Julia's dish, is named after the many Julia's in her family." "My sister, my daughter, my grandmother, and my granddaughter. If I disclose my special seasoning, people go home to make it, then call me to say it doesn't taste the same!" The meal also includes ham, sausage, or bacon, "always grits," homemade biscuits, and oat bran, blueberry, or pecan muffins.

Pecan trees grace the grounds, but we didn't bestir ourselves to pick the nuts. Mostly we sat on the long front porch and vegetated. Mary has a photograph of the house, taken in 1899, with the exact same line-up of chairs sitting on the porch. Sure gave us a laugh!

How to get there: Take exit 116 off I–35; go east about 1 mile on Highway 30 (11th Street) to signal light on Avenue M. Turn left onto Avenue M; go 2 blocks; driveway of inn is on the left, and there is a sign.

Pride House
Jefferson, Texas
75657

Innkeeper: Ruthmary Jordan
Address/Telephone: 409 East Broadway; (903) 665–2675
Rooms: 10, including 1 suite (6 in main house, 4 in annex); all with private bath; 1 room for handicapped.
Rates: $65 to $100, double, EPB.
Open: All year.
Facilities and activities: Front porches, swings, rocking chairs, and reading material everywhere. Nearby: historic homes to tour, Jefferson Museum, railroad baron Jay Gould's railroad car, restaurants, and antiques shops.

Pride House was the first bed-and-breakfast inn in Texas, and a national magazine has called it "one of the 23 most romantic spots in America," so we were eager to see it. We weren't disappointed! To begin with, the hospitality of the Old South comes naturally to innkeeper Ruthmary Jordan. "Wonderful people come through my life," she says. "They share with me their family, their insights, their interests—as I do in return." They also share the inn that is one of the prides of Jefferson.

Outstanding are the stained-glass windows in every room of the house; red, blue, and amber pieces frame the clear glass centers. Ornate woodwork, gingerbread trim on the porch, long halls, and steep staircase make this house a treasure.

214

The parlor has an antique piano that the Historical Society asked Pride House to keep for them. Over it Ruthmary has hung a wonderful old gilt mirror from her husband's family, "who were riverboat people, you know." Well, we didn't know, but it was exciting to learn that riverboating was big business on Jefferson's Big Cypress Bayou until the Civil War. Now you can take a ghostly trip on the bayou, seeing sights like an old square building that once stored gunpowder for the Confederate Army.

In the Main House, the Golden Era Room next to the parlor commemorates the Golden Era of the town, when tens of thousands of people lived in Jefferson instead of today's 2,000 some. It's a lovely golden room with a romantic 9-foot half-tester bed and a large stained-glass bay window, but we were just as happy in the large Blue Room with its Victorian slipper chairs and king-sized bed.

The Green Room has antique white wicker furniture, the West Room has rich red walls and an Eastlake walnut full bed, and the Bay Room, which Ruthmary calls her "lusty Victorian," is furnished with Eastlake Victorian furniture. A romantic surprise in the Bay Room—gold stars shine down on you from the ceiling!

Six guest rooms are in the main house; the remaining four are at the rear of the property in what Ruthmary has named Dependency. The box house is so named because it was once the servants' quarters, and "the folks in the main house were dependent on their work, you know," she says.

A refreshing contrast to the Victoriana is the plant-filled common room at the rear. Large and bright, with a wall of windows lighting up the chic black-and-white tile floor, it's a popular gathering place in the inn.

Breakfast always features one of the innkeeper's famous recipes, from her days as owner of Ruthmary's Restaurant. Oh, her crème brûlée fruit parfait! Indescribably delicious! With it, bran muffins delicately redolent of almond, croissants with strawberry butter and melon preserves, and two kinds of sausage, mmm-mmm! Another morning we were served her special baked pear in French cream sauce. If you catch her in a whimsical mood, there may be Not Eggzactly Benedict, a wonderful takeoff on the popular egg dish.

How to get there: Highway 49 becomes Broadway as it heads east into town. The Pride House is on the northwest corner of Broadway and Alley Street.

La Borde House
Rio Grande City, Texas
78582

Innkeepers: Crisanto Salinas and Armandina Garza
Address/Telephone: 601 East Main Street; (512) 487–5101
Rooms: 21; all with private bath.
Rates: $59, double, historical rooms; $40, double, modern rooms; EP.
Open: All year.
Facilities and activities: Restaurant open for lunch and dinner Monday to
  Thursday, 11:00 A.M. to 2:00 P.M.; Friday, Saturday, and Sunday, 11:00
  A.M. to 9:00 P.M. Nearby: hunting, fishing, bird watching, International
  Bridge to Mexico, historic Fort Ringgold.

We were delighted and surprised to find this New Orleans Cre-
ole mansion here on the Texas–Mexico border. The La Borde House
is elegant, no doubt about it, and we soon discovered why: It was
designed by French architects in Paris (France, not Paris, Texas!).
Way back in 1899, leather merchant Francois La Borde had his inn
designed at Paris's Beaux Arts School. It was his combined home,
storehouse, and inn, and his guests were often cattle barons, who
sold their herds on the nearby Rio Grande River docks, or military
officers en route to California. La Borde brought to life his visions of
European grandeur, and we reveled in the faithful reconstruction. I
felt like a Southern belle with my cavalier in attendance.

Restoration (in 1982) was authentic, established from original
records and photographs. The inn was originally built by both Euro-

pean and Rio Grande artisans, and the brick used in the restoration work was purchased from the same brickyard in Camargo, Mexico, that made the originals.

We were entranced by the inn's opulence—the collector-quality oriental rugs and the English Axminster carpets, the luxurious furnishings in the main house. It was intriguing to read in old ledgers the records of such fancy purchases, made way back when this was pretty raw territory. Each posh bedroom in the historical section is furnished with antique furniture and authentic wallpapers. Many of the papers and fabrics are duplicates of those used in the 1981 restoration of the Texas Governor's Mansion up in Austin.

"It tells the whole history of the Border, it's that simple," say the innkeepers. "We really get a joy out of the smiles we see on people's faces as they reminisce about old times here in the Valley."

What the old-timers reminisced about for our benefit was the days of Fort Ringgold, named for the first army officer killed in the battle that began the Mexican-American War. It's not easy to see how such an important event could happen in the sleepy little town Rio Grande City is nowadays, but evidently Fort Ringgold was pretty important in those yesterdays. We visited historic Lee House, which was occupied by Robert E. Lee when he commanded here, before he was called for action in the Civil War. Fort Ringgold is one of Texas' best-preserved old military posts, so it's something to see.

Back at the inn with a good appetite, we found that the restaurant is the place for special Border cuisine. The Mexican Plate of tacos, enchiladas, tamales, beans, and rice has a special Valley flavor, just right for lunch.

For dinner over candlelight we tried the Chicken Cilantro, sautéed in butter and seasoned with the savory south-of-the-border herb for which it is named. Served on a rice bed, it was delicious. We topped it off with fried ice-cream, a neat treat of frozen ice cream dipped in batter and deep-fried in a hurry!

Seafood lovers usually may choose from three selections, but the two favorites are shrimp and the catfish.

How to get there: From Highway 281 take Highway 83 west, which becomes Main Street in town. The inn is on the corner of Main and Garza.

E: *This duet of France and south-of-the-border adds up to a wonderfully romantic getaway for two!*

Thee Hubbell House
Winnsboro, Texas
75494

Innkeepers: Laurel and Dan Hubbell
Address/Telephone: 307 West Elm Street; (214) 342–5629
Rooms: 5, including 2 suites; all with private bath. No smoking inn.
Rates: $65 to $150, per room, EPB.
Open: All year.
Facilities and activities: Dinner by reservation. Nearby: Lake Bob Sandlin, Cypress Springs Lake and twenty-two other lakes within a 30-mile radius; Autumn Trails Festival, Christmas Festival, spring and summer festivals.

We felt sentimental about the Good Old Days at Thee Hubbell House just as soon as we asked if it was safe to take a walk outside. The Hubbells, who take their peace and safety for granted, were gently amused.

"Of course you can walk here, even at night," Dan said with a twinkle. "The front door of the inn is open so that guests can come and go as they please," he added as we took off like little school kids, giggling and holding hands. We walked all of the two and a half blocks downtown, where we found antiques shops and at least three churches.

What we thought was pretty romantic about this inn was our discovery that East Texas was more pro-Confederate than not back in Civil War days. Quite a few mansions testify to the antebellum influence. Thee Hubbell House is a true East Texas Southern belle, with its white Georgian colonial facade catching our eye as we came down the street. The porches and upstairs gallery sport swings and rockers, and, as Dan Hubbel says, "it's amazing how people love to sit out and rock. If they're my age, or older, they remember what it was like to sit out on the porch and rock."

We enjoyed staying around, rocking and loafing, and the Hubbells seemed to enjoy it, too. Part of our pleasure stemmed from the fact that Dan is the Mayor of Winnsboro. "We meet and greet our guests on a kind of official level," he says with a chuckle. "It seems to add a sort of prestige to our guests, to have the Mayor serve them coffee." We sure enjoyed being impressed!

The centuries-old mansion has pine floors, square handmade nails, and original glass in its windows—at night our reflections in the wavy panes had a fun-house look! Cabinets now surround a solid-oak pie safe so heavy that it took three men to lift it. The banister posts were made at former owner Colonel Stinson's sawmill; it was his daughter Sallie who married Texas's first governor, Jim Hogg, so there was some historical romance for us. The inn has some lovely English antiques, and Dan's grandmother's sewing chair and Laurel's grandmother's washstand testify to their native Texas roots.

Breakfast is bountiful, to say the least. We began the feast with a baked apple stuffed with mincemeat. Next came shirred eggs, baked ham, buttermilk biscuits, grits and cream gravy, wheat raisin muffins, coffee, and juice. "We call it a Plantation Breakfast," Laurel told us. They served it in the dining room at 8:30, and we didn't rise from the table until 11!" Laurel and Dan joined us for breakfast since there were less than eight guests. When there are more guests than that, "we don't eat at all, but we have coffee with our guests," says Laurel.

Talk about Southern hospitality: On Mondays all Winnsboro restaurants are closed, so the Hubbells might ask you "if you enjoy a good stew with just crackers and a glass of milk, well, come and sit down."

How to get there: Winnsboro is on Highway 37 between I–30 and I–80. Highway 37 becomes Main Street. Turn west on Elm to 307.

Rocky Mountain Region

by Doris Kennedy

In an attempt to select the most romantic inns from the many hundreds I have visited, I first asked myself what I would look for when choosing such an accommodation for my husband and myself. Next I interviewed friends and colleagues, questioning them as to the qualities they would seek in their ideal hideaway for two.

I discovered most of us pretty much thought the same, with the main difference being in the order of preference.

As for me, I would look for a secluded place, private, with soothing sounds in the form of birdsong, the steady chirp of crickets, the rush of a river, or the distant call of coyotes at dusk.

Luxurious or rustic, either would be fine; but if a turret room were available, I would absolutely have to have it, for here we would leisurely sip morning coffee and take turns reading aloud. I would like a fireplace and perhaps a four-poster canopied in ruffles and lace, or one made of rough-hewn logs and covered with billowy quilts.

No phones, please. And if a television must be present, let it be hidden away in an armoire.

Blessed is the innkeeper who is attentive yet discreet. Guests seeking a romantic rendezvous want to be greeted warmly, then graciously left alone. Let the innkeeper spin his or her magic by leaving treats and morning coffee outside the door and, while we are out, a fresh rose on the bed, a pitcher of ice water spiked with floating fresh strawberries, and a love poem or a sachet of potpourri under the pillows.

Flowers, candles, adjustable soft lighting, and a nearby wood or a park for wandering hand in hand would be nice.

Most of all, let it be peaceful, where hushed conversations proceed without interruption, where secrets are shared and promises made, and where cherished memories have their beginnings.

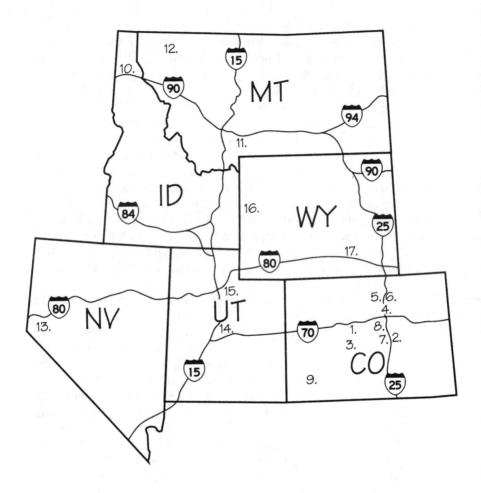

Rocky Mountain Region

Numbers on the map refer to towns numbered below.

Sardy House
Aspen, Colorado
81612

Innkeeper: Jayne Poss
Address/Telephone: 128 East Main Street; (303) 920–2525 or (800) 321–3457
Rooms: 20, including 6 suites; all with private bath and TV, most with
  whirlpool bath, suites with VCR, stereo, and dry bar. No air conditioning (elevation 7,908 feet).
Rates: $155 to $380, double, summer and fall; $265 to $560, double, winter
  and early spring; EPB. High-end rates are for suites. Rates will vary
  some, depending on season.
Open: Mid-June to mid-October and from Thanksgiving to mid-April.
Facilities and activities: Sunday brunch. Concierge service. Bar, heated outdoor pool, sauna, Jacuzzi. Nearby: restaurants, shopping, art galleries,
  free ski shuttle, all within walking distance; summer music festivals,
  hiking, fishing, river rafting, downhill and cross-country skiing, ice
  skating.

If your ideal romantic getaway leans toward turreted, Victorian
mansions, perhaps this is the inn for you: a red-brick masterpiece
with original oak staircases and sliding parlor doors, round reading
rooms tucked away in a turret, gourmet breakfast set upon pearl
gray linen centered with fresh flowers, and fine dining in the
evenings as well.

Soft plum carpeting with pale pink roses, made in Ireland
especially for the Sardy, is used throughout the building, and wallpaper of subdued gray cloaks the walls. The guest rooms have thick

terry his and her robes, heated towel racks, down comforters with Laura Ashley duvets, and televisions hidden in walls or armoires. Except for two units with antique tubs, all have whirlpool baths.

We have a thing about carriage houses, and that is where we chose to stay, in a beautifully appointed complement to the main mansion. Our room had a vaulted, many-angled ceiling; natural wicker table, chairs, and writing desk; a cherry-wood, high-off-the-floor bed with feather-filled comforter and five fluffy pillows; and a bay window that looked out on Aspen Mountain and the ski slopes. The almond-scented lotion, shampoo, and bath gel were another nice touch. If you add just a few drops of bath gel to your whirlpool bath you'll both disappear into a myriad of boundless bubbles!

Our breakfast was a Brie-cheese omelet topped with sautéed cinnamon apples, nut bread, a garnish of fresh fruit, coffee, and orange juice. Crabtree & Evelyn preserves from London were on every table.

With the glow of candlelight reflecting softly off the silver, crystal, and china, our evening meal featured filet mignon with a sauce of pink peppercorns and cream and Colorado rack of lamb with fresh herbs, an extensive wine list, unusual hors d'oeuvres, and fancy desserts. For those who prefer the privacy of their room, the Sardy House will serve either or both breakfast and dinner in your guest room.

How to get there: Sardy House is on the corner of Main and Aspen streets in downtown Aspen.

D: *The Sardy House is a popular place for small weddings, receptions, and private dinners. It was recently awarded the Mobil 4 Star rating: "Outstanding . . . worth a special trip."*

Holden House 1902
Bed & Breakfast Inn
Colorado Springs, Colorado
80904

Innkeepers: Sallie and Welling Clark
Address/Telephone: 1102 West Pikes Peak Avenue; (719) 471–3980
Rooms: 5; all with private bath and air conditioning. No smoking inn.
Rates: $60 to $90, double, EPB, turn-down service, chocolates on pillows, printout on history of house, bottled spring water in guest rooms. Special breakfast on Sundays. Inquire about 2-day romance package.
Open: All year.
Facilities and activities: Nearby: historic Old Colorado City, Pikes Peak, cog railroad, Garden of the Gods, Cave of the Winds, Air Force Academy, Will Rogers Shrine of the Sun, Royal Gorge, restaurants, shopping, hiking, fishing, ice skating, cross-country skiing.

In 1902, Isabel Holden, wealthy widow of rancher, property owner, bank president, and stockholder Daniel M. Holden, had this gracious Colonial Revival–Victorian home and carriage house built for herself and her six children. After her death in 1931, the fine old house was allowed to deteriorate and crumble.

Enter Sallie and Welling, who spent twelve months laboriously installing a new foundation, plumbing, heating, wiring, and landscaping and otherwise refurbishing and loving this fine old structure back to life. Recently, they totally renovated the carriage house, creating two guest rooms, a sitting room, and a front parlor. The Clarks then filled both facilities with family heirlooms, lovely antiques, and genuine hospitality.

The guest rooms are named after Colorado mining towns: Aspen, Cripple Creek, and Leadville are located in the main house, while Silverton and Goldfield share the carriage house.

The romantic Aspen, Silverton, and Goldfield suites all boast fireplaces. The Goldfield has a Roman marble oversized tub and 4-foot skylight for stargazing, and the Aspen, with an open Victorian turret over a queen-sized brass bed and private sitting area, contains a luxurious brass-appointed eighty-gallon tub for two in a garden-like setting. I suggest you request the "Romance Package," available to guests staying two nights or more. For an additional $10 charge, a specially prepared "Sweetheart Breakfast" will be brought to your door on the morning of your choice.

Breakfast at the Holden House is extensive. A typical menu might include eggs fiesta, topped with sour cream and salsa with a touch of fresh herbs from the garden; blueberry corn muffins; fresh fruit with a fruit-yogurt topping; amaretto coffee, specialty teas, and orange juice. The morning meal is served on the front veranda during summer and in the formal dining room in winter.

The Victorian parlor has an oak fireplace with marble hearth, pink-and-blue wallpaper sprinkled with birds and flowers, and furniture grouped for reading or quiet conversation. Mingtoy, the friendly resident cat, is the inn's official greeter.

For dinner choices, check the brass basket full of menus in Sallie and Welling's parlor. Historic Old Colorado City is within walking distance and features many restaurants in addition to boutiques and antiques shops.

How to get there: From I–25, take exit 141 west on Highway 24. Take the first right onto 8th Street. Turn left onto West Colorado Avenue and proceed for 3½ blocks to 11th Street. Turn right onto 11th Street. The inn is on the corner of 11th Street and West Pikes Peak Avenue.

Crested Butte Club
Victorian Hotel & Spa
Crested Butte, Colorado
81224

Innkeeper: Joe Rous

Address/Telephone: 512 Second Street (mailing address: P.O. Box 309); (303) 349–6655

Rooms: 7, including 1 suite; all with private bath, cable TV, phone, and working fireplace. No air conditioning (elevation 9,000 feet). No smoking inn.

Rates: $60 to $155, double, depending on room and season, continental breakfast.

Open: All year.

Facilities and activities: Sports Pub, weight gym, lap pool, racquetball court, aerobics area, Nordic ski shop, two whirlpools, two steam baths, ski tuning bench, conference room. Nearby: restaurants, shopping, shuttle to ski slopes, hiking, mountain biking, wildflower meadows, championship golf course, tennis, horseback riding, jeep tours, downhill and cross-country skiing, Aerial Weekend (hot-air ballooning, skydiving, hang gliding, stunt pilots), Chamber Music Festival, Slavic Harvest Festival, wildflower and photography workshops.

A stay at the Crested Butte Club is a taste of luxury that everyone should experience at least once and, preferably, many, many times. All the guest rooms are beauties but the romantic elegance of the Presidential Suite is nonpareil. I had decided on this room, sight unseen, when making a reservation by phone. I couldn't have made a better choice.

As I opened the door, I caught my breath—it was that overwhelming. A rich royal blue carpet, strewn with peach and yellow roses and gold curlicues, spread before me. A French Provincial four-poster, which I later discovered to be an exceptionally comfortable waveless waterbed, stood against the far wall. Fresh flowers graced the coffee table in front of a white brocade love seat. To my right was a gleaming wet bar with copper sink and brass fixtures, and chilling in a bucket of ice was a bottle of champagne.

Ah, but there was even more opulence to discover. In the bathroom, dark wood wainscoting met cream-colored wallpaper sprinkled with tiny blue flowers; twin pedestal sinks, imported from Italy, sat beneath oak cabinets; an oak pull-chain commode hid in one corner; and, best of all, a sloped-to-fit copper tub with hammered-brass feet beckoned me to break out the bubble bath.

Imagine lying in bed and watching the flickering firelight glimmer against the brass and candlestick chandelier. Too warm or too much light? All one has to do is reach for the remote control on the bedside table to lower or extinguish the flames.

Other rooms feature oak or white-iron-and-brass beds; televisions hide in armoires or above fireplace mantels; two rooms have decks; and all chambers have gas fireplaces and copper tubs.

Honeymooners and anniversary couples receive champagne, with a choice of labels. In addition, newlyweds are given a gift copy of the *Colorado Cookbook*, with a personal note of congratulations and best wishes. Horse and carriage rides from the hotel to one of many romantic restaurants can be arranged.

How to get there: From Gunnison, about 220 miles southwest of Denver, take Highway 135 north to Crested Butte. When you reach Crested Butte, take Elk Avenue into town. Turn left onto Second Street. The inn is on the left.

D: *The Crested Butte Club has a first-class spa with complimentary use for inn guests. It also is open to the public, but guests have private after-hours privileges.*

Castle Marne
Denver, Colorado
80206

Innkeepers: Jim and Diane Peiker
Address/Telephone: 1572 Race Street; (303) 331–0621
Rooms: 9; all with private bath and phone. No air conditioning (not needed; walls are 20 inches of solid stone). No smoking inn.
Rates: $80 to $155, double, EPB plus Victorian tea.
Open: All year.
Facilities and activities: Candlelight dinners, with advance reservations; game room with pool table and exercise equipment; gift shop. Nearby: business and financial districts, Colorado State Capitol, U.S. Mint, Center for the Performing Arts, restaurants, convention center, museums, recreation centers, shopping facilities, professional sporting events, hiking, fishing, biking; downhill and cross-country skiing approximately 50 miles away.

For those of us not lucky enough to grow up in a castle amidst opulence and grandeur, the Castle Marne provides a wee glimpse of what we missed. The exterior is stunning. For years, passersby have paused to admire the medieval-looking rusticated stone structure. Now they come to spend the night.

Inside, one can't help but marvel at the glowing woodwork, original fireplaces, and exquisitely decorated rooms. The parlor, blessed with a baby grand piano and treasured family antiques, lends itself nicely to the intimate Victorian tea served each afternoon on heirloom porcelain china and silver.

230

There's something hopelessly romantic about climbing the stately oak staircase, past the resplendent beveled-crystal and stained-glass Peacock Window, to your guest room. Our favorite chamber is the Presidential Suite, an elegant affair featuring a king-sized brass-and-white-iron tester bed with rose bed cover peeping through ecru lace. This room is further enhanced by a tiny fireplace, an antique gentleman's dresser, and a cozy turret room surrounded by five lace-paneled windows. French doors lead to a private solarium with a large whirlpool tub and a balcony overlooking downtown Denver.

The Conservatory also caught our fancy. This light and airy room has a queen-sized bed, a wicker armoire and love seat, and creamy walls sprinkled with cabbage roses.

Extraordinarily good breakfasts come from Jim and Diane's kitchen. A fresh fruit plate is followed by wonderful homemade breads, muffins, and cinnamon sticky buns. Perhaps you will choose one of their many waffle varieties with real maple syrup, an innovative quiche, or a hot-from-the-oven breakfast casserole.

How to get there: From East Colfax Avenue, turn north onto Race Street. Proceed for almost 1 block. Inn is on southeast corner of Race Street and Sixteenth Avenue.

D: *Imagine a private candlelight dinner in the Castle Marne's formal dining room amid the gracious ambience of days long past. Soft music accompanies your conversation, and you scarcely notice the striking of the wall clock as you dine on chilled marinated shrimp and Cornish game hen with apricot glaze and fruit and nut stuffing, followed by chocolate mousse and café au lait. Later you climb that wonderful oak staircase, soak in the oversized Jacuzzi with balcony doors open to the stars and, eventually, sip a cup of wine or tea in your own tiny turret hideaway. Every couple should have just such an evening at least once in their lifetime. Hopefully, many, many times.*

Queen Anne Inn
Denver, Colorado
80205

Innkeepers: Chuck and Ann Hillestad
Address/Telephone: 2147 Tremont Place; (303) 296–6666 for information; (800) 432–INNS for reservations
Rooms: 14; all with private bath, air conditioning, and stereo chamber music. No smoking inn.
Rates: $64 to $159, double, continental-plus breakfast, afternoon refreshments.
Open: All year.
Facilities and activities: Innkeepers will arrange horse-and-carriage rides, catered candlelight dinners, musicians for private serenading, and just about anything else your imagination (or theirs) can come up with. Nearby: business and financial districts, Colorado State Capitol, U.S. Mint, Center for the Performing Arts, convention center, museums, shopping, restaurants (several five-star), all within walking distance; hiking, fishing, biking; downhill and cross-country skiing approximately 50 miles away.

This circa-1879 Queen Anne Inn proudly reigns amid a row of lovely Victorians in downtown Denver's Clements Historic District. While you relax in the beautifully appointed parlor, you are apt to witness a breathless couple arriving by horse and carriage, she still in her long, white wedding dress, he nervously trying to avoid stepping on same. Or the newest arrivals might be a middle-aged pair, with bottle of champagne in hand, bent on escaping their lawn-mowing, car-polishing neighbors for a romantic weekend getaway. They've come to the right place.

Every guest room is different, and each one is special in its own way. The Fountain Room, overlooking Benedict Fountain Park, boasts a four-poster with frilly, white-ruffled arched canopy, soft-peach walls, a blue-and-peach love seat, and a black-tiled sunken tub tucked away in one corner. A more romantic room would be hard to find.

While the Tower Room, with European carved king-sized bed and bay window love seat, is exceptionally inviting, the Aspen Room is definitely the most unusual. Located in the turret, it features a hand-painted, wraparound mural of an aspen grove. If you lie on the bed and look up at the ceiling, you will gradually see the forest come alive until the aspen leaves seem to quake in the alpenglow.

The grounds are positively lovely. A series of latticework arbors leads to an enclosed backyard garden bordered by brick and flagstone planters filled with flowers and greenery. Ornate, white-iron tables and chairs and a center fountain beckon couples to linger awhile.

Numerous publications, including *Bride's* magazine, *Romantic Hideaways, Bridal Guide, Country Inns, Travel Holiday,* and *Vacations,* have raved about the Queen Anne's romantic qualities. Ann and Chuck have printed a small "Guide for Brides" with "50 Great Tips for a Stress-free Wedding," available from the inn. They also have prepared an in-room leaflet with more than 100 suggestions for romantically enhancing your relationship. It can be purchased for $4. A small price to pay for many, many years' worth of romantic ideas!

How to get there: From East Colfax Avenue, take Logan Street north to 20th Avenue. Turn left onto 20th Avenue and proceed to 21st Street. Turn right onto 21st Street and then immediately right again onto Tremont Place. Inn is on the left.

❁

D: *According to Chuck, "Six out of ten rooms have been simultaneously filled with beaming brides. Sometimes there is a literal traffic jam of white satin and lace around here."*

233

The Anniversary Inn
Estes Park, Colorado
80517

Innkeepers: Don and Susan Landwer
Address/Telephone: 1060 Mary's Lake Road, Moraine Route; (303) 586–6200
Rooms: 4, plus 1 cottage; all rooms with private bath, cottage with private
   bath, whirlpool tub, and fireplace. No air conditioning (elevation 7,600
   feet). No smoking inn.
Rates: $70 to $120, double, EPB and evening refreshments.
Open: All year.
Facilities and activities: Picnic lunches available. Sun porch, library. Nearby:
   Rocky Mountain National Park, Lake Estes, Historic MacGregor Ranch,
   restaurants, shopping, hiking, fishing, sailing, mountain climbing,
   horseback riding, golf, tennis, rafting, sledding, snowshoeing, cross-
   country skiing.

The emphasis here is on romance. This lovely turn-of-the-century
log cabin inn can become a wedding chapel, a honeymoon haven, or a
place to celebrate your anniversary and renew your vows. Don and
Susan specialize in romantic getaways for couples.

All guest rooms are named after Strauss waltzes. On the main
floor, the Emperor's Room boasts a king-sized bed, plum-colored
balloon shades, lace curtains, and off-white walls with stenciled
trim.

Upstairs, Rosewood is cozy with pretty wallpaper, while Vien-
na Woods sports a queen-sized cast-iron bed, lace curtains, and sev-

234

eral antique pieces. My choice of rooms was the Blue Danube. An upholstered fainting couch sits in one corner, and a beautiful mountain view is as close as the window. A little nook with an antique writing desk, a sloped ceiling, a queen-sized brass bed, blue wainscoting, white walls, and blue, red, and green hand-stenciling all add to the charm of this room.

After a great night's sleep (don't forget to open your window to hear the quiet rustling of the pine trees), wake to the wonderful aroma of fresh-baked breads and brewing coffee.

The dining area, small library, and living room with moss rock fireplace are all for guest use. Breakfast is served on the enclosed wraparound sun porch and varies from a cheese blintz soufflé with blackberry cassis sauce to berry pancakes, accompanied by muffins and breads and fruits and juices. Other specialties include home-made cinnamon rolls and apricot-banana smoothies.

In the evening you are invited to sit back and enjoy light refreshments before a warm fire.

Located about 50 feet from the inn is the new, wonderfully romantic Sweetheart's Cottage. Having come a long way since it sufficed as the servants' quarters, it features a queen-sized four-poster bed, wing chairs in front of the fireplace, and a whirlpool tub for two.

How to get there: Going west on Elkhorn Avenue, Estes Park's main street, turn left onto Moraine Avenue and proceed 4 blocks. At first stoplight, turn right onto Highway 36. At stoplight (1¹/₅ miles) turn left onto Mary's Lake Road. Watch for Anniversary Inn sign on left, just across the bridge.

D: *This inn is picture-book perfect: Nestled among tall fir and pine, at the end of a tree-lined lane, it is surrounded by wildflowers in the spring and summer and snowcapped like a whipped cream–topped gingerbread house in winter.*

River Song Inn
Estes Park, Colorado
80517

Innkeepers: Gary and Sue Mansfield
Address/Telephone: Mary's Lake Road (mailing address: P.O. Box 1910); (303) 586–4666
Rooms: 4 in main inn, 1 carriage house suite, 4 deluxe cottages; all with private bath. Two rooms in 1 cottage with wheelchair access. No air conditioning (elevation 7,522 feet). No smoking inn.
Rates: $85 to $160, double, EPB.
Open: All year.
Facilities and activities: Candlelight dinner and box lunches by reservation. Located on twenty-seven acres of land with easy hiking trails. Nearby: Rocky Mountain National Park, restaurants, shopping, hiking, fishing, sailing, mountain climbing, golf, tennis, wildlife seminars, cross-country skiing, snowshoeing.

The River Song recently added a wonderfully secluded two-unit cottage, with guest quarters separated by a foot-and-a-half-thick wall to ensure privacy. Named "Wood Nymph" and "Meadow Bright," the two chambers nestled on the mountainside (easily accessible) near a rushing stream and tranquil, trout-filled pond, with a spectacular view of the snow-capped peaks of Rocky Mountain National Park. Both have fireplaces, canopy beds (Wood Nymph's is handmade of river birches, and Meadow Bright's is a massive hand-hewn log affair), decks, and radiant-heated floors. Wood Nymph has a Jacuzzi whirlpool tub and Meadow Bright features a fireside jetted tub and a waterfall shower. Both rooms have wheelchair access.

Another of our favorite rooms at this inn is Chiming Bells. A shiny brass bed gleams above the emerald green carpet; a moss-rock fireplace fills one corner; and skylights open the pine-planked cathedral ceiling to the sun and stars. In the small parlor, one finds a crimson Victorian settee and walnut platform rocker; in the bathing area, a sapphire-blue oversized, recessed soaking tub and redwood-paneled double shower with skylight.

The Mansfields have added a huge whirlpool tub for two in front of the fire in the carriage house. This accommodation also has an oversized shower and skylight. Wonderfully romantic. But, if you are looking for something unique and also romantic, you really should ask for the River Song's most requested accommodation: Indian Paintbrush. A charming cottage sequestered among tall pine trees, it is tastefully done in southwestern decor and features a love seat, handwoven Navajo wall hangings, an oversized bathtub, and, best of all, a swinging, queen-sized bed suspended from the ceiling by heavy white chains in front of a rose-tiled fireplace.

Sue is an excellent cook and makes many delectables such as apple pandowdy, blueberry cobbler served with vanilla yogurt, and corn fritters topped with genuine Vermont maple syrup. Elegant candlelight dinners, served in style with heirloom silver, crystal and china, are available with prior notice.

Plush off-white couches and a soft-blue carpet add luxuriance to the living room, where one entire side is a window with a magnificent view of tall pines and mountains. Books line two walls, a warm fire crackles in the fireplace, and the grandfather clock periodically chimes the hour. All's well at River Song.

How to get there: Going west on Elkhorn Avenue, Estes Park's main street, turn left onto Moraine Avenue and proceed 4 blocks. At first stop sign, turn right onto Highway 36. At stoplight (1½ miles) turn left onto Mary's Lake Road. Watch for River Song Inn mailbox just across bridge. Turn right and proceed for ⅘ mile. The road ends at River Song.

The Lovelander
Bed & Breakfast Inn
Loveland, Colorado
80537

Innkeepers: Marilyn and Bob Wiltgen
Address/Telephone: 217 West 4th Street; (303) 669–0798
Rooms: 9; all with private bath, air conditioning, and phone, 1 with
   whirlpool bath. No smoking inn.
Rates: $80 to $110, double, EPB, complimentary beverages.
Open: All year.
Facilities and activities: Meeting and reception center. Nearby: restaurants,
   shopping, art galleries, museums, concerts, performing arts, lectures,
   theater, outdoor and indoor swimming pools, outdoor and indoor
   Jacuzzis, hiking, biking, fishing, boating, cross-country skiing, llama
   farm, Rocky Mountain National Park.

Loveland, Colorado, is known nationwide as the Sweetheart
City, where one can send his or her valentines to be postmarked by
hand and mailed from "Loveland." What better way to impress that
special someone?

The Lovelander Bed and Breakfast Inn fits right into the
scheme. Its Victorian elegance definitely lends itself to romance. A
wide veranda wraps around the front and one side of this lovely
circa-1902 inn; inside, gleaming woodwork, an ornate organ from
the late 1800s, a corner fireplace, and plush overstuffed furniture

add to the inviting glow of the parlor.

Lace-curtained bay windows spread soft light into the dining room, where one can always find coffee or tea and genuine, home-made Victorian vinegar cookies on the sideboard. Breakfast is served either at tables set for two or at the large oval dining room table.

And the two of you are in for a treat when you come down to breakfast. Baked eggs Florentine, cinnamon-raisin breakfast pudding, stuffed French toast with strawberry-tangerine sauce, almond scones, banana oatmeal pancakes, gingered melon with honey, and strawberry-banana smoothies are only a few of the specialties Marilyn cooks up in her kitchen.

The private and secluded guest rooms are tucked away in downstairs corners and upstairs gables. Sloped ceilings and lots of nooks and crannies, along with antique writing desks, armoires, carved walnut and oak and brass and iron beds, and claw-footed bathtubs, add to the charm of these chambers.

Among our favorites are the Country Garden Room with its queen-sized bed covered with a pale aqua floral spread, oak desk, and indoor window box filled with cheerful wooden tulips, and the Columbine, with king-sized bed, writing desk, love seat, and elegant bath with 6-foot whirlpool tub.

The Lovelander dedicates the entire month of February to romance. Guest chefs create gourmet candlelight dinners, musicians entertain, and lovers receive commemorative valentines and complimentary boxes of chocolates. During the rest of the year, Marilyn will arrange romantic dinners for two at area restaurants, with limousine service, if desired.

How to get there. From I-25, turn west onto Highway 34 to Garfield Avenue. Turn left onto Garfield to West 4th Street. Turn right onto West 4th Street. Inn is on the right.

D: *What better place to get married or repeat your vows than in Loveland? The Lovelander has a separate facility especially designed for that purpose. It also will nicely handle small receptions.*

Red Crags Bed & Breakfast
Manitou Springs, Colorado
80829

Innkeepers: Carrie and Kevin Maddox
Address/Telephone: 302 El Paso Boulevard; (719) 685–1920
Rooms: 7; all with private bath and fireplace. TV available. No air conditioning (elevation 6,400 feet). No smoking inn.
Rates: $75 to $150, double, EPB, afternoon tea.
Open: All year.
Facilities and activities: Solarium, outdoor Jacuzzi, picnic area with barbecue. Nearby: Pikes Peak Cog Railway, Garden of the Gods, Cave of the Winds, Air Force Academy, Florissant Fossil Beds, May Natural History Museum, spa, limited-stakes gambling at town of Cripple Creek, hiking, fishing, white-water rafting, cross-country skiing.

Whether for a honeymoon stay or a weekend getaway, this inn sets the stage where fantasy and romance intertwine.

Innkeeper Carrie Maddox dons Victorian attire to welcome guests to her elegant, three-story mansion. On overcast days, she might wear a black satin dress, at Christmastime a red velvet formal, while honeymoon couples merit an heirloom lace wedding gown.

Thus do visitors step into a past era when the Red Crags operated as a healing center more than 120 years ago. Original skeleton keys unlock doors that still bear a patient number. Each room has a corresponding call bell to the nurse's station, now a private dining area for two.

Today names designate guests' quarters, most with king-sized European-style feather beds. The Dr. Bell Room pays homage to the founder of Manitou Springs and the builder of Red Crags.

It's hard to resist the lure of the Honeymoon Suite, also known as the Teddy Roosevelt Room, where the Rough Rider himself stayed in 1901. It's fun to lie on the king-sized bed, listen to the crackling fire in the copper fireplace, and imagine how life was way back then. Teddy's room surely was not as delightful as it is now, for Carrie has added many decorative touches: a profusion of dried and fresh flowers, potpourri sachets, and a white embroidered duvet bed cover with matching ruffled skirt. French doors swing open onto an oversized bath with claw-foot tub and a glass wall looking out toward Pikes Peak. The private deck is the perfect place for early-morning coffee or late-evening hushed conversations.

The breakfast site is subject to guests' fancies: in rooms, on the deck, or in the formal dining room with elaborate cherry Eastlake fireplace. Entrees range from macadamia-nut waffles to egg, cheese, and broccoli soufflé topped with ham in the shape of a heart, Carrie's trademark. Nut breads and fruit muffins, along with fresh fruit, decoratively share the plate. In season, an edible blossom from the mansion's gardens embellishes the arrangement.

Complimentary afternoon tea features cake or breads and a specialty, Teddy Roosevelt cider, poured from one of a collection of unusual teapots. As a special service, the Maddoxes later transport guests to the restaurant of their choice in a sleek '55 Jaguar.

How to get there: Take Highway 24 west from Colorado Springs to the Manitou Springs Business exit. Turn right onto Manitou Avenue. The Red Crags is prominently situated on a bluff on the right. At Buena Vista, turn right, then right again onto El Paso.

Meadow Creek
Bed & Breakfast Inn
Pine, Colorado
80470

Innkeepers: Pat and Dennis Carnahan, Judy and Don Otis
Address/Telephone: 13438 U.S. Highway 285; (303) 838–4167 or (303)
838–4899
Rooms: 7, including 1 cottage; all with private bath. Limited wheelchair
access. Air conditioning in Grandma's Attic and Sun Room (elevation
8,200 feet).
Rates: $69 to $120, double, EPB. Two-night minimum stay on weekends
preferred.
Open: All year.
Facilities and activities: Dinner available, with twenty-four-hour advance
reservation, Wednesday through Saturday, $15 to $18 per person. Hot
tub, sauna, gazebo, gift shop, picnic table, fire pit in old brick silo for
marshmallow roasts, thirty-five acres of woods to roam, toboggan hill.
Nearby: restaurants, mountain towns, shopping, hiking, fishing, golf,
cross-country skiing, one hour to downhill skiing.

Our idea of a perfect couple of days would be to hide away in
this inn's new Room in the Meadow, a delightful cottage set in a
grassy meadow and blessed with a fireplace, Jacuzzi for two, brass
king-sized bed, private deck, microwave, and fridge. We would
spend time outdoors, too, wandering through the woods in search
of wildflowers and forest critters, listening to the wind rustle

through the aspen, fir, and pine, and having afternoon lemonade in the gazebo, all the while absorbing the peace and quiet of the countryside.

This inn was once the summer home of a prince, and in my opinion it's still fit for a king and queen. The two-and-a-half story stone structure was built in 1929 for Prince Balthasar Gialma Odescalchi, a descendant of nobility from the Holy Roman Empire. When the prince left Colorado in 1947, the residence was absorbed into a 250-acre ranch; more recently, it has been transformed into a lovely country inn.

Among other guest accommodations are the Wild Rose Room, where a lop-eared cousin of Flopsy, Mopsy, and Cottontail, dressed in pink taffeta, sits on a queen-sized bed covered with white lace, and the cheery Sun Room, featuring a white wicker bed and love seat.

I recommend that you make dinner reservations at the time you book your room. The night we were there the fare was marinated, grilled chicken with mandarin orange sauce, homemade bread, tossed green salad, pecan pie, ice cream turtle pie, and, an inn specialty, mountain mud slide, a cookie crust filled with layers of cream cheese and chocolate mousse, whipped cream, and chocolate bits.

A full breakfast is provided at the inn, or a couple may take a continental-style repast of homemade pastries, fruit, and juice to their room the night before if they don't care to come down to the inn for breakfast in the morning.

How to get there: Take Highway 285 (Hampden Avenue) south from Denver to Conifer. From the traffic light at Conifer, continue on Highway 285 for exactly 5³/₁₀ miles. Turn left, follow road past school and take next left onto Douglas Drive at Douglas Ranch. Turn right onto Berry Hill Lane and continue to inn.

San Sophia
Telluride, Colorado
81435

Innkeepers: Gary and Dianne Eschman
Address/Telephone: 330 West Pacific Avenue (mailing address: P.O. Box 1825); (800) 537–4781
Rooms: 16; all with private bath, cable TV, and phone. No air conditioning (elevation 8,745 feet). No smoking inn.
Rates: $85 to $175, double, EPB, afternoon refreshments. Rates slightly higher during festivals and Christmas holidays.
Open: All year except for 1 month in spring and 1 month in fall. Phone for exact dates.
Facilities and activities: Concierge service, covered parking, individual ski and boot storage, observatory, library, gazebo with sunken Jacuzzi. Nearby: restaurants, shopping, hiking, mountain biking, fishing, golf, horseback riding, mountain climbing, downhill and cross-country skiing; world-renowned festivals honoring film making, dance, jazz, bluegrass, chamber music, hang gliding, wine tasting, and mushrooming.

The minute we stepped into this inn of many gables, we knew we were going to like it here. The San Sophia was designed and built specifically to be an inn, with guest comfort and pleasure as a top priority. The most hospitable elegant inn in the valley, it offers both plenty of privacy and ample opportunity to mingle with other guests.

The full buffet breakfast features a hot entree of pancakes, French toast, quiche, or perhaps the house specialty, eggs Taos.

244

Additional breakfast items include hot and cold cereal, fresh fruit, muffins, bagels, and homemade poppyseed or cappuccino coffee cake. In the late afternoon, the sideboard is spread with a complimentary assortment of cheese, sausage, and crackers, along with beer, wine, and soft drinks.

The cozy parlor is the perfect place to enjoy a quiet conversation before a crackling fire. Or climb up the stairs to the third-floor observatory, where you'll find a 360-degree panorama of the village, the mountains, and the valley. Padded benches and pillows provide a great place to share an early-morning cup of coffee, a bedtime glass of wine, or perhaps a bit of stargazing.

Although the guest rooms are named after the gold and silver mines that dot the area, they contain luxuries that Telluride's miners could only have dreamed of. Each room has special touches such as etched-glass light fixtures and mirrors, gleaming brass beds covered with handmade quilts, and bathtubs built for two. Some guest rooms boast stained-glass or bay windows, built-in VCRs, and king-sized beds. All rooms have tiled baths and plush carpeting. I especially like the Gold King room with its queen-sized white-iron-and-brass bed, knotty pine armoire, and white wicker chairs and table. The unique feature in this chamber is the 6-foot oval bathtub sitting in its own little alcove. Different, and very romantic.

All of the above, plus a gazebo with sunken Jacuzzi, ski lockers and boot racks fitted with air dryers for drying sports gear, terry robes, enormous bath blankets, cosmetic baskets, and fax service, add up to one luxurious country inn.

Not only is the San Sophia a destination for numerous newly-weds, it also hosts many wedding ceremonies. Gary and Dianne's good friend, the town's local judge, conducts the proceedings while they often act as witnesses. During the winter, many couples choose to be married on the "Ski Forever" ski run. After skiing out the back door of the San Sophia, they catch the ski lift to the top of the mountain where the wedding takes place at 12,000 feet before a spectacular vista of mountain ranges.

How to get there: Take Highway 145 into Telluride. Highway 145 turns into Colorado Avenue, Telluride's main street. Turn right onto Aspen Street. The inn is on the left at the corner of Aspen Street and West Pacific Avenue.

The Blackwell House
Coeur d'Alene, Idaho
83814

Innkeepers: Kathleen Sims and Margaret Hoy
Address/Telephone: 820 Sherman Avenue; (208) 664–0656
Rooms: 8, including 3 suites; 6 with private bath.
Rates: $75 to $119, double, EPB and late-afternoon refreshments, champagne in room for special occasions.
Open: All year.
Facilities and activities: Catered luncheons, dinners, weddings, and receptions. Minister on staff. Music room with grand piano, large yard with gazebo and barbecue, within walking distance to downtown. Nearby: Lake Coeur d'Alene, "World's Longest Floating Boardwalk," Tubb's Hill nature trails, shopping, restaurants, hiking, fishing, boating, bicycling, downhill and cross-country skiing, snowmobiling.

People passing by with no intention of spending the night cannot resist ringing the doorbell and asking if they can see the interior of this stately mansion. From the attractively appointed parlor to the music room with its antique grand piano, from the sweeping staircase to the upper floors of absolutely picture-perfect guest rooms, this inn is a designer's showcase—the perfect place for a wedding. And wouldn't you just know—there's a minister on call to perform the ceremony!

Built by F. A. Blackwell in 1904 as a wedding gift for his son, this magnificent, three-story structure was allowed to deteriorate over the years to the point that, when Kathleen bought it in 1982,

246

it took nine months, one hundred gallons of paint remover, 282 rolls of wallpaper, nineteen tons of sod, and unmeasured amounts of laughter and tears to help bring it around to the masterpiece it is today.

The morning repast is served in the Breakfast Room, where French doors open out onto the patio and spacious lawns. A fire in the fireplace removes the early-morning chill, fresh-ground Irish cream coffee warms the tummy, large bowls of fruit center the round, cloth-covered tables, and baskets of huckleberry muffins soon appear hot from the oven. Lunch and dinner can be catered just for two in the formal dining room.

The second-floor Blackwell Suite is a pink-and-white dream with oak-spool bed; white wicker settee, table, and chairs; white ruffled curtains with pink tiebacks; white eyelet-trimmed comforter and bed ruffle; pink floral wallpaper; dusty-rose carpet; and claw-footed bathtub sequestered in its own little alcove.

But, before you decide on this one, you must also see the former servants' quarters and children's playroom on the third floor. Smaller but ever so cozy, the three rooms share a sitting area with love seat, and they, like the others, are exquisitely decorated.

The hospitality here even extends to your friends, who are welcome to join you for late-afternoon tea and cookies or wine and munchies. If you haven't yet tried staying at country inns, The Blackwell House would be a great place to start.

How to get there: From city center, go east on Sherman Avenue (main street) for approximately 5 blocks. Inn is on the right.

Cricket on the Hearth
Coeur d'Alene, Idaho
83814

Innkeepers: Al and Karen Hutson
Address/Telephone: 1521 Lakeside Avenue: (208) 664–6926
Rooms: 5; 3 with private bath, all with air conditioning.
Rates: $45 to $75, double, EPB.
Open: All year.
Facilities and activities: Game room, deck, large yard, croquet. Nearby: Lake
Coeur d'Alene, "World's Longest Floating Boardwalk," Tubb's Hill
nature trails, shopping, restaurants, live theater, hiking, fishing, boat-
ing, golf, downhill and cross-country skiing, snowmobiling.

Finding a cricket on your hearth is said to be a sign of hospitality and good fortune. Well, I've seen those little critters, and I think
I'll settle for the brass variety on Al and Karen's fireplace hearth.

Staying at this inn, the longest-operating inn in Coeur d'
Alene, is a delightful experience. The guest rooms are individually
designed, and it's difficult to choose a favorite.

The Victorian-motif guest room on the main floor is perfect for
newlyweds or not-so-newlyweds. Outfitted with a gleaming brass
bed covered with a pink-and-red homemade quilt, a scarlet claw-
footed bathtub snugged into one corner of the room, and a private
porch with swing, this hideaway is a favorite of romantics.

Also downstairs, the Lilac Room is a breath of springtime. Decorated in delicate shades of orchid and lavender, it boasts lace cur-

tains, white wicker furniture, a queen-sized bed, and a private bath.

The Navajo Room carries a Southwestern theme with hand-crafted lodgepole pine furniture, Native American artifacts, and a splendid mix of soft pastels and bold textures. This room also has a private bath.

Upstairs, in the Pine Room, Mr. and Mrs. Teddy Bear recline atop a handmade quilt on the whitewashed pine queen-sized bed. This room is large and has a wonderful dormer window. The next-door Tulip Room is smaller but oh, so cozy with a brass bed and pink tulip motif. These two rooms share a most unusual little bath-room snuggled under the eaves and a small sitting room at the top of the stairs, perfect for reading or chatting.

Breakfast is part of the fun because you never know where you will be seated. Sometimes it's in the formal dining room, but it might be on the deck, in the game room, or at the umbrella table in the garden. You will find fresh-ground specialty coffee, juice, and fresh-baked muffins and breads. Karen makes a very special PANDA bread: P for pumpkin, A for apple, N for nuts, D for dates, and another A for applesauce. This one's a winner. She also serves a main dish of deep-dish French toast or Finnish pancakes, with fresh huckleberry or raspberry sauce in season, or quiche, or potato pie. Cinnamon pull-aparts are another of her specialties.

I'm not convinced that we can give Mr. Cricket all the credit, but this is definitely a hospitable inn, and it will be your good fortune, indeed, if you plan a stay here.

How to get there: From Sherman Avenue (main street), turn north onto 16th Street and proceed 1 block to Lakeside. Inn is on the corner.

D: According to Al and Karen, "No whispering or tiptoeing is allowed. The inn is not a library or museum—guests are encouraged to be themselves." A good approach to innkeeping, I think.

The Voss Inn
Bozeman, Montana
59715

Innkeepers: Bruce and Frankee Muller
Address/Telephone: 319 South Willson; (406) 587–0982
Rooms: 6; all with private bath, some with air conditioning, fans available
for others.
Rates: $65 to $75, double, EPB, afternoon tea, nightcap.
Open: All year.
Facilities and activities: Airport pick-up if requested in advance. Nearby: Lewis
and Clark Caverns, Museum of the Rockies, Bridger Bowl and Big Sky
ski areas, restaurants, shopping, hiking, fishing in blue-ribbon trout
stream, downhill and cross-country skiing; personalized daytrips into
Yellowstone National Park and other points of interest, including
gourmet breakfast and picnic lunch.

Often referred to as one of Montana's most romantic bed and
breakfasts, The Voss Inn is located in Bozeman's historic district.
Many a couple, bent on a blissful weekend, walks hand in hand
through this inn's English cottage perennial garden, up the steps,
past Victorian wicker furniture on a porch ablaze with geraniums,
and into the lovely parlor. And it only gets better from here.

As meticulously scrubbed, starched, pressed, and polished as
an Easter-morning Sunday School class, The Voss Inn exudes perfection. Antique beds, private sitting areas, breakfast nooks, and bay
windows all add to the charm of this stalwart, red-brick Victorian.
Every room I peeked into was captivating. The Sartain Room on the

main floor features a provocative tub and bathing alcove; the front parlor is graced with an ornate, etched-glass chandelier; the Chisholm Room, a favorite with honeymooners, boasts a magnificent 9-foot brass headboard with an antique brass lamp hanging from it, a claw-footed bathtub, and an antique gas fireplace.

Flowered wallpaper banks the staircase leading to the immaculate upstairs guest rooms. I entered my favorite, Robert's Roost, by descending three steps into a bright and cheerful garden of white wicker, deep-green walls sprinkled with tiny white blossoms, white ruffled curtains, and a private balcony. The bed, brass and iron, has a white eyelet spread and is embellished with dark green, rose-flowered pillows. A miniature bottle of liqueur and two small glasses waited on the bedside table.

Frankee tiptoes upstairs and leaves early morning coffee and tea in the hallway. Then, a little later, she brings fresh fruit, orange juice, homemade cinnamon rolls and muffins, and wonderful egg-soufflé dishes to the hall buffet. She has twelve different breakfast entrees that she chooses from, and, even if you stay a week, you will not get a repeat performance. Breakfast is taken to tiny tables in the guest rooms, and that's a definite plus because you'll want to spend as much time as possible in your newfound hideaway.

How to get there: From I–90, take exit 306 into Bozeman. Turn south onto North 7th Avenue, left onto Main Street, and proceed to South Willson. Go south on Willson for approximately 3½ blocks to the inn.

D: Breakfast rolls are kept hot in a uniquely styled bun warmer built into the circa-1880 upstairs radiator. This type of warming oven is rare, indeed, at least in this part of the country, and The Voss Inn's is only the second one we've seen in all our gypsying about.

Izaak Walton Inn
Essex, Montana
59916

Innkeepers: Larry and Lynda Vielleux
Address/Telephone: Off Highway 2 (mailing address: P.O. Box 653); (406) 888–5700
Rooms: 31; 11 with private bath, 20 share several baths. No air conditioning (elevation 3,860 feet).
Rates: $65 to $85, double, EP. Caboose: $350 for 3 nights; $600 for 7 nights, based on 4-person occupancy; EP. Five- and 7-day packages, including meals, available. Personal checks preferred.
Open: All year.
Facilities and activities: Full-service dining room, bar, sauna, laundromat, gift shop with Montana-made items; Amtrak flag stop # E.S.M., train activity, train memorabilia; cross-country ski rentals, guided cross-country ski tours into Glacier National Park. Nearby: Glacier National Park and Bob Marshall Wilderness Area, constituting more than a million acres of wilderness; fishing, hiking, horseback riding, rafting, wildlife viewing, photography, cross-country skiing.

For couples seeking seclusion and total privacy, a stay in one of this inn's cozy "little red cabooses" would be a great choice. Genuine Great Northern cabooses, now resting on the hillside overlooking the inn, have been totally remodeled with pine interior and accented with blue-and-white pinstripe bedding and red pillows and include a mini-kitchen, private bath, and deck. If you prefer complete isolation, you can forego the meals offered in the inn's dining room by requesting, in advance and for an additional fee, that your tiny cupboard and fridge be stocked in anticipation of your arrival.

Built in 1939 to accommodate service crews for the Great Northern Railway, whose enormous task it was to keep the mountain track open during winter, the inn is still very much involved in the railroad business. It is here that "helper" engines hook onto lengthy freight trains and help push them over the Continental Divide. The inn is also a designated flag stop, with Amtrak passing through daily. If you decide to arrive via Amtrak, inn personnel will meet you at the platform to help with luggage.

Fifteen to twenty freight trains pass by the front door of the inn each day; and, whether resting in one of the charming guest rooms, playing volleyball in the playfield, or downing a few in the Flag Stop Bar, one is hard-pressed to keep from running outdoors like a kid to watch as the massive trains chug by.

The Izaak Walton is packed with signal lanterns, vintage photographs, and all sorts of train memorabilia. In the Dining Car Restaurant, you may be seated next to a striped-capped engineer from the train waiting out on the tracks or share a meal and spirited conversation with members of an international rail fan club.

Highlights of our stay at the Izaak Walton: lovely accommodations, light and fluffy breakfast crepes filled to overflowing with huckleberries; a dinner of honey-glazed chicken sautéed with orange slices and onions; the sighting of whole families of shaggy, beautiful mountain goats zigzagging their way down the hillside to a salt lick; and spotting a yearling bear cub peacefully munching his way along the side of the road.

How to get there: Inn is ¹/₂ mile off of Highway 2, on southern rim of Glacier National Park between East and West Glacier. Watch for sign for Essex turnoff.

D: *Wildlife photographers can have the time of their lives here: black bears, mountain lions, mountain goats, spawning salmon, and, from early October to early November, a sometimes large migration of bald eagles.*

Gold Hill Hotel
Gold Hill, Nevada
89440

Innkeepers: Bill Fain and Carol DeKalb
Address/Telephone: Highway 341 (mailing address: P.O. Box 304, Virginia City, NV 89440); (702) 847–0111
Rooms: 11, plus 2 guest houses; 9 rooms and guest houses with private bath. Second-floor guest rooms with wheelchair access.
Rates: $45 to $125, double, continental breakfast. Full breakfast available at additional charge.
Open: All year except January.
Facilities and activities: Full-service dining room with wheelchair access, closed Mondays; Great Room lounge; Tavern Bar, weekly lectures by local historians. Nearby: restaurants, saloons, gambling casinos, excursion train, mine tours, hiking, fishing, exploring; downhill and cross-country skiing at Lake Tahoe, approximately 35 miles away.

Bill and Carol took a courageous and gigantic step when they decided a few years ago to try to transform a decaying six-room, one-bath hotel and bar into a charming and luxurious country inn. Bill, with a Ph.D. in physics, and Carol, with restaurant management background, just couldn't resist the challenge. In the fall of 1986 they bought the old hotel and settled in to life out West.

Built during the gold rush to the Comstock Lode in 1859, the hotel served a bustling community that received as many as fifty scheduled trains a day, hauling commodities in and ore out. The stone section of the building still stands, and a new wooden addition has been added to replace that which disappeared sometime before 1890. It is the oldest operating hotel in Nevada.

A walk through this comfortably elegant hotel proves beyond a doubt that Carol and Bill accomplished their goal with smashing success.

All the guest rooms boast period furnishings and lovely decor, but our choice, and often that of newlyweds, was Room 6, with a private balcony; stone fireplace; a beautiful circa-1850 half-tester bed; marble-topped dresser and bedside tables; wet bar; fine-print blue wallpaper; and an extra-large bath. The pink-draped corner windows look out to the Sierra Nevada mountain range.

In the hotel's Crown Point Restaurant, the tables are clad with white linen and set with crystal stemware and fine china. Soft-rose drapes and upholstered chairs, sea-green carpet, and an antique sideboard contribute to the elegance of this room. There is an extensive wine list featuring wines from France, Germany, California, and Washington state.

How to get there: From Reno, take Highway 395 south to Highway 341 turnoff to Virginia City. At Virginia City, continue south for 1 mile to Gold Hill. Hotel is on the right.

D: *You are welcome to join the regular members of the Gold Hill Ladies' and Gentlemen's Back Road Almost Daily Hiking and Exploration Club. Ask at the hotel for details.*

Manti House Inn
Manti, Utah
84642

Innkeepers: Beverly and Charles Futrell
Address/Telephone: 401 North Main Street; (801) 835–0161 or (800)
   288–1893
Rooms: 6, including 2 suites; all with private bath. No smoking inn.
Rates: $45 to $95, double, EPB.
Open: All year.
Facilities and activities: Lunch available daily except Sundays; dinner served
   Thursday, Friday, and Saturday evenings, reservations required. Ice
   cream parlor, gazebo, hot tub, summer outdoor concerts. Nearby:
   horse-drawn carriage rides, hiking, fishing, hot-air ballooning, golf,
   tennis, swimming, museum; Mormon Miracle Pageant, largest outdoor
   pageant in the U.S., performed each July.

   This inn is one of our favorites, and we can't decide if it's the
country charm of hand-stitched quilts (two on every bed!), hand-
crafted furniture (superbly executed pie safe stands in the upstairs
hallway), the inn's culinary creativity, or perhaps the warm welcome we received at this English vernacular masterpiece, built of
limestone in 1868.
   All the rooms are exquisitely done: tiny printed wallpapers,
gigantic four-posters, and claw-footed bathtubs.
   We stayed in the bridal suite, and we heartily recommend that
you reserve ahead for this one with its raspberry-sherbet carpet,
white-railinged stairway leading down to the hot tub, private bal-

cony, tiny window seat, and massive four-poster, so high it takes a two-step platform to climb into bed.

Lace-covered French doors partition off the built-for-two, rose-colored tub and Jacuzzi with wraparound mirrors and ruffled burgundy drapes.

If it hadn't been for the aroma of bacon and oven pancakes, made with lemon and nutmeg from an old family recipe, we'd probably still be in that lovely room.

Breakfast here is wonderful, but dinner is even better because that is when the chef really has the opportunity to exhibit his expertise. A three- or five-course affair, the meal may begin with an appetizer of crab-stuffed tomato, continue with either French onion or potato soup, fresh-fruit salad with pineapple topping, corn pudding, and prime rib au jus, and conclude with a strawberry torte or raspberry mousse. Dinner is served on Thursday, Friday, and Saturday evenings, and reservations are a must.

Lunch is served daily, except on Sunday, in the Ice Cream Parlor amid white wrought-iron tables and chairs. The menu lists homemade soup, sandwiches, and wonderful ice cream concoctions ranging from the usual shakes and sundaes to the "John D. T. McAllister," named after a prominent Mormon church member and Utah citizen. This extravaganza consists of two and a half pounds of ice cream, three sauces, bananas, whipped cream, nuts, and cherries. As the menu says, "Enough for a family of five."

How to get there: From I–15 at Provo, take Highway 89 southeast to Manti. From I–70 at Salina, take Highway 89 north to Manti. Inn is on the main street of town.

Washington School Inn
Park City, Utah
84060

Innkeepers: Nancy Beaufait and Delphine Covington
Address/Telephone: 543 Park Avenue (mailing address: P.O. Box 536); (801)
  649–3800 or (800) 824–1672
Rooms: 15, including 3 suites; all with private bath. Wheelchair access. No
  air conditioning (elevation 7,000 feet).
Rates: $75 to $120, double, spring, summer, and fall; $100 to $240, double,
  winter; EPB, afternoon refreshments.
Open: All year.
Facilities and activities: Lunch for groups of ten or more. Hot tub, Jacuzzi,
  sauna, steam showers, concierge services. Nearby: restaurants, golf,
  tennis, hiking, fishing, horseback riding, sailboarding, sailing, waterski-
  ing, Park City Ski Area, Park West Ski Area, Deer Valley Ski Resort,
  downhill and cross-country skiing.

Although the perfect hideaway for grown up childhood sweethearts, there's no more "readin', `ritin', and `rithmetic" at the old
Washington School. The three Rs now more accurately stand for
"romance," "rendezvous," and "resplendent." Built in 1889, the
structure served as a public school for forty-two years, became a
social hall during the '30s, and lay vacant from the '50s until 1984.
The hammered-limestone exterior, bell tower, dormer and class-
room windows, and curved entry porticos have been retained, thus
qualifying the inn for the National Register of Historic Places.

The entry hall still has the feeling of an old-fashioned schoolhouse, with exposed original timbers supporting the three-story bell tower. A library/mezzanine overlooks the elegant living room, where complimentary beverages await your arrival and refreshments are served during the afternoons.

Each morning, an antique sideboard in the formal dining room is lavishly spread with breakfast items such as eggs Florentine or cheese strata served with bacon, ham, or sausage; fresh fruit and lemon-nut bread; homestead pumpkin bread; Grandma Anderson's brown bread; or, perhaps, Utah beer bread.

All guest rooms are elaborately custom-decorated and bear the names of former school teachers. "Miss Thatcher" has a brick fireplace, king-sized bed, rose carpet, and, heavens to mercy!, a pink-flowered love seat and a wet bar. "Miss Thompson" has a green iron-and-brass bed, fireplace with round windows on either side, and, also, a love seat and wet bar. Our favorite room was "Miss Urie." Bright and sunny, it has pink and blue flowers sprinkled on yellow wallpaper, a chatting corner, and a writing alcove. A pine chest sits at the foot of a pine four-poster with burgundy pillows plumped on the lemon yellow bedspread. An antique book acts as doorstop.

Couples especially enjoy the lower level of the inn which features a wine cellar and a luxurious whirlpool spa with stone floor, bent-willow furniture, dry sauna, and steam showers. Wouldn't the Misses Thatcher, Thompson, and Urie have loved this as their "Teacher's Room"?

How to get there: From I-80, take Highway 224 south to Park City; 224 turns into Park Avenue at Park City. Inn is on the right side of street.

The Wildflower Inn
Jackson, Wyoming
83001

Innkeepers: Sherrie, Ken, and Jessica Jern
Address/Telephone: Off Teton Village Road (mailing address: P.O. Box 3724); (307) 733–4710
Rooms: 5; all with private bath and TV. No air conditioning (elevation 6,200 feet). No smoking inn.
Rates: $110 to $120, double, EPB. Inquire about off-season rates.
Open: All year.
Facilities and activities: Solarium, hot tub, deck. Nearby: Yellowstone National Park, Grand Teton National Park, National Elk Refuge, restaurants, art galleries, artist studios, museums, Old West Days, Mountain Man Rendezvous, Jackson Hole Arts Festival, Grand Teton Music Festival, Dancers Workshop, summer theater, acting workshops, rodeo, chuckwagon dinner shows, stagecoach rides, covered wagon trips, photography, wildlife viewing, hiking, fishing, biking, golf, tennis, climbing, horseback riding, llama treks, rafting, ice skating, sleigh rides, snowmobiling, dog sledding; downhill, helicopter, snowcat, and cross-country skiing.

Made of glowing lodgepole pine inside and out, with balconies, gables, and, everywhere, wildflowers, this inn is at once both elegant and country. In the expansive sitting room, Native American rugs hang on log walls, a freestanding wood stove stands before a massive river rock wall, and the polished wood floor is centered with a colorful braided rug. This room, along with the solarium and dining room, looks out onto a wooded three acres of aspen and cottonwood trees, a creek-fed pond, and a meadow where horses graze. Just the day before we visited, a mama duck and her baby ducklings had paddled into the pond, lingered a while, and then ventured on downstream.

The guest rooms have a secluded feeling and all five are beautifully decorated. Indian Paint Brush has a cathedral ceiling and private deck. The queen-sized hand-hewn pine log bed, made by Ken, sports a bed ruffle made of blue-and-white ticking and a red print down comforter. Red-and-white checked curtains flank the windows, and red plaid Ralph Lauren towels brighten the private bath.

Sherrie is a master of spontaneous, creative cooking and serves a full outdoorsman's breakfast, including homemade granola, fresh fruit, oatmeal muffins, and either buttermilk pancakes, French toast, or an egg dish. She will see to it that you don't leave hungry.

Besides romantics, this inn is popular with outdoor enthusiasts. Ken is a ski instructor and climbing guide, and both he and Sherrie are authorities on what to do in the Jackson Hole area.

After a day of hiking or skiing, put your sports gear in the separate storage area, pile into the hot tub, relax, and watch the day fade to twilight over misty fields and distant mountains.

How to get there. From Jackson, go west on Highway 22 toward Wilson. Before the town of Wilson, turn right onto Teton Village Road. Turn left onto first road past Jackson Hole Racquet Club (also called The Aspens). Inn is at end of roadway.

✦

D: *Sherrie confided to us that she and Ken dream of one day saving an evening just for themselves. They plan to choose their favorite guest room, pack the well-used champagne bucket with ice, take along the crystal glasses etched with wildflowers, gaze at the stars from the private deck, and hear nothing but the melancholy vocalizing of happy frogs. Now how could you go wrong with romantic innkeepers like these?*

The Historic Virginian Hotel
Medicine Bow, Wyoming
82329

Innkeepers: Vernon and Vickie Scott
Address/Telephone: Main Street of Medicine Bow (mailing address: P.O. Box 127); (307) 379–2377
Rooms: 21; 4 suites with private bath, 17 rooms share baths. Pets permitted with prior arrangements. No air conditioning (elevation 6,563 feet).
Rates: $17.50 to $65, single; $19.50 to $70, double; EP.
Open: All year.
Facilities and activities: Full-service restaurant, saloon, ice water brought to rooms in antique pitchers. Nearby: museum, tours of world's largest wind generator, world's largest dinosaur find; Fossil Cabin, said to be the oldest building on earth; ghost town, hiking, fishing, downhill and cross-country skiing.

If Medicine Bow, Wyoming, is not on your route, you might consider adding it to your itinerary, because you may never have a better chance to experience a truer example of an elegant Old West hotel.

As we sat on a red velvet settee in the Virginian's upstairs parlor, I wished for a long skirt, ruffled blouse, and high-top shoes to replace my jeans and Nikes. A visiting gentleman paused to ask incredulously, "Can you really *stay* here? Do they actually take in *guests*?" That's how authentic the furnishings and decor are in this 1911, National Historic Landmark hotel. It's like a "hands-on" museum where you can not only touch but actually sleep in the beautiful, many-pillowed beds, bathe in one of the oversized claw-footed tubs, sip a cup of tea in a plush parlor, and feel like wealthy turn-of-the-century honeymooners.

The three-story building is named after Owen Wister's 1902 novel *The Virginian*, of "When you call me that—smile" fame. The walls of the Shiloh Saloon are covered with memorabilia from the novel and the movie of the same name; and signed photographs of Wister and his best friend, Theodore Roosevelt, who encouraged the author to write such a story, are in several rooms.

The Owen Wister Suite features a lace-canopied bed and a sitting room, enhanced by a matching, ornately carved, red velvet settee, rocker, and chair set, all in mint condition. This is a chamber meant for fantasizing, where it's easy to imagine that you are the heroine of a romance novel, an adored bride recently wed to a cattle baron or to the owner of a rich gold-producing mine. Such a room must have witnessed many a scene like this; these walls, could they talk, would have wonderful stories to tell.

An abundance of doilies, pillows, quilts, and comforters contributes to the inn's cozy feeling, and an original sign in Room 30 advertises OATS FOR HORSE 1 CENT A GALLON. HORSES STABLED FREE. LIQUOR 6¼ CENTS A GLASS, WINE 25 CENTS A GALLON.

The Eating House serves light lunches, and The Owen Wister Dining Room offers plentiful fare, such as 10-ounce lobsters and 16-ounce steaks. Less hearty meals of chops and seafood are also available. This hotel sits out on the "lone prairie" where, indeed, the antelope still roam, and it is a must for anyone wanting a true glimpse of Old West elegance.

How to get there: From I–80 at Laramie, take Highway 30 north. Or, from I–25 at Casper, take Highway 220 south to 487, then drive south on Highway 487 to Medicine Bow. Hotel is on the main street.

West Coast

by Julianne Belote

Julianne Belote once facetiously told a friend that the secret of her forty-two-plus years of marriage to the same man was never to have a meaningful conversation. She now concedes there *is* another factor: frequent visits to romantic country inns.

Who can deny the spell cast by precisely the right ambience? For some couples, a Jacuzzi tub and champagne breakfast in bed rates a ten on their romance scale. Other equally romantic couples want to walk beside windswept surf or dine by candlelight in an intimate, beautifully appointed dining room.

This collection reflects a range of lodgings from simple to splendid, all of them for true romantics. The old Rodgers and Hart song says, "My romance doesn't need a castle rising in Spain." Right. But it is also worth noting that these west coast inns are undoubtedly a lot more comfortable than most castles.

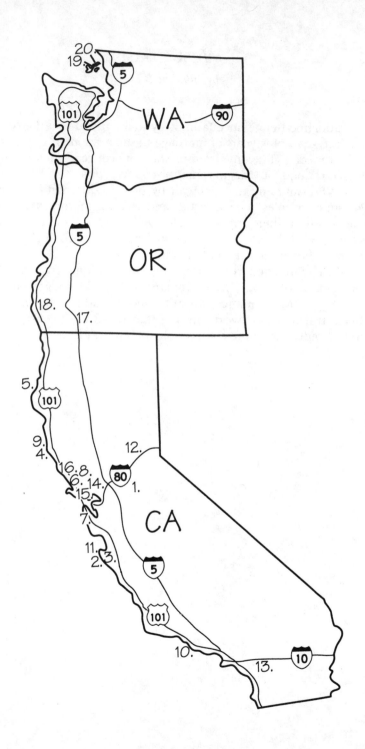

West Coast

Numbers on map refer to towns numbered below.

Olive Metcalf

Imperial Hotel
Amador City, California
95601

Innkeepers: Bruce Sherrill and Dale Martin
Address/Telephone: Highway 49 (mailing address: P.O. Box 195); (209) 267–9172
Rooms: 6, all with private bath, air conditioning. No smoking in rooms.
Rates: $60 to $90, double occupancy, continental breakfast. Two-night minimum when Saturday is involved.
Open: All year.
Facilities and activities: Full bar, restaurant; Sunday brunch and dinner every night. Wheelchair access to dining room. Nearby: antiques and specialty shops in town; attractive opportunities for photographers in town and nearby mines; many wineries; seasonal events include fall Miwok Big Time Days at Indian Grinding Rock State Park, Daffodil Hill's spring blooms, Amador City's Calico Christmas.

I am smitten with this new addition to gold-country lodgings. The 1879 red-brick building with a painted white balcony stretching across the top story sits at the end of the main street running through tiny Amador City, population about 179 citizens. The entire scene reeks of Western nostalgia—it's old, authentic, and romantic.

The outside of this venerable hotel is thoroughly old-fashioned, but inside you'll find it has been stylishly renovated with all the modern amenities and a first-class restaurant. First stop should be the beautiful, old full bar, not a reproduction but the real McCoy. In addition to the usual spirits, they stock a large selection of beers and California wines. The friendly service you find here is indicative of the atmosphere throughout the hotel.

The dining room has a certain touch of elegance with high ceilings, white tablecloths, and fresh flowers, yet it is welcoming and casual. The intimate room (seats fifty-five) has a changing display of local artwork that stands out beautifully against white walls. Dine in your traveling clothes, by all means, but you won't feel out of place if you want to dress for a special occasion, either.

The dinner chefs offer a menu that is both continental and California fresh. The appetizers are so good that it takes careful planning to save room for the entree. Roasted garlic with Brie and Polenta Crostini topped with prosciutto were the two we chose. The main event was a roast pork loin in prune sauce followed by an excellent salad with a house dressing I wish I could duplicate. The pastry chef had several hard-to-pass offerings, and after all her work, how could we skip a poppy-seed butter-cream tart with fresh raspberries? Eating it seemed the only kind thing to do.

Six bedrooms upstairs are not large, but unexpectedly comfortable and whimsically decorated. One has an Art Deco feeling with Maxfield Parrish prints and a ceiling fan. One has a vivid hand-painted headboard over the king-sized bed and bright folk art on the walls. Rooms One and Two are slightly larger than the others and open onto the front balcony. (The traffic going by fades away by 10:30 or 11:00.) Each room has a radio and a sparkling white tile bathroom that sports a hair dryer and heated towel bar.

Two balconies are upstairs, one at the back and one at the front of the hotel. A small library is at one end of the hall, with a desk, telephone, and door opening out to the balcony.

In the morning the innkeepers place coffee and newspapers in the hallway outside the guest rooms for early risers. Breakfast is a full, fresh meal prepared with the same skill as the dinner menu. Guests have the option of eating in their rooms, on the second floor balcony, or downstairs in the dining room.

How to get there: Amador City is 2¹/₂ hours from San Francisco on Highway 49.

olive Metcalf

Ventana Inn
Big Sur, California
93920

Innkeeper: Robert E. Bussinger
Address/Telephone: Big Sur; (408) 667–2331 or in California, (800) 628–6500
Rooms: 60; all with private bath and television, most with fireplace, some
with private hot tub on deck.
Rates: $155 to $775, double occupancy, continental breakfast and afternoon
wine-and-cheese buffet.
Open: All year.
Facilities and activities: Restaurant serves lunch, dinner; cocktail lounge. Hot
tubs, saunas, swimming pool. Nearby: hike, picnic, Ventana general
store.

The Big Sur Coast has always welcomed the offbeat, and even
this sybaritic paradise was designed as a "different" kind of place: no
tennis, no golf, no conventions, no Muzak, no disco delights.

What it does offer is a window (*ventana* means "window" in
Spanish) toward both the Santa Lucia Mountains and the Pacific
Ocean from a redwood and cedar lodge on a magnificent slope. This
is the ultimate hideaway, a tasteful, expensive world of its own har-
monizing with the wilderness surrounding it. For activity there are
two 75-foot pools (heated all year) and two separate bathhouses
with luxurious Japanese hot tubs, one of them with saunas. And
there are walks over grassy slopes, through the woods, or on the
beach. From every point your eyes go to the spectacular Big Sur

Coast, where boulders send white foam spraying into the air.

Some rooms in the cottages clustered around the lodge look down into a canyon of trees; others face the ocean. Their uncluttered blend of natural fabric and design makes each room seem to be the best one. Every detail—folk baskets holding kindling, window seats, quilts handmade in Nova Scotia, private terraces—has been carefully conceived.

A gravel path leads to the restaurant, with the opportunity of seeing native wildflowers and an occasional deer or bobcat on the way. The food is colorful California cuisine: fresh fish, veal, chicken, creative pastas, and a good wine list. The place to be at lunch is the expansive terrace with a 50-mile view of the coast. Dinner inside is a candlelight and pink linen affair. If you've walked the hills enough, indulge in a chocolate torte the *Washington Post* called "celestial."

At breakfast, a continental buffet accompanied by baroque music is spread in the lodge lobby by the rock fireplace: platters of melons, papayas, strawberries—whatever is fresh—pastries and breads baked in the Ventana kitchen, honey and preserves, yogurt and homemade granola. An afternoon wine and cheese buffet has an incredible array of domestic and imported cheeses.

The Store by the restaurant (books, baskets, mountain clothing, handmade knives, bird whistles) is as intriguing as its staff—all of whom seemed to be bilingual and have fascinating histories.

How to get there: On State Highway One, Ventana is 311 miles (about a six-and-a-half-hour drive) north of Los Angeles. The inn's sign is on the right. From San Francisco, the inn is 152 miles, 28 miles south of Carmel.

J: *If "trickle down economics" has dropped a little gold on you, this is the place to liberate your plastic for a romantic splash.*

olive Metcalf

Robles Del Rio Lodge
Carmel Valley, California
93924

Innkeeper: Glen Gurries
Address/Telephone: 200 Punta Del Monte; (408) 659–3705
Rooms: 31, including some cottages; all with private bath and cable TV, some with fireplace and kitchenette. Wheelchair access.
Rates: $80 to $250, double occupancy, generous continental breakfast.
Open: All year.
Facilities and activities: Exceptional restaurant, The Ridge, serves lunch and dinner; Cantina serves wine and beer. Swimming pool, tile hot tub with Jacuzzi, sauna, tennis. Nearby: golf, horseback riding, 12 miles to ocean beaches, surrounding woodlands to hike, ten minutes to Carmel attractions.

How does a hilltop hideaway sound, one that is just outside one of the west coast's most romantic towns? Driving the twisting road up to Robles Del Rio gives you a feeling that you're deep in the heart of California countryside, though it's only a ten-minute drive from Carmel. The lodge looks just right for its rustic setting. Surrounded by live oak trees and perched on the mountaintop (well, high hill) surveying the valley below, this is true country-inn feeling. A tree-shaded flagstone terrace extends from the lodge with flowers in profusion and a pool, Jacuzzi, and an outdoor fireplace to be enjoyed night and day.

It was built in the 1920s, the oldest resort still operating in the

Carmel Valley. The lodge is now owned by the Ron Gurries family with son Glen and his wife Adreena as resident managers. Former longtime owner Bill Wood lives just across the road. He ran the place for over forty years and approvingly watches the renovations and improvements going on. He can reminisce about the early days of the lodge, when Arthur Murray would check in for a month or so, when Alistair Cooke visited after the war, and how the swimming pool was dug with horse and plow because they couldn't get a tractor up the crooked road.

Six rooms are in the main lodge; the other more private accommodations are in separate buildings scattered over nine acres. These rooms are unpretentious but entirely comfortable, and the views are wonderful. Some have a rustic board-and-batten decor, and others have a more contemporary country look using Laura Ashley fabric. Expandable options available in the cottages with outfitted kitchens and fireplaces are convenient for longer stays.

Beginning with a bountiful breakfast buffet set in the main lodge living room, good food is a big part of the Lodge's appeal. With a crackling fire going to chase away the morning chill, much of the original 1920s furniture still in place, and wide views of the valley, this room has a good feeling.

Lunch or dinner in The Ridge restaurant, also in the main lodge building, is a dining experience equal to the best available in Carmel or Monterey. Chef David Allen has extensive credentials from the East Coast, but he's now a California specialist. He relies on Monterey agriculture for daily deliveries of whatever is freshest and best.

His wine list, too, has a deliberate regional focus. (Did you know more grapes are grown in the Monterey region now than in Napa?) Notice the hand-painted china, the fresh flowers, the broad deck overlooking the valley. What a seat to watch a fog bank form over Carmel and quietly roll in. A fresh rockfish soup and a chicken breast stir-fry with ginger, bell pepper, and tomatoes were pretty impressive, too.

How to get there: From Highway One at Carmel, drive east on Carmel Valley Road about 13 miles to Esquiline Road. Turn right and follow the signs up the hill to the lodge, about 1 mile.

Olive Metcalf

Harbor House
Elk, California
95432

Innkeepers: Helen and Dean Turner
Address/Telephone: 5600 South Highway One (mailing address: Box 369);
(707) 877–3203
Rooms: 10, including 4 cottages; all with private bath, 5 with private deck, 9
with fireplace.
Rates: $155 to $230, double occupancy, breakfast and dinner. Ask about
midweek winter rates. No credit cards.
Open: All year.
Facilities and activities: Dinner by reservation. Private beach, fishing, ocean
kayaking with guide. Nearby: Mendocino shops, galleries, restaurants,
forest walks, local wineries; golf, tennis, horseback riding.

The windswept solitude of this stretch of Northern California's
shore is one of nature's tens. And for an inn on the bluffs above the
rocky coast, Harbor House has all the ingredients I consider necessary in a romantic inn for grown-ups: a dramatic location, fresh
decor, fine food, and a quiet, quiet atmosphere.

The house was built in 1916 entirely of virgin redwood by the
Goodyear Redwood Lumber Company as a place to lodge and
entertain their executives and guests. In the 1930s it was converted
to an inn and has variously faded and flourished over the years. The
inn's newest owners are warm hosts who understand exactly what
a spell this inn casts.

The large living room, completely paneled in redwood with a high-beamed open ceiling, sets the tone: quiet and unpretentious. Comfortable sofas and a piano are grouped on a rich Persian rug before a huge fireplace, with books and a stereo nearby. (Christmas here sounds wonderful—the redwood room glowing in firelight, a giant tree, roasting chestnuts, festive dinners, and music from local musicians.) Bedrooms and cottages are freshly decorated, many with pastel watercolor prints by a local artist of flowers and birds indigenous to the area.

Ocean views from the dining room are breathtaking. On blustery North Coast days, some guests choose to spend the day in this redwood-paneled room watching the churning surf. It's comforting to know you don't have to leave this warm atmosphere to find a restaurant. Wonderful food is in store for you here.

The Turners subscribe to that old verity of California cooking: Use only the freshest, best ingredients possible, and keep it simple. Many ingredients are plucked right from the inn's own garden. What they don't grow, they purchase from the finest local sources, like baby potatoes and the locally raised lamb. Fresh fish is often featured, prepared with Harbor House nuances. All the breads and breakfast pastries are homemade. Desserts also tend to reflect whatever is fresh. Typical are poached pears with raspberry sauce, or a sweet flaky pastry stuffed with apricots and cream. A fine California wine list and a good selection of beers are available. Dinner is a fixed menu, changing every night, but with advance notice, they'll try to accommodate any special dietary needs.

Mendocino's attractions are only twenty minutes farther north, but I'm all for staying right here. Walking the beach, discovering the secluded patios and paths—one leads to a waterfall and grotto—these are the inn's quiet seductions. If you're in during the day, a bottle of local wine and a cheese platter from the kitchen are available to hold body and soul together until dinner.

How to get there: From the Bay area, take Highway 101 to Cloverdale, then Highway 128 west to Highway One. The inn is 6 miles south on the ocean side of Highway One.

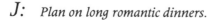

J: *Plan on long romantic dinners.*

olive Metcalf

Hotel Carter
Eureka, California
95501

Innkeepers: Mark and Christi Carter
Address/Telephone: 301 L Street; (707) 444–8062
Rooms: 20, including 2 suites; all with private bath, television, telephone, 8
    with whirlpool baths, suites with fireplace. Smoking in lobby only.
Rates: $95 to $250, including full breakfast, evening wine and hors d'oeuvres.
Open: All year.
Facilities and activities: Restaurant serving elegant cuisine Thursday through
    Sunday. Lobby and dining-room showcase of contemporary art. Near-
    by: walk along brick pathway bordering marina, through restored Old
    Town with specialty shops, restaurants; hundreds of restored Victorian
    homes, many art galleries in town.

Ever since first hearing Rodgers and Hart's "There's a Small
Hotel," I've thought the song—and small hotels—were the
quintessence of sophisticated romance. In Eureka's charmingly
restored Old Town district, the Hotel Carter brings the essence of
that lovely song to mind. It is a perfect rendezvous—intimate, glamorous, and serving some of the most elegant food and wines available north of San Francisco.

Most first-time visitors assume that Mark Carter restored the
yellow Victorian-style building, but it is newly constructed, modeled after a nineteenth-century Eureka hotel. It blends the exterior
look and ambience of the past era with today's luxurious conve-
niences. Everything is done with Carter's impeccable taste in detail-

ings and furnishings. (He also built from scratch the magnificent Victorian-style B & B across the street.)

You may very well fall in love with the hotel the minute you step into the lobby. Fourteen-foot-high ceilings here and in the adjoining dining room create an aura of Old-World elegance. Plump sofas and chairs look both chic and inviting, and the work of local Humbolt County potters and painters is showcased brilliantly against the salmon-colored walls. The Carters set out fine regional wines and hors d'oeuvres before a marble fireplace here each evening.

But your outstanding taste treats will come at breakfast and dinner in the intimate dining room. Since the days when Christi Carter, while managing two babies, cooked at their B & B what came to be known as the famous Carter Breakfast, she has always taken the lead in searching for the best chefs, the finest ingredients, and true cutting-edge cuisine. The Hotel Carter has become the right place to see that concern for truly excellent cooking come to fruition.

Our dinner one night began with baby greens dressed with a strawberry vinaigrette, fresh, grilled swordfish with lemon butter, three perfect vegetables grown in the Carters' garden, a new small grain (something akin to couscous), and crusty baguettes. A local chardonnay and a pinot noir *had* to be sampled. A scrumptious apple-walnut tart served with homemade ice cream and coffee saw us off to our room impressed with the quiet service and fine food.

The twenty guest rooms are decorated in pale earth colors, with peach and white linen, and are furnished with handsome antique pine furniture combined with appointments we appreciate—telephones, remote-controlled televisions hiding in wardrobes, and whirlpool tubs. Our suite on the second floor with a fireplace, window seat, and view of Humbolt Bay was a spot we would love to return to often.

How to get there: From Highway 101 in downtown Eureka, proceed west on L Street through Old Town to the hotel.

J: *You may think of Eureka as logger/fisherman country, a perception that makes this elegant hideaway all the more surprising. If it weren't that the Carters are such nice people, I'd say, "keep it a secret."*

Olive Metcalf

Applewood, An Estate Inn
Guerneville, California
95446

Innkeepers: Darryl Notter and Jim Caron
Address/Telephone: 13555 Highway 116; (707) 869–9093
Rooms: 10; all with private bath, television, telephone. No smoking inn.
Rates: $115 to $185, double occupancy, full breakfast. Two-night minimum on weekends.
Open: All year.
Facilities and activities: Fixed-price dinner available some evenings. Swimming pool, spa; facilities for private parties, small business seminars. Nearby: restaurants, golf, tennis, horseback riding; canoeing and other river activities; Guerneville shops; many local wineries; Sonoma Coast beaches. Armstrong Redwood State Reserve.

Applewood, formerly called The Estate, is an unexpected taste of glamour in the forested hills hugging the Russian River. As it twists through the Guerneville area, the river's beautiful natural setting has long been a popular choice for "resorts," cabins, cottages, and campgrounds. But . . . this is something quite different.

It's not always easy to relax in handsome surroundings, but that's not the case in this Mission Revival–style house. It was built as a private residence in 1922 by a financier, Ralph Belden, and you know what grandiose ideas the wealthy in those days had when it came to building even their vacation homes. This one is imposing, but it remains an inviting country home. On the main floor, a large rock fireplace divides the living room from a many-windowed solarium. On the lower level, bedrooms open to still another comfortable sitting room.

The decor is *Architectural Digest*—with warmth. Darryl studied design in San Francisco, and the house shows it. There's no one "look," but rather an individual, personal style. He's designed stylish slipcovers for some of the chairs and smart duvet covers for the beds. There are fine antiques among some just comfortable furniture. Both he and Jim are always looking for interesting pieces, but they admit that as much as they've bought, it seems to disappear in the large house.

Bedrooms are wonderfully romantic, and there's not a Laura Ashley in the lot. Billowing cotton draperies at an expansive bow of casement windows graced Number 4, our room. ("Cute" room names are out, says Darryl.) A sitting area had two cushy lounge chairs, a settee, and a fresh bouquet of roses. The room had everything for comfort: television and telephone, down pillows and comforters, even the rarest of all inn appointments—good reading lights. When we returned from dinner, the drapes were drawn, bed turned down, and our robes laid out.

Breakfast was prepared and served as elegantly as everything is done around here. On a terrace by the pool a table set with heavy silverware, linen napkins, silver coffeepot, and newspaper at hand was the right place to be on the sunny morning of our visit. The beautiful fresh fruit, hot muffins, and a bacon-avocado-tomato-sour-cream omelet were perfection.

This is a terrific place to entertain one other person or a party. If you have four or more, the innkeepers will sometimes cater special lunches or dinners. They're working hard to make this classic house a class-act inn by applying a simple philosophy: only the best of everything.

How to get there: From 101 north, take River Road/Guerneville exit just past Santa Rosa; go west 14 miles to Guerneville. At the stop sign at Highway 116 and River Road, turn left, cross the bridge over River Road. The inn is ¹/₂ mile beyond the bridge on the left. Local airport pickup.

Olive Metcalf

Old Thyme Inn
Half Moon Bay, California
94019

Innkeepers: Simon and Anne Lowings
Address/Telephone: 779 Main Street; (415) 726–1616
Rooms: 7; all with private bath, 3 with Jacuzzi and fireplace.
Rates: $65 to $210 for suite, double occupancy, breakfast and early-evening
   beverage. Reduced rates for weekdays and extended stays.
Open: All year.
Facilities and activities: Nearby: 1 mile to state beach; Fitzgerald Marine
   Reserve; whale watching, elephant seal reserve, hiking, horseback rid-
   ing, fishing fleet at Princeton Harbor and pier, Main Street with shops
   and restaurants, Spanishtown Art Center, many annual events including October Art and Pumpkin Festival.

Medical experts would surely agree that a two-day dropout
from routine can refresh spirits and do more for good marital rela-
tionships than an entire season of watching Dr. Ruth. In addition, it
only gently dents a budget. All of which should have Bay Area residents, especially, zipping down to the small coastal community of
Half Moon Bay. This short getaway destination is just forty-five
minutes from the heart of San Francisco and a jog off the highway—an unpretentious, pleasantly unchic, and, best of all, semi-
undiscovered historic little town.

For lodging comfort, The Old Thyme Inn beautifully fits the bill
for such a low-key holiday. The house is picturesque, dating back to

1899; it's freshly renovated, delightfully decorated, and sits right on the town's historic Main Street. You need not get in your car again until it's time to go home. (Stop by Zabella House, the oldest standing house in Half Moon Bay, and just 4 blocks away, to see still another inn beautifully restored by the Lowings.)

Actually, meeting Anne and Simon Lowings is reason enough to check into the Old Thyme. They're two of the most charming innkeepers you'll ever know. To my Anglophile ear, it helps, of course, that they speak English with a British accent—probably due to being born there. They restored this old house (and some of their stories about *that* enterprise sound like episodes from *Fawlty Towers*), Anne planted an herb garden, and Simon learned to cook. The whole family has become familiar with the joys of tide-pooling at the local Fitzgerald Marine Reserve, with the elephant seals that come ashore near here, and with walking and riding the hills and beaches all about them. You're quite likely to catch their enthusiasm for the area.

They've given a lot of care to the decorating, which has an herb theme. Each room has pretty wallpaper, comforters, English antiques, and an understated charm. The Thyme Room has a fireplace and a whirlpool tub (Simon denies it's the "Wild Thyme Room"). A Garden Suite has a whirlpool tub for two under a skylight, a four-poster bed, a fireplace, a television/VCR, and even the cachet of an English butler (Simon) who will bring breakfast in bed.

A comfortable, homey sitting area ("lounge" to us Anglophiles) has a wood-burning stove and English appointments and memorabilia. I especially liked sitting down to breakfast in the adjoining dining area under a portrait of the young Victoria. The menu would have pleased the old girl, I'm sure: fresh juice, homemade hot scones with marmalade, cold meats, and English cheeses, all topped off with a French cherry flan.

How to get there: From San Francisco, take Highway 280 south to Highway 92 and head west. At Main Street, turn left. The inn is on your left.

J: *Please understand . . . innkeepers do like to change menus. Simon tells me everyone who stays as a result of reading this guide comes "expecting those damned scones!"*

olive Metcalf

Madrona Manor
Healdsburg, California
95448

Innkeepers: John and Carol Muir
Address/Telephone: 1001 Westside Road (mailing address: Box 818); (707)
    433–4231, or fax (707) 433–0703
Rooms: 18 and 2 suites; all with private bath, telephone, and air condition-
    ing, 18 with fireplace. Wheelchair access.
Rates: $110 to $200, double occupancy, full breakfast, Sunday through
    Thursday. $190 to $280, for two, Friday, Saturday, and holidays, MAP.
Open: All year.
Facilities and activities: Dinner nightly, Sunday brunch. Swimming pool.
    Nearby: golf, tennis, hiking, canoeing, fishing, winery tours, picnics,
    bicycling.

Country inns continue to spring up in northern California faster than yuppies are going out of style, but Madrona Manor stands alone. First, it is a truly dramatic Victorian mansion sitting in the midst of landscaped grounds and eight wooded acres. But even more notable is its outstanding California restaurant, the only one in Sonoma County rated three stars by *Chronicle* food critic Patricia Unterman.

Approaching the Italianate mansion up the long driveway brings feelings of pleasant anticipation. Elegant accommodations await inside: antique furnishings, period wallpapers and rugs, and rooms with original plumbing and lighting fixtures. The third floor has renovated rooms with fireplaces, queen-sized beds, and antique reproduction furniture from Portugal. Less opulent but more modern rooms are in two other outbuildings and the Carriage House, where a fireplace has been added to the lounge.

The fine cooking is served in two high-ceilinged, attractive dining rooms. Former Chez Panisse cook Todd Muir runs the kitchen. He and his staff work in a modern kitchen (contrasting with the rest of the 1881 setting) complete with a mesquite grill and a smokehouse in back that produces smoked trout, chickens, and meats. The gardens produce all the flowers for the dining room and guest rooms as well as herbs and specialty produce for the kitchen.

An a la carte menu of salads, pastas, and grilled main courses, or an elegant prix-fixe dinner ($40 at this writing for weekend guests on the Modified American Plan) are available seven nights a week. My first course of individual goat-cheese soufflé was perfectly crusty on top with a softly oozing middle. Every element of the meal, down to dessert of amaretto-soaked cake with chocolate-ricotta filling, was meticulously prepared.

The wine list is both extensive and reasonably priced, which, even though this is the heart of the wine country, is not always true up here. Some selections from small local wineries are at near-retail prices.

Breakfast for guests is as carefully done as dinner. It includes their wonderful house bread, toasted; a perfectly timed soft-boiled egg; loads of seasonal fruit; oatmeal and granola; ripe, room temperature cheeses; and house-smoked meats. When the weather allows, take this meal outside on the palm terrace.

How to get there: From San Francisco, drive north on Highway 101, 12 miles north of Santa Rosa; take the Central Healdsburg exit; follow Healdsburg Avenue north to Mill Street, turn left, and it becomes Westside Road. Inn is ³/₄ mile on the right. From the north, take Westside Road exit from Highway 101; turn right. Inn is ¹/₂ mile on the right.

J: What a beautiful place for a special celebration.

Olive Metcalf

Agate Cove Inn
Mendocino, California
95460

Innkeepers: Sallie McConnell and Jake Zahavi
Address/Telephone: 11201 North Lansing Street (mailing address: P.O. Box
   1150); (707) 937–0551; in Northern California, (800) 527–3111
Rooms: 10; all with private bath, ocean view, and cable television. No smoking in rooms.
Rates: $75 to $175, including full country breakfast. Ask about cash dis-
   count rates, midweek rates.
Open: All year.
Facilities and activities: Accommodations for weddings and special occasion
   parties. Nearby: short walk to Mendocino Village galleries, Art Center,
   restaurants, specialty shops. Hiking, canoeing, horseback riding, tennis,
   golf accessible.

   A friend of mine who pursues a lively romantic life insisted
that she had discovered a jewel in Mendocino that I had missed.
"Fabulous views," she raved. "Best breakfast I ever had at an inn,"
she went on. "It was simply the most low-key, fresh . . . romantic
place I've been in ages!" Being an election year, I was ready to for-
give a little exaggeration, but I was also prepared to be under-
whelmed. Score one for my friend.
   Agate Cove Inn is indeed a jewel. Sitting above and behind
Mendocino Village on a bluff above the ocean, it appears to be an
old farmhouse. That is just what the main house is, built in the
1860s by Mathias Brinzing, who established the first Mendocino

284

brewery. Some of the original candlestick fence still runs through the beautiful old-fashioned garden.

Scattered through the grounds are the cozy cottages, each with views of the ocean (except for one room where you have to make do with only a lovely garden view), a fireplace, a decanter of sherry, and a private deck for watching the sea.

The rooms have king- and queen-sized four-poster or canopy beds, handmade quilts, and country decor that goes for comfort rather than excessive cuteness. The luxury cottages have large double showers or oversize tubs, and considering California's water problems, it would be a crime to use one of them alone.

The main house has a spacious living room for guests to enjoy. A red-brick fireplace, colorful wing chairs, love seats, quilts, antiques, and books all bring a country warmth. The room opens onto the breakfast room, with stunning ocean vistas. For some of us breakfast really begins with the morning San Francisco newspaper on the doorstep . . . and that's the way they do it at Agate Cove, too. A short walk through the garden to the main house leads to great food. Select your juice and fresh fruit and choose a table, already set with fresh, home-baked bread and jams. You must divide your view between your entree being cooked on an antique wood stove nearby and the drama out the window of crashing waves on the rocks.

Mendocino is an enchanting seaside village, but it is not undiscovered. Agate Cove puts you close to all the village attractions but just enough removed to feel you're in a very special, romantic hideaway. For quiet, uncrowded—some say the most beautiful times— come during the winter season.

How to get there: About a three-hour drive from San Francisco via Highway 101 and 128. When your each Mendocino, take the Lansing Street exit after the traffic light. The inn is $1/2$ mile north of the village.

olive Metcalf

San Ysidro Ranch
Montecito, California
93108

Innkeeper: William Shoaf, general manager
Address/Telephone: 900 San Ysidro Lane; (805) 969–5046, fax (805) 565–1995
Rooms: 44; all with private bath, TV, telephone, fireplace, porch, and stocked refrigerator.
Rates: $195 to $375 for cottage rooms; $425 to $625 for cottages with private Jacuzzi; double occupancy; breakfast included with Sunday-through-Thursday-night stays.
Open: All year.
Facilities and activities: Breakfast, lunch, dinner, Sunday brunch. Horses, guided rides, swimming pool, tennis courts, golf.

Admittedly, the San Ysidro is not inexpensive, but I think you'd have the curiosity of a turnip if you didn't want to see the place where John and Jacqueline Kennedy honeymooned, where Laurence Olivier and Vivien Leigh married, and where Winston Churchill and John Galsworthy relaxed and wrote.

The San Ysidro has been around since 1893, always a premier hideaway and favorite of celebrities and writers. I admit being worried when I heard about its new corporate ownership, but the blue business suits have wisely not changed the unique feeling at this gorgeously situated inn. There are more elegant room appointments now—televisions, telephones, and fresh decor—but I was relieved to see the ranch has not gone California chic. Those infamous cheery signs announcing I AM A CATALPA TREE or LATE CHECK-OUTS WILL BE CHARGED AN ARM AND A LEG have disappeared, but the special low-key ambience, elegant but not slick, still prevails.

Privacy, in a setting of great natural beauty, was and still is the story of the ranch's appeal. The soft foothills of the Santa Ynez Mountains offer miles of riding trails with breathtaking views. You can disappear into one of the cottages and not see another soul for days, though the innkeepers claim if a guest doesn't come out for twenty-four hours, they do force-feeding.

There is no typical room in the buildings scattered around the lush grounds. Some are parlor suites with patio or deck; some are individual cottages. They're not all equally spiffy, it must be admitted. There's the odd piece of antique plumbing or worn upholstery, but luxury appointments aren't what have attracted people here for so long.

A kind of "we're all country gentlemen here" atmosphere is also part of the charm. Take the stocked refrigerators in every room—they are honor bars. Mix your own and keep tabs. Very upper class, don't you think?

One other major lure is the outstanding food at the Stonehouse Restaurant. From alfresco breakfasts on the deck to candlelit continental dinners in the beautiful white-stuccoed dining room, the cuisine ranges from Western to sophisticated. The manager calls it "American Regional." The important fact is that its reputation attracts even diners who aren't ranch guests.

How to get there: From Highway 101, take San Ysidro Road exit in Montecito, 4 miles south of Santa Barbara. Follow signs to San Ysidro Ranch, 2 miles toward the mountains.

J: *John Galsworthy wrote, of San Ysidro Ranch, "The loveliness of these evenings moves the heart; and of the mornings, shining, cool fragrant."*

Olive Metcalf

Old Monterey Inn
Monterey, California
93940

Innkeepers: Ann and Gene Swett
Address/Telephone: 500 Martin Avenue; (408) 375–8284
Rooms: 10; all with private bath, most with fireplace. Smoking in garden only.
Rates: $160 to $220, double occupancy, full breakfast and afternoon tea with homemade cookies. No credit cards.
Open: All year.
Facilities and activities: Accepts small executive retreats winter weekdays. Nearby: short walk to historic district of Monterey, Fisherman's Wharf, shops, restaurants; Monterey Bay Aquarium; short drives to Carmel, Pebble Beach, Point Lobos State Reserve, Big Sur coastline.

Let's discuss romantic lodgings for persnickety people. Does the word *rustic* give you a headache? When the phrase "Victorian charm" is mentioned, do you have an acute attack of nausea? Do you feel that anything built after World War II is faintly tacky? Have I got an inn for you!

The Old Monterey Inn is an elegant architectural gem built in 1929 and until recently had always been a private residence. It's a half-timbered, Tudor-style house sitting on an oak-studded hillside in a quiet residential neighborhood. More than an acre of astonishingly beautiful gardens surround it and give each room a view of begonias, fuchsias, hydrangeas, and wooded banks of ferns and rhododendrons.

Ann and Gene Swett are the proprietors of this paradise, the family home where they raised their six children. Their hospitality and these beautifully appointed rooms are all the most discriminating guest could want. Choose any room and you can't go wrong, but the Library captured my heart with book-lined walls, a stone fireplace, and a private sun deck overlooking the garden. Everyone who stays in the Ashford Suite plots a return to this triumph of refined chic: a sitting room, separate dressing room, and large bedroom in antique pine and Ralph Lauren fabrics.

Eight of the ten rooms have wood-burning fireplaces. All of them have luxuries like elegant linens, goosedown comforters, the gleaming wood of period furniture, family antiques, and bathroom items you might have forgotten. Other personal touches include soft challis robes in each room, a refrigerator stocked with complimentary juices and soft drinks, and the loan of an outfitted picnic basket for a day's outing. The Swetts include a list of the best delis, the most interesting picnic sites, and directions for getting there.

Another fireplace is in the elegant step-down dining room where breakfast is served. You can have breakfast sent to your room, but it's awfully grand to sit around the long antique table with your hosts and meet the other lucky people who are here. Fresh fruit compotes and things like strata soufflé, Belgian waffles, or Orange Blossom French toast are featured.

In the evening a fire burns in the living room, and the Swetts join their guests for wine and cheese. It's another lovely room, with oriental rugs and fine furniture. The ultimate standard of good taste runs throughout the house: comfort and quality, without pretension.

How to get there: Take Munras Avenue exit from Highway One; make an immediate left on Soledad Drive, then right on Pacific. Continue ³/₅ of a mile to Martin Street on the left. Inn is on your right at number 500.

J: *If checking into an inn is buying a bit of magic for your life, get ready to be enchanted.*

Olive Metcalf

The Red Castle Inn
Nevada City, California
95959

Innkeepers: Mary Louise and Conley Weaver
Address/Telephone: 109 Prospect; (916) 265–5135
Rooms: 8; 6 with private bath. Third- and fourth-floor rooms air conditioned. Smoking on verandas and in garden.
Rates: $70 to $110, double occupancy, full breakfast and afternoon tea. Two-night minimum Saturdays April 1–December 31.
Open: All year.
Facilities and activities: Saturday morning carriage rides, historical narratives and poetry readings, Victorian Christmas dinner and entertainment, picnic baskets by advance request. Nearby: walking path to downtown shops, restaurants, antiques; local theater, musical events; swimming in mountain creek; cross-country skiing twenty minutes away.

It's little wonder the current owners fell in love with this Victorian brick mansion when they first visited back in the seventies. Looking for all the world like the cover background for a Victorian romance novel, The Red Castle has an undeniably romantic appeal.

Hanging on a hillside nestled among dense trees, The Red Castle is an impressive sight from many places around Nevada City. The Gothic-revival mansion is wrapped in rows of white, painted verandas and lavished with gingerbread trim at roofline and gables. From the private parking area, you walk around a veranda, with stylish canvas draperies tied back at each pillar, to the front of the house, where you can survey the historic mining town's rooftops and church steeples.

Since it was built in 1857, the castle has had a succession of caring owners who have maintained it without compromising its elegant period character. The Weavers have brought not only their respective professional skills in architecture and design but also some impressive art, including several Bufano sculpture pieces, and fine furniture. Eight guest rooms range over the four floors, each one of them a vibrantly decorated, tasteful delight. Most furnishings are Victorian, but not fragile or frilly. An explosion of color from wallpapers, fabrics, and rugs has an engaging effect in combination with the dramatic architecture. Two garret rooms on the top floor share a sitting room, bath, and balcony. It was from here that the original owner's son used to serenade the town with impromptu trumpet concerts.

A cozy sitting room off the entry hall has cushy upholstered sofas, wingback chairs, and an inviting collection of gold-rush history and art books. We helped ourselves to an elegant tea spread here and took it outside. Three small terraced gardens, one with a fountain and pond, are idyllic sitting and strolling areas. A path through cascading vines leads down to Nevada City's main street.

The Weavers are proud of their vintage inn and are enthusiastic about Nevada City. They'll arrange a horse-drawn carriage tour through the town's historic district. They always have good suggestions for restaurants and local events. Their own Victorian Christmas celebration sounds like a truly memorable feast.

The lavish breakfast buffet is a splendid sight—all of it homemade. Ours was typical, but the menu varies every day: juice, poached pears, glazed fresh strawberries, a baked egg curry with pear chutney, cheese croissants, banana bread, jams, Mary Louise's grandmother's bread pudding (what a treat!) with a pitcher of cream, and, of course, great coffee.

How to get there: From Highway 49 at Nevada City, take Sacramento Street exit to the Exxon station; turn right and immediately left onto Prospect Street. The driveway takes you to the back of the house. Walk around the veranda to the front door.

Olive Metcalf

Villa Royale
Palm Springs, California
92264

Innkeepers: Monika and Stephen Maitland-Lewis
Address/Telephone: 1620 Indian Trail; (619) 327–2314, fax (619) 322–4151
Rooms: 31 suites and rooms; all with private bath, TV, telephone, and some
 with fireplace, kitchenette, and private spa. Limited wheelchair access.
Rates: $75 to $300, double occupancy, continental breakfast. Lower sum-
 mer rates and for longer stays.
Open: All year.
Facilities and activities: Restaurant serves lunch and dinner; full bar and piano
 lounge. Two swimming pools, bicycles, spas, courtyards with foun-
 tains, outdoor fireplaces. Nearby: golf, tennis, horseback riding, Palm
 Springs shops, restaurants, aerial tramway ride up Mt. San Jacinto.

Only a few blocks from slick downtown Palm Springs with
glamorous hotels lining the main drag, a heartwarming alternative
lies low on the desert plain just waiting to beguile you. Everything
conspires at Villa Royale to make you think you're in an old European resort. Winding brick paths connect a series of courtyards with
ancient-looking pillars under the red-tile roofs of surrounding
rooms. Shade trees are everywhere, as are pots of flowers, exotic
vines and palms, and small gardens and fountains. And on a March
visit, the cascading bougainvillea was dazzling.

From the blazing Palm Springs sun, you step into a lobby/sit-
ting room with a cool brick floor and squashy sofa and chairs. Just

outside the door in the courtyard are bicycles ready for guests to borrow for sightseeing around the quiet residential streets or touring the shopping plazas. On request, the kitchen will pack you a picnic basket to take along. Owners Monika and Stephen and their well-trained staff are always ready to help. There aren't just *two* bikes; there are lots of them. You don't get just *one* extra towel for the pool; you get big thick ones, as many as you need.

The variety of accommodations at Villa Royale is only one of its attractions. Whether you take a standard guest room or splurge on a deluxe studio with kitchenette, private patio, and spa, the colorful ambience of flowers, fountains, and dramatic views of the San Jacinto Mountains is available to everyone. Every room, large or small, is decorated in an individual international style, the result of the former owners' frequent buying trips to Europe. Each one has interesting treasures: woven hangings and table covers, wall carvings, bright pottery, sculpture, pillows, and antique furniture.

Across the first courtyard is the dining room with a glass-enclosed casual area where breakfast is served looking out at the pool. The brick floor extends into a more formal interior room with a wonderful ambience. Armchairs with rush seats and cushions surround tables skirted with dark floral cloths to the floor and topped with lighter color linen. The walls are a rosy adobe, and in the soft lighting, with beautiful china and glassware, it's an atmosphere I would like to get used to. Our dinner was an attractively presented, relaxing experience: tortellini soup, green salad, scampi, and a marvelous fresh mango sherbet with fresh peaches and raspberries.

As visually rich as the days are here, relaxing in the sunshine surrounded with colorful flowers, wait 'til you see it at night! Dozens of small ornate brass lanterns hanging from trees and vines gleam with tiny lights and cast light and shadows throughout the courtyards. If you aren't enchanted, check your pulse.

How to get there: Proceed through downtown Palm Springs on its main street, North Palm Canyon. When it becomes East Palm Canyon, look for Indian Trail, just past Indian Avenue. Turn left to the inn on your right.

Olive Metcalf

The Gables
Santa Rosa, California
95404

Innkeepers: Michael and Judy Ogne
Address/Telephone: 4257 Petaluma Hill Road; (707) 585–7777
Rooms: 6, plus 1 cottage; all with private bath, 3 with wood stove. No smoking inn.
Rates: $95 to $155, double occupancy, full country breakfast and afternoon refreshments.
Open: All year.
Facilities and activities: Sun deck and gardens. Nearby: restaurants, Sonoma and Russian River wineries, Luther Burbank Center for Performing Arts, Burbank home and gardens, Bodega Bay, Russian River, bicycling, tennis, golf, hot-air ballooning.

If you have time to explore only one area of California's wine country, I say choose Sonoma County. This region north of San Francisco has everything that makes people feel passonate about the wine country—rolling hills and meadows bordered on the west by one of the most spectacular stretches of coastline anywhere; wildflowers, redwoods, colorful historic towns, and throughout the area some of the finest wineries and vineyards in the world.

The Gables is a lodging that does justice to the peaceful feeling of Sonoma. The beautiful rose-painted mansion with burgundy shutters sits on three and one-half acres in a rural setting. It was built in 1877 by one of the few California gold miners who didn't lose his money. Instead, he built this ornate example of High Victorian Gothic architecture with 12-foot ceilings, three Italian marble fireplaces, and a splendid mahogany spiral staircase. The name of the house comes from its most striking detail, the fifteen gables crowning the unusual keyhole-shaped windows.

The house couldn't have had a happier fate than being rescued by the Ognes. Every room is invitingly fresh and tastefully decorated in fine fabrics and romantic color schemes. The spacious bedrooms are appointed with lovely antiques (but not so many they clutter the room), private baths, goose-down comforters, freshly cut flowers, and a good selection of books.

William and Mary's Cottage is a separate accommodation next to Taylor Creek. Its sleeping loft, wood stove, and kitchenette make it particularly pleasant for a longer-than-overnight stay.

The atmosphere at this fine country house will invite you to stay around and relax right here. There's a great old (about 150 years) barn on the property with a resident owl family, and a three-holer outhouse . . . strictly for academic inspection. You can stroll through the kitchen gardens, cross the footbridge over Taylor Creek into the meadow, or take a cup of coffee out to the big sun deck and soak in the countryside.

Wonderful restaurants abound in the surrounding area. Michael and Judy are ready to recommend according to your food favorites and will make the necessary reservations at the most "in" places. With your evening meal booked, you can skip lunch and abandon yourself to the big, all-fresh country breakfast the Ognes provide. Besides an ever-changing entree, you always find fresh juice and fruits and freshly baked breads and pastries. Breakfast is served in the dining room at separate tables, or you can join other guests at one long table.

How to get there: About an hour north of San Francisco, exit Highway 101 east at Rohnert Park Expressway to Petaluma Hill Road. Turn north to The Gables on the left. Fly-in: Sonoma County Airport.

J: *I arrived at The Gables and asked to be shown around just as the Ognes were expecting a group of innkeepers and winery association guests for lunch. Being busy didn't diminish their hospitality one whit. They showed the kind of friendly, gracious style that separates real innkeepers from the amateurs.*

olive Metcalf

Casa Madrona Hotel
Sausalito, California
94965

Innkeeper: John Mays
Address/Telephone: 801 Bridgeway; (415) 332–0502 or (800) 288–0502
Rooms: 34; all with private bath, some with fireplace, private deck, water view.
Rates: $95 to $200, double occupancy; cottages, $140 to $160; 3-room suite, $325; continental breakfast and wine and cheese social hour.
Open: All year.
Facilities and activities: Dinner, wine and beer bar nightly; lunch Monday through Friday; Sunday brunch. Outdoor Jacuzzi. Nearby: Sausalito's shops and galleries, ferryboat rides across the bay, fine dining, hiking, bicycling.

John Mays knows how to create an atmosphere. He's turned this luxurious old mansion perched on a hill above Sausalito into one of the most romantic inns you'll find. Of course, he has a lot going for him with a town almost too winning for words and spectacular views of the yacht harbor.

Casa Madrona is more than one hundred years old. Time had taken its toll on the former residence, hotel, bordello, and boardinghouse when John Mays rescued it in 1978. It nearly slid off the hill during the rains of '82, but renovations already begun saved it from gliding away.

Since then Mays has added an elegant tumble of cottages that dot the hillside down to Sausalito's main street. Each one is different, with dormers, gables, peaked roofs, and hidden decks. Amazingly, the whole gray-blue jumble lives perfectly with the old mansion.

You've seen "individually decorated" rooms before, but these beat all. Each of Mays' new hillside cottages was designed by a different Bay Area decorator. The range of their individual styles resulted in rooms with themes from nautical to equestrian (The Ascot Suite) to a Parisian Artist's Loft. Most have private decks and superb views. And since it *is* in fabled, sybaritic Marin County, there are luxurious tubs for two (sometimes elevated and open to the room), refrigerators stocked with fruit juice and mineral water, and fresh flowers. (But no peacock feathers.)

If you're indifferent to unique rooms surrounded by lush gardens, exotic bougainvillea and trumpet vine spilling over decks and walkways, perhaps elegant food will ring your bell. A beautiful wine bar and uncluttered dining room in the old house on top of the hill are lighted and decorated to enchant. Only white linen on round tables and fresh flowers compete with the view of the bay and Sausalito Yacht Harbor . . . that is, until the food is served.

We began with what I thought was a California cuisine standard but that has become a part of American cuisine: radicchio and Belgian endive salad with baked chèvre (goat cheese). Perfection. Our waiter was agreeable when I ordered another first course (angel hair pasta with roasted peppers and mussels) instead of an entree. (I love places that encourage you to order by *your* appetite instead of *their* rules.) Others at our table raved about linguine with Parma prosciutto, roasted shallots, baby turnips, and balsamic vinegar cream, and rack of lamb with minted gremolata and roasted garlic glaze. The meal could not have been lovelier.

How to get there: Cross the Golden Gate Bridge; take Alexander Street exit to center of town. San Francisco Airport pickup available. Ferry service from San Francisco.

❦

J: *If this inn can't rekindle a dying ember, no place can.*

olive Metcalf

Timberhill Ranch
Timbercove, California
95421

Innkeepers: Barbara Farrell, Frank Watson, Tarran McDaid, Michael Riordan
Address/Telephone: 35755 Hauser Bridge Road, Cazadero 95421; (707) 847-3258
Rooms: 10 secluded cottages; all with private bath, fireplace, minibar. Handi-capped access. Smoking restricted to designated areas.
Rates: $350, double occupancy, Friday, Saturday, Sunday; $325, double occupancy, weekdays; breakfast and six-course dinner included.
Open: All year.
Facilities and activities: Lunch. World-class tennis courts, swimming pool, outdoor Jacuzzi, hiking. Nearby: 4 miles to ocean beach; Salt Point State Park, Fort Ross, The Sea Ranch public golf course.

When your stress level hits an octave above high C and you can't bear making one more earth-shaking decision . . . when you want to seclude yourself with nature (and a close, close friend) for some spiritual renewal . . . when you demand the best in fine food, service, and amenities . . . then head for Timberhill Ranch.

This classy resort on a very intimate scale is off the beaten track, perched high in the hills above the Sonoma coast. Once you've checked in at the reception and dining area, you're shuttled to your cottage in a golf cart, and not a telephone or a discouraging word will ruffle your brow until you grudgingly conclude it's time to go home.

Sonoma's fabulous climate, rugged beauty, unspoiled high meadows, and redwoods are undisputed. What's surprising is to find an inn with such luxury blending into these surroundings. All credit must be given to the two innkeeping couples who planned and built 80 percent of the resort themselves. Their vision accounts for keeping the ranch an underdeveloped oasis of tranquility; for only ten cottages, despite eighty acres of land; for building their world-class tennis courts far from the swimming pool, because "when you're lounging quietly by the water you don't want to hear tennis chatter."

The spacious, cedar-scented cottages are situated for maximum privacy. Each has a stocked mini-bar, a fire laid, a well-appointed tile bath, handmade quilt on the queen-sized bed, comfortable chairs, good lights, and a radio. In the morning, breakfast is delivered to your door to enjoy on your private deck as you look out at a stunning view.

What more? Superb food served beautifully in an intimate dining room with windows overlooking hills and forest—but without reservations, hurry, hassle, or check to interrupt. (Breakfast and dinner are included in the rate.) The six-course dinners, for inn guests only, are what you might expect in one of San Francisco's finest restaurants. Here's a sample of one recent night: chilled artichoke with lemon mayonnaise, beef barley soup, salad with hearts of palm, raspberry sorbet, loin of lamb with red-pepper butter (among five other entree choices), and a dessert selection including puff pastry blackberry torte.

The four owners are hands-on innkeepers, always giving a level of personal attention far removed from a slick resort atmosphere. One told me, "We really like taking care of people and giving them the kind of service and privacy *we* looked for when *we* used to get away." As I watched the reluctant farewell of one couple, the hugs and promises to be back soon, I decided that Timberhill has all the right stuff, including a warm heart.

How to get there: From Highway One north of Fort Ross, turn east on Timber Cove Road. Follow to Sea View Ridge Road. Turn left, follow to Hauser Bridge Road and inn sign on the right.

olive Metcalf

Mt. Ashland Inn
Ashland, Oregon
97520

Innkeepers: Jerry and Elaine Shanafelt
Address/Telephone: 550 Mt. Ashland Road; (503) 482–8707
Rooms: 5, including 1 suite with Jacuzzi for two; all with private bath, queen- or king-sized bed, and individual thermostat. No smoking inn.
Rates: $80 to $130, double occupancy, full breakfast and beverages. Special rates November through April, excluding holidays and weekends.
Open: All year.
Facilities and activities: Meeting room for small gatherings with sitting area and audiovisual equipment, VCR for guests. Light suppers available in winter by prior arrangement for additional charge. Hiking, sledding, cross-country and downhill skiing. Nearby: river rafting, Ashland Shakespeare Festival February through October, Britt Music Festival June to September in Jacksonville.

A late April snow was falling as we drove up the road to Mt. Ashland, making the passing scenery all the more breathtaking. At 5,500 feet, just 3 miles from the summit, the beautiful Mt. Ashland Inn sits nestled in the Siskiyou Mountains 16 miles south of Ashland, a snug haven of outstanding craftmanship and hospitality.

The cedar log structure was handcrafted by the Shanafelts from lumber cut and milled on the surrounding property. But don't picture a cottage in the woods improvised by a couple with some land and a chain saw. Jerry's remarkable design and woodworking skills are apparent everywhere your eyes rest—in hand-carved mountain scenes on the doors, the decorative deck railing, log archways, stained-glass windows, and a unique log-slab circular staircase. Most amazing to us were the twelve Windsor chairs he made one winter, each one a smooth, perfect piece of art.

The peeled log walls of a common room draw you in with the warmth of cushy furniture, brilliant oriental rugs, mellowed antiques, and a stone fireplace. Can you imagine how the fire, music playing softly, and hot spiced cider can hit you on a cold afternoon? Right. It's nap time in the mountains.

Each of the guest rooms upstairs has a view toward Mt. Shasta, Mt. McLoughlin, or some part of the Cascades. The Sky Lakes Suite on the ground floor has a Jacuzzi for two, a rock wall with trickling waterfall (operated by the guests), a rock patio, a wet bar, and a view of Mt. McLoughlin.

When we looked out the window in the morning, the fir trees were thickly frosted with snow, and I felt like Heidi in Oregon. But pretending we were roughing it in the wilderness just wouldn't fly in the face of all the comforts: big chairs with reading lights by the windows, a queen-sized bed topped with a handmade quilt, and the woodsy aroma of cedar filling the air.

Breakfast in the dining room was fresh juice and fruit and a tasty entree of puffy orange French toast. Daffodils on the table were picked that morning as they popped through the snow.

If you must stir from this comforting cocoon, a cross-country skiing path that ties into old logging roads is out the back door. Three miles up the road, Mt. Ashland offers fairly demanding downhill skiing. For hikers, the Pacific Crest trail passes right through the property. The premier attractions in the area are the Ashland theaters, about a twenty-five-minute drive (to good restaurants, also) from here.

A bonus of being up the mountain is that when Ashland is covered in clouds and fog, you're often in a pocket of sunshine here.

How to get there: North on Highway 5 take Mt. Ashland exit 6; turn right under the highway. At stop sign turn left, parallel highway ½ mile. Turn right on Mt. Ashland Road to ski area. Inn is 6 miles from the highway.

olive Metcalf

Tu Tú Tun Lodge
Gold Beach, Oregon
97444

Innkeepers: Dirk and Laurie Van Zante
Address/Telephone: 96550 North Bank Rogue; (503) 247–6664
Rooms: 16, including 2 suites each accommodating 6; all with private bath.
Wheelchair access.
Rates: $115 to $155 for river-view rooms; $159 to $169 for suites; $189 for
garden cottage; double occupancy; meals extra. Daily rate for two
including dinner and breakfast: $190 to $200.
Open: April 27 to October 27. Two suites with kitchens available all year.
Facilities and activities: Breakfast, lunch, dinner for guests or by reservation,
full bar. Swimming pool, 4-hole putting green; jet boat white-water
Rogue River trips; salmon and steelhead fishing, seasoned guides available. Nearby: scenic flights over Siskiyou Mountains, hiking, beachcombing, scenic drives, legalized gambling in Gold Beach.

Here is a hideout for those couples whose romance never
glows more brightly than when they're fishing together, but dims
when it comes to the gritty realities of camping. In case you have
the mistaken notion that the Northwest consists only of fir trees
and lumberjacks, consider the motto of Tu Tú Tun Lodge: "Casual
elegance in the wilderness on the famous Rogue River."

That's summing it up modestly, for this is a very special blend
of sophistication and an outdoors-lover's paradise. Top-notch
accommodations and superb food are those of a classy resort, but
the young owners create a friendly atmosphere that's more like that

302

of a country inn.

Guest rooms are situated in a two-story building adjacent to the lodge. Each has comfortable easy chairs, extra-long beds, a dressing area, and a bath with tub and shower. Special touches that make wilderness life civilized aren't forgotten—fresh flowers, good reading lamps, and up-to-date magazines. Two recently redecorated rooms now have Japanese-style soaking tubs in their outdoor area. The suites can accommodate up to six persons each. No telephone or television intrudes as you watch the changing colors of the Rogue's waters at sunset from your private balcony or patio.

A bell at 6:30 P.M. calls guests to the lodge for cocktails and hors d'oeuvres. Dirk and Laurie introduce everyone, and by the time they seat you for dinner at round tables set for eight, you'll feel you're dining with friends. The set entree dinner they serve is outstanding. It always features regional specialties, frequently grilled over mesquite. Fresh chinook salmon, a soup, crisp salad made from locally grown greens, freshly baked bread or rolls, and a raspberry sorbet is a typical dinner.

After dinner, guests usually gather around the two fire pits on the terrace overlooking the river to enjoy an after-dinner drink, inhale the scent of jasmine, and take in the beauty all around. There's much to talk about as you share ideas for the next day's plans. If those plans call for an early-morning rising for fishing, a river trip, or hiking, breakfast and lunch baskets will be ready for you.

One adventure almost every visitor to the lodge tries is the exciting 104-mile white-water round trip up (and down) the river. Jet boats stop at the lodge's dock to pick up passengers in the morning and stop for a wonderful lunch at an old farmhouse up the river.

How to get there: Driving north on Highway 101, pass through Gold Beach, cross bridge, and watch for signs on right to Rogue River Tavern. Turn right and drive 4 miles to tavern; follow signs another 3 miles to lodge on the right.

J: *This is my idea of keeping the romance in roughing it. Was that the cocktail bell?*

Clive Metcalf

Edenwild Inn
Lopez Island, Washington
98261

Innkeeper: Susan Aran
Address/Telephone: Lopez Road (mailing address: P.O. Box 271); (206) 468–3238
Rooms: 7, all with private bath, some with fireplace; garden and water views. Handicapped facilities. No smoking inn.
Rates: $90 to $140, double occupancy, full breakfast and afternoon aperitif. Ask about winter rates November through April.
Open: All year.
Facilities and activities: Facilities for small weddings and small conferences. During winter season, lunches and Saturday night ethnic dinners by reservation. Nearby: Lopez Village shops, hiking, bicycling.

When your request for a reservation is answered with a map of an island, a ferry schedule, and the assurance that ferry landing, sea plane, and airport pick-up is available, I say you're on your way to an adventure. The Edenwild Inn on Lopez Island is such a place. Just getting there is a romantic adventure.

The island slopes gently up from the ferry landing to reveal rural nature at its most picturesque. Pasture, fields, and farms are interspersed with dense woodland, and the shoreline is notched with bays and coves.

The recently built inn is about 4¹/₂ miles from the ferry landing. A broad porch dotted with chairs wraps around three sides of the large house, giving it an inviting, traditional look. Dozens of antique rose bushes and a green lawn brighten a brick patio and pergola to the parking area. Inside is a spacious, casually elegant country house with pale oak floors and fresh bouquets. Bright fabrics cover sofas and chairs grouped before the fireplace. An old upright piano sits here, and the work of some wonderful local artists is displayed here and all through the inn. Breakfast and other meals are served in the adjoining dining room.

Each one of the seven bedrooms appealed to us. It could be because they are new and fresh, or perhaps it is the comfortable built-in beds, or the terrific-looking black-and-white tile bathrooms, or the views—Fisherman's Bay, garden, or San Juan Channel. From Room 5, we thought our view of the main garden and the Channel was the best view in the house . . . until we watched a magnificent sunset that beat them both.

In addition to a full, family-style breakfast for house guests, Susan offers wintertime island visitors (November through April) her version of a soup kitchen. Her collection of great soup recipes is the source for lunches of a bowl or cup of homemade soup, freshly baked bread from an island bakery, and desserts. Susan is also having fun during the winter months with Saturday-night ethnic dinners—anything from Chinese to Cajun. The only thing certain is that you'll need a reservation. This energetic innkeeper and her staff will see that you eat well and have a good time.

An unexpected bit of excitement occurred as we were packing the car to leave. An awfully attractive man helped put our bags in the trunk and then blushed becomingly when we recognized his well-known face. When he's at the inn, this first-rate actor is strictly Susan's husband.

How to get there: From the Lopez Island Ferry Landing, proceed 4¹/₂ miles to Lopez Village Road. Turn right.

J: *This is a wonderful island for bicycling. You might consider buying a "walk-on" ferry ticket (much cheaper than bringing a car), bring just your bikes and luggage, and arrange for an inn pick-up.*

Olive Metcalf

Turtleback Farm
Orcas Island, Washington
98245

Innkeepers: Bill and Susan Fletcher
Address/Telephone: Crow Valley Road (mailing address: Route 1, Box 650, Eastsound); (206) 376-4914
Rooms: 7; all with private bath, king- or queen-sized or double beds, and individual heat control. Wheelchair access. No smoking inn.
Rates: $65 to $135, winter; $65 to $155, May 1 to November 1; double occupancy; full breakfast and afternoon beverage.
Open: All year.
Facilities and activities: Farm; pond stocked with trout. Nearby: hiking trails in Moran State Park; bicycle and moped rentals; swim, picnic at Lake Cascade; fishing, kayaking, sailing; good restaurants.

When an escape from the fast track is high on your list of romantic priorities, a picturesque inn on the San Juan Islands is an ideal choice. Set back from a country road, Turtleback Farm looks like an attractive, well-kept old farmhouse, a big, green, two-story clapboard building. Featured in numerous articles, it is usually booked months in advance, despite its remote location. This may well be the gem lodging of Orcas Island.

The reasons are clear once you settle in. This is a first-rate, impeccably maintained inn. It delivers the quiet country charm that so captivates inngoers but with all the comforts you could ask for.

Once an abandoned farmhouse being used to store hay, the

inn is now restored from the ground up. There are seven guest rooms, a parlor, a dining room, and a tree-shaded deck that runs the length of the house. This is a wonderful place to sit on a warm day and enjoy looking out at acres of meadow with mountains beyond. We're talking idyllic, tranquil setting.

Even if the weather turns dismal, the comforts of this house will keep you charmed. The decor is tasteful and nonfussy, with muted colors, mellow wood trim and floors, and open-beam ceilings. Each guest room has a modern bath appointed with antique fixtures, claw-footed tub, pull-chain toilet, and wall shower. The pedestal sinks came from the Empress Hotel in Victoria. There's a cozy parlor where you can curl up and read before a fire. (The custom here is, "If you find a book you can't put down, take it with you and just return it when you finish.")

The dining room is still another place to enjoy the view and have a cup of tea or a glass of sherry. An outstanding breakfast is served here, course by course at individual tables on bone china. The menus change, but a typical morning would bring juices, local berries, granola, an omelet with ham, and English muffin. Seconds are always offered.

What do you do on an 80-acre farm if you're fresh from the city? If you're smart, you settle yourselves on the deck with blades of grass between your teeth, big hats tipped down over your noses, and think things over—very, very slowly. Then there are the exhausting demands of critter watchin'. There are ducks and blue heron, sheep, chickens, a rambunctious brown ram named Oscar, and visiting Canada geese. You're welcome to fish the large pond by the main house—it's stocked with trout. If you're picnic fans, the paths leading to private little spots will be irresistible. The Fletchers make every effort to acquaint you with all that the island offers. They'll make arrangements for you to charter a boat, rent a moped, play golf, or whatever sounds good to you.

How to get . tere: From Orcas Island ferry landing proceed straight ahead on Horseshoe Highway to first left turn; follow to Crow Valley Road. Turn right and continue to the inn, 6 miles from ferry landing. Fly-in: Eastsound Airport.

Indexes

Alphabetical Index to Inns

Inns on or near Lakes

Inns at or near the Seashore

Inns with, or with Access to, Swimming Pools

Inns with Downhill or Cross-Country Skiing Nearby

Inns with, or with Access to, Golf or Tennis Facilities

Inns That Forbid or Restrict Smoking